THE PEACEFUL TRANSFER OF POWER

Miller Center Studies on the Presidency

Guian A. McKee and
Marc J. Selverstone, Editors

THE PEACEFUL TRANSFER OF POWER

An Oral History of America's
Presidential Transitions

David Marchick and Alexander Tippett

with A. J. Wilson

Published in association with the Partnership for Public Service and the
University of Virginia's Miller Center of Public Affairs

University of Virginia Press • *Charlottesville and London*

University of Virginia Press
Printed in the United States of America on acid-free paper

First published 2022

9 8 7 6 5 4 3 2 1

Library of Congress Cataloging-in-Publication Data

Names: Marchick, David Matthew, author, interviewer | Tippett, Alexander, author. |
  Partnership for Public Service.
Title: The peaceful transfer of power : an oral history of America's presidential
  transitions / David Marchick and Alexander Tippett ; with A.J. Wilson.
Description: Charlottesville : University of Virginia Press, 2022. | Series: Miller Center
  studies on the presidency | Includes bibliographical references and index.
Identifiers: LCCN 2022010858 (print) | LCCN 2022010859 (ebook) | ISBN
  9780813947761 (hardcover) | ISBN 9780813947778 (ebook)
Subjects: LCSH: Presidents—United States—Transition periods—History. |
  Historians—United States—Interviews. | Politicians—United States—Interviews. |
  Political consultants—United States—Interviews.
Classification: LCC JK516 .M347 2022 (print) | LCC JK516 (ebook) | DDC 352.230973—
  dc23/eng/20220427
LC record available at https://lccn.loc.gov/2022010858
LC ebook record available at https://lccn.loc.gov/2022010859

PARTNERSHIP
FOR PUBLIC SERVICE

Cover art: istock.com/sassy1902

CONTENTS

III. Policy

Illustrations follow page 178

FOREWORD

HISTORY DOES not repeat itself. It never has, and it never will. But sometimes, as Mark Twain supposedly said, it rhymes.

In the 118 days between Abraham Lincoln's election in 1860 and his swearing-in on March 4, 1861, seven Southern states seceded. Assassins closed in on the president-elect. A mob attempted to disrupt the certification of Lincoln's victory, only to be repelled by Capitol security officers. The incumbent president, James Buchanan, was paralyzed with indecision, overseeing a cabinet that included Southern sympathizers and insurrectionists. Less than a month after Lincoln took office, Confederate troops fired on Fort Sumter.

And while no set of challenges has ever stacked up to those that President-elect Lincoln faced, history certainly rhymed in the 2020–21 transition of power.

No states seceded in 2020 or 2021, but President-elect Joe Biden took office during one of the most difficult moments in American history. The Covid-19 pandemic peaked, leaving more than 10 million Americans unemployed. Protests flared in the wake of police killings of George Floyd and other African American citizens. Amid the turmoil, President Donald Trump refused to recognize Biden as the legitimate winner, delayed the launch of the formal transition, and became the first president not to attend his successor's swearing in since Andrew Johnson in 1869. As in 1860, a violent mob attempted to impede the certification of the election, on January 6, 2021.

The foundations of our democracy were bent but did not break. And the United States continued its unbroken 224-year streak of presidential transitions, one that began with George Washington handing the reins to John Adams in 1797. It may not have been smooth. It may not have been peaceful. But power was transferred. That unbroken 224-year streak remains unique in world history. We have a duty to see that it persists.

LINCOLN'S FIRST inaugural address included, to my mind, one of the most poetic sentences ever written. It implores the mostly Southerners in his audience not to go to war.

The mystic chords of memory, stretching from every battlefield and patriot grave to every living heart and hearthstone all over this broad land,
will yet swell the chorus of the Union, when again touched, as surely they
will be, by the better angels of our nature.

To stir those better angels is the mission of this book. Its contributors
understand that history is one of the great teachers, enabling us not only
to place our current moment in perspective but also to remain hopeful,
even during trying times. Not content merely to document the history of
presidential transitions, this book seeks to put history's lessons to use in
improving future handoffs from one president to another.

As well as an important historical record and a guide for future transitions, this book highlights the important work of the Partnership for
Public Service's Center for Presidential Transition and contributes another important resource to the treasure trove on presidential history
kept by the University of Virginia's Miller Center. I hope that students,
historians, policymakers, and citizens can enjoy and benefit from its
publication.

My approach to documentary filmmaking has, at its core, always
been grounded in storytelling, on the principle that great stories unlock
history and make it accessible. Similarly, this book is enlivened by some
of the great storytellers who appeared on the Partnership for Public Service's podcast *Transition Lab* during the 2020–21 transition. In its pages,
readers will find tales of Abraham Lincoln's history-changing thirteen-
day train ride; of Herbert Hoover's efforts to strangle Franklin Delano
Roosevelt's presidency in the crib; of how Presidents Bush and Obama
cooperated to navigate a perilous transition during war and financial
crisis.

In a wider sense, this book serves to amplify a truth that should should
be self-evident: that a smooth and peaceful transition from one president
to another is and will remain foundational to our democracy. As Lincoln
learned in peril of his life, and as many of his successors have experienced, the all-too-short period between election and inauguration represents one of the most vulnerable and precarious times for our country. To
navigate those risks requires effective planning and, above all, cooperation between administrations of opposing parties. At this time of vocifer-
ous partisanship, a spirit of cooperation is too often in short supply. All

the more reason why we the people must with one voice demand that, when it comes time to transfer power, politicians leave their swords at the door and work together for the good of the country. The stakes are simply too high not to.

KEN BURNS
Walpole, NH
April 2022

ACKNOWLEDGMENTS

FOR SOMEONE with an interest in history, politics, management, and effective government, it is hard to imagine a more invigorating and interesting project than to study and help improve the art of presidential transitions. Icing on the cake was the opportunity to work with the extraordinary team at the Partnership for Public Service and the bipartisan community of experts and former officials devoted to smooth transitions of power in the United States.

Since 2008, the Partnership for Public Service has devoted substantial resources and expertise to studying, documenting, and, most importantly, improving the effectiveness of presidential transitions. After all, the start of any presidency will have a disproportionate impact on whether, and how, an incoming president delivers for the American people.

When we launched the *Transition Lab* podcast, we sought to create a public record of various aspects of the peaceful transfer of power, including the history of this sacred handoff, enabling those who ran, helped drive, or studied presidential transitions to share their stories and history. Little did we know that 2020 would bring one of the most complicated and contentious transitions in US history. Nor did we know that the podcast would become a must-listen in Washington during this period.

Historians and research institutions have studied and documented almost every other aspect of the American presidency. But few have studied and written about presidential transitions. It therefore was a privilege to work and collaborate with the University of Virginia Press and the Miller Center, the world-class center of excellence for presidential scholarship, to contribute to the historical record on an important aspect of the modern presidency.

It would be impossible, in this short space, to adequately thank all those who worked with the Center for Presidential Transition, on the podcast, and on this book. Here is a try:

First, Max Stier, the CEO of the Partnership for Public Service, deserves sainthood for his two decades of working to build a better government and a stronger democracy, a passion that includes improving presidential transitions. When I joined the effort for the 2020–21 cycle, Max and many of his colleagues at the Partnership poured their considerable expertise, experience, and energy into this important mission, just as several had done in previous cycles. They include Kristine Simmons, Troy Cribb, Austin Laufersweiler, Tina Sung, Katie Bryan, Chrissy Carroll, Samantha Donaldson, Jill Hyland, and Loren DeJonge Schulman. The Partnership's outstanding board of directors was deeply engaged in the transition work, and I particularly benefited from the wisdom and engagement of Tom Bernstein, Scott Gould, Dina Powell McCormick, Tom Nides, Steve Preston, Sean O'Keefe, Kevin Sheekey, Dan Tangherlini, and Neal Wolin.

The Center for Presidential Transition's Advisory Board was an additional source of strength, energy, and engagement. Josh Bolten, as described throughout the book, set the gold standard for presidential transitions as Chief of Staff for President George W. Bush, played a critical role in the 2020 transition, and was often my first call of the day. Penny Pritzker brought her considerable expertise in both business and government to the table. Governor Mike Leavitt's calm demeanor belies his fierce commitment to improving transitions; he has been a trusted advisor to candidates and transition teams regardless of political party. And Mack McLarty, a friend and mentor of thirty years, stepped up to any request or challenge, including playing an important leadership role during the tumultuous delay of the formal launch of the transition.

The Center's staff executed their work with skill and grace, worked nights and weekends, and met every demand in a pressured environment. The standard for excellence was set by my partners running the project, Shannon Carroll and Ann Orr. Other key contributors to the Center's work included Dan Hyman, Chantelle Renn, Livi Logan-Wood, Dan Blair, Christina Condreay, Paul Hitlin, Kayla Shanahan, Jaqueline Alderete, Amelia Ziegler, Carter Hirschhorn, Emma Jones, Amanda Patarino, and, of course, Alex Tippett.

AJ Wilson and Alex Tippett were incredible collaborators on this book. Their drafting, editing, and research shaped not only the organization of the book but also its contents and prose. AJ's outstanding writing skills helped the manuscript overcome my deficiencies. Alex demonstrated research skills that will enable him to excel at the University of Chicago, where he is pursuing his PhD. On top of that, they were fun and easy to work with throughout the last two years. Isabella Epstein, formerly an intern at the Center and now an aspiring lawyer, made extraordinary contributions to this book, including drafting, editing, and perfecting the interview transcripts. Shannon Carroll, Dan Hyman, and the current Director for the Center for Presidential Transition, Valerie Smith Boyd, also edited several turns of the manuscript, improving every iteration.

At UVA Press, Nadine Zimmerli, the editor for history and politics, was simply incredible throughout the process. Part editor, part advisor, part counselor, Nadine kept the book moving, shepherded the peer review process, made immeasurable improvements in the draft manuscript, and became a good friend. Special thanks to UVA Press Director Suzanne Moomaw and to Senior Project Editor Wren Morgan Myers. Susan Murray copy-edited the book with skill and precision and Katie Mertes expertly prepared the index. Jason Coleman and Clayton Butler lent their expertise to marketing the book.

My former State Department colleague, friend of twenty-five years and esteemed Director of the Miller Center, Bill Antholis, was the first person I called with the idea of a book. Luckily, Bill supported the idea and facilitated an introduction to UVA Press. Under Bill's leadership, the Miller Center has solidified its position as a world-class research and policy institution and hosts the most extensive oral history on the US presidency anywhere. Marc Selverstone, who chairs its Presidential Recordings Program, has been an outstanding partner, facilitator, and supporter of this book, as has Guian McKee, who also works on the presidential recordings and, along with Marc, edits the Miller Center Studies on the Presidency series at UVA Press.

Ken Burns has been and remains a hero to me. It therefore is a thrill that he wrote the foreword to this book and appeared not once but twice on the podcast.

Finally, I would be remiss for not thanking Pam Kurland, my wife of twenty-three years, for putting up with me, and my two adult children, Hannah and Zach, for allowing me to continue to embarrass them.

I hope readers learn from this book and enjoy the stories. I also hope that in some small way, it contributes to strengthening the manner in which the peaceful transfer of power takes place in the future.

THE PEACEFUL TRANSFER OF POWER

INTRODUCTION

The orderly transfer of authority as called for in the Constitution routinely takes place, as it has for almost two centuries, and few of us stop to think how unique we really are. In the eyes of many in the world, this every-four-year ceremony we accept as normal is nothing less than a miracle.

—President Ronald Reagan

There won't be a transfer, frankly. There'll be a continuation.

—President Donald Trump

JANUARY 6, 2021, is a day that, like December 7, 1941, will "live in infamy." The world cannot forget the images: a mob, stirred by inflammatory rhetoric, stormed the Capitol Building with the express aim of stopping the peaceful transfer of power from one president to the next. The "violent insurrection," in the words of Republican Senate leader Mitch McConnell, led to human tragedy as five Americans died, including a Capitol Police officer. It was a tragedy, too, for democracy. Never before in a presidential transition had troops been alerted and shots fired. But it happened that day.

Indeed, the fraught 2020–21 transition epitomized larger trends in the United States—political polarization, suspicion of the most sacred of institutions, and the infection of politics in what traditionally has been a purely nonpartisan affair. The modern American presidential transition had increasingly been cooperative, nonpartisan, and collaborative. That trend broke down in the Trump to Biden transition.

Even before the horrific events of January 6, we knew that the 2020–21 transition would be challenging.

First, those of us working at the nonpartisan, nonprofit Partnership for Public Service and its Center for Presidential Transition knew that the results would be delayed. Thanks to the COVID-19 pandemic, voters had cast an unprecedented number of mail-in ballots—too many to count on election night. But sure enough, four days after the 2020 election, former vice president Joseph R. Biden was declared the winner by all major news outlets.

Second, we knew that President Trump might not accept the results. Traditionally, a unanimous declaration by news organizations would trigger a concession speech from the unsuccessful candidate. Even in extremely tight races, the loser has conceded promptly. Richard Nixon, no paragon of virtue, did so within hours in 1960, despite a razor-tight margin of 118,000 votes, because he did not want to put the country through an ordeal or compromise John F. Kennedy's first six months.

Moreover, by any standard, the 2020 outcome was *not* close. Biden garnered eighty-one million votes—the most ever for a presidential candidate—representing a seven-million-vote margin and a clear electoral college majority. Nevertheless, President Donald Trump refused to concede, tweeting with regard to Biden's win: "He only won in the eyes of the FAKE NEWS MEDIA. I concede NOTHING! We have a long way to go. This was a RIGGED ELECTION!"

Third, we anticipated that the formal launch of the transition might not occur quickly. Indeed, General Services Administration (GSA) Administrator Emily Murphy refused to "ascertain" Biden as the "apparent winner" of the 2020 election, putting the formal transition process on ice.[1] The nation waited. Pressure built. Briefing books collected dust. The Biden transition team was locked out of key national security briefings and prevented from ensuring continuity on such life-or-death policy matters as the response to COVID-19, which was at that moment reaching its peak in terms of the daily death toll.

One by one, federal courts tossed out Trump's lawsuits. Clamor grew. Red-state governors and GOP senators called on the GSA to allow the formal transition to begin. The terms "transition" and "ascertainment," previously obscure, suddenly entered the daily vocabulary of millions of Americans. Still, under apparent pressure from President Trump, Murphy did not move.

Against the backdrop of national security threats, economic turmoil, protests against racial injustice, and a pandemic in which thousands of Americans were dying every day, this was a true crisis for American democracy in the modern era. Why? Because in a presidential transition, time is tight and the stakes for the country are almost incomprehensibly high.

EVEN DURING the best of times, an incoming administration faces a gargantuan task. The president-elect's team must not only understand the complexity of the massive federal government; it must be ready to take charge of it and steer it in a direction that helps deliver on the president-elect's promises. A new president's team needs to draw up legally viable executive orders, a management agenda, a budget proposal, and a wish list of legislation. It must formulate a strategy for communicating effectively with the federal workforce, political appointees, Congress, the media, and, of course, the American people themselves. A president-elect must also move quickly to appoint the senior White House staff, the cabinet, and the senior leadership of all the major agencies, before turning to a vast number of other presidential appointments—some four thousand in all.

To make matters still more complex, the handover of power constitutes a time of peak vulnerability for the nation. Crises do not stop happening because a transition is in progress; the 1993 World Trade Center bombing, the 9/11 attacks, and many of the darkest days of the 2008–9 financial crash all happened within a year of a new president's first inaugural. Indeed, in some cases, the timing of events may be more than happenstance, for America's global adversaries know the dangers inherent in transfers of power and are not afraid to use them against us.

Of course, presidential transitions have been taking place since George Washington passed the torch to his vice president, John Adams, in 1797. The modern transition process dates back to Jimmy Carter in 1976. The nation now has more than four decades of accumulated wisdom (and, as we will see, more than a few avoidable mistakes) to draw upon for modern transition planning.

Despite this, institutional knowledge on transitions has historically been in short supply. Hundreds of thousands of books have been written on the presidency, including fifteen-thousand-plus volumes on Lincoln alone. But only a few scholars and practitioners have studied the modern presidential transition. Towson University political science professor Martha Kumar chronicled the 2008–9 Bush-Obama transition, widely considered the smoothest in history.[2] Mitt Romney's transition team, headed by former Utah governor Mike Leavitt and business executive Chris Liddell, published a record of their own experiences.[3] Michael Lewis, author of such smash hits as *Moneyball* and *The Big Short*, chronicled the extensive efforts made by Obama administration officials in 2016–17 to help the incoming Trump team, and President-elect Trump's unwillingness to take the process seriously, in his 2018 bestseller *The Fifth Risk*.[4]

But the transition process as a whole, including its history and major themes, has rarely been addressed in a way that is accessible to practitioners, students, and the public. The number of scholarly books on presidential transitions can be counted on two hands, and the two major academic treatments of the subject at large are twenty-two and thirty-six years old, respectively.[5]

Similarly, the subject lacks a repository of documents. The National Archives and Records Administration and presidential libraries accumulate presidential documents, but since transitions are not considered government enterprises, no similar repository exists for them. In attempting to learn what it could from its predecessors, the 2008 Obama transition team, led by John Podesta and Chris Lu, collected boxes of documents from a closet at the office of Jim Johnson, who served as transition chair for the 2004 Democratic nominee, John Kerry. Mike Leavitt, Mitt Romney's 2012 transition chief, tells a similar story about a cardboard box of documents disinterred from the basement of somebody involved in the Reagan transition in 1980.

That was the reality that Max Stier—president and CEO of the Partnership for Public Service—his colleague Katie Malague, and others encountered in 2008, when they began initial efforts to focus attention on presidential transitions, a natural extension of the Partnership's goal of creating a more effective, better-functioning federal government. Administrations succeed in getting elected, often get off to a slow start, and then stumble because of last-minute and poor transition planning.

To draw attention to this critical issue and spur rigorous advance planning, about six months before the 2008 election, the Partnership invited the three candidates still in the race—John McCain, Barack Obama, and Hillary Clinton—to send campaign representatives to a conference where they could exchange ideas with each other, with outgoing Bush administration officials, with those who had overseen past transitions, and with a handful of academic experts like Martha Kumar (whose interview is included in this volume). Since then, the Partnership and its Center for Presidential Transition, formally created in 2016, have offered support to the major campaigns every election cycle, developed an impressive resource library and learning system to help guide them, and helped draft and pass federal legislation to improve the transition process.

That makes me a relative latecomer to the scene. In the summer of 2019, Max Stier and I had breakfast at the Silver Diner in Washington, DC. Max first asked if I could recommend anyone to run the Center for the next election cycle. Then, knowing that I had recently retired from the Carlyle Group, he said, "You aren't busy—why don't you do it?"

A few months later, I was digging in at the Center for Presidential Transition, reading books, talking to experts, absorbing everything I could about the subject. The rest of the team was already well into its preparation for the next cycle. In fact, several staff members, including Kristine Simmons, Shannon Carroll, Dan Hyman, and Chantelle Renn, had been working for almost three years to improve transition planning based on their experiences during the 2016–17 transition.

When Katie Bryan, a communications expert at the Partnership, raised the idea of a podcast on the history and art of transitions, we were intrigued. Done right, such a project would yield an oral history of presidential transitions that might prove invaluable for future administrations-in-waiting. But in pressure-testing the idea with several friends and transition veterans, most were skeptical. Too boring, they said. Too technical. Too wonky. Who would listen?

Nevertheless, we decided to give it a shot. We debated titles. My early favorite was *Lost in Transition*. Sadly, it turned out there was already a television show with that name about people undergoing gender confirmation surgery. That would not work. Eventually, Paul Hitlin, a researcher at the Partnership, and his brother came up with the name *Transition Lab*, and it stuck. Alex Tippett, a research associate, provided comprehensive research and topics for each episode, working tirelessly and showing keen intellectual curiosity. Paul "Woody" Woodhull and Makenna Chester of District Productive produced every episode, and Carter Hirschhorn joined as an intern and later became a staff member, contributing greatly to our work.

To my delight, our first two interviews were bipartisan affairs. In episode 1, we heard from Rich Bagger and Ed Meier, the executive directors, respectively, of the Donald Trump and Hillary Clinton transition teams. Denis McDonough and Josh Bolten, accomplished chiefs of staff for Presidents Barack Obama and George W. Bush respectively, taped episode 2. By the time of Joe Biden's inauguration, we had recorded well over forty episodes featuring former chiefs of staff, transition chairs, and cabinet secretaries, alongside eminent historians, journalists, and transition scholars. We offered deep dives on every modern presidential transition since Jimmy Carter; discussed the best and worst transitions with noted historians like Ken Burns; and covered every aspect of transition planning including cabinet selection, the vetting of potential appointees, and the important role of career agency officials.

Despite the skepticism we encountered early on, the overall size of our audience grew consistently. But what was even more gratifying was the makeup of that audience: current and former transition team members, White House and agency officials, and leading members of the press. *Washingtonian* magazine remarked with approval that while most in DC were focused on polls, the podcast focused on the transition.[6] *Politico* said it was its favorite podcast of the election cycle.[7]

With these interviews, we compiled what we believe is the largest and most comprehensive oral history of presidential transitions. Now, with this book, we aspire to help future transitions run better, faster, and more smoothly. But equally, we hope we can educate a broad audience on the importance of presidential transitions to our country. And we are honored to make a small contribution to the University of Virginia's Miller Center's work to chronicle and analyze the American presidency.

THIS BOOK is not intended as a work of scholarship. Instead, it presents the viewpoints of various academics, public servants, and journalists. Each interview distills some of the most important insights collected in our podcast alongside some commentary to place these experts and their views in context. The guests also share some wonderful and fun stories, highlighting how personalities and relationships shape events. The work is organized into three parts. In part 1, "History," five historians set the stage by discussing general trends and examples of striking past transitions. Part 2, "Memory," presents the recollections of key participants in every presidential transition from Carter to Biden, plus the planned 2012 transition to Romney that never happened. In the final part, "Policy," experts share their experience of particular aspects of the presidential transition and give recommendations for improving those aspects.

We hope the wisdom collected here will help future transitions ensure a smooth handoff from one president to another and enable the incoming president to hit the ground running on day one. Five major lessons learned stand out:

First, transition planning must start early. Candidates and their teams should begin the process by spring of the election year, if not earlier. In today's increasingly complex world, it is no longer enough to leave the heavy lifting until after the nominating conventions, let alone until after the election. A delayed transition can really hurt. Critical positions may be left empty, policy decisions unresolved. George W. Bush's 2001 transition was held up by a contested election; the 9/11 Commission later found that empty seats at key agencies likely contributed to the country's lack of readiness to deal with this horrific terrorist attack.

Second, transition teams must learn from their predecessors. As we will see, too many have repeated the mistakes of the past. For example, Clinton, like Carter, failed to sufficiently focus on the White House staff; while Trump, like Clinton and Carter, failed to effectively integrate the campaign with the transition. I hope that this book will help make it easier for transition practitioners to learn about the pitfalls.

Third, a candidate must hire the right team, starting with the transition chair. For example, Trump's choice for that role, former New Jersey governor Chris Christie, enjoyed the candidate's trust but lacked the confidence of key people on the campaign. A good transition chair should have both, along with a plan for avoiding a postelection blowup like the one from which the Trump administration never recovered. Throughout the book, we will outline the qualities of an ideal transition leader.

Fourth, transition teams must prioritize the selection, vetting, and training of political appointees. A number of our interviewees said words to the effect of "people are policy"—meaning that no president can hope to execute their agenda without the right people in place. Besides, as we indicated above, there are a *lot* of appointments to be made. The new administration's core leadership (the White House senior staff, the cabinet, and a handful of key personnel for each major agency) must be ready to go at noon on Inauguration Day, with White House appointments taking priority over the cabinet. The White House chief of staff should generally be the first appointment announced postelection.

Fifth, incumbent administrations must help their successors, as well as engage in planning for a second term if seeking reelection. The handoff by an outgoing president is frequently choppy, even when there is no change of party—as the interview with Andy Card on the transition between Ronald Reagan and George H. W. Bush makes clear. When incumbents actively seek to hinder their successors, as Donald Trump did with Joe

Biden and Herbert Hoover did with Franklin Delano Roosevelt (FDR), the results are invariably negative. But when they do offer cooperation, as did George W. Bush with Barack Obama, the country reaps enormous dividends. The transition is one area of politics in which opponents really must leave their swords at the door.

THOSE WHO thought the Bush-to-Obama handoff would solidify cooperation as a model were disappointed in 2016—and horrified four years later. Thankfully, the bumpy Trump transitions in and out of office represent only half the story. Between November 2020 and January 2021, while turmoil played out in the White House and on Capitol Hill, perhaps the best-organized, best-resourced, and most experienced transition team in history guided President-elect Biden into office. Biden's team, led by Ted Kaufman, Jeff Zients, and Yohannes Abraham, was bolstered by a flurry of Partnership-backed, bipartisan amendments passed by Congress during the 2010s that created stronger government support for transitions earlier in the process.

The presidential transition process therefore stands at a critical juncture. What will future transitions look like? Orderly and by the book, or chaotic and lawless? The answer remains to be seen, but the choices legislators and federal officials make over the next few years will determine the future of this most vital of institutions. The better informed we all are, the more positive the outcome will be.

Ever since George Washington chose to leave office at the end of his second term, the peaceful transfer of power has been a jewel in the crown of American democracy. Nothing should ever threaten that legacy again. As we will see repeatedly in the pages to follow, the stakes are simply too high.

Notes

1. Kevin Freking, "Trump Tweets Words 'He Won'; Says Vote Rigged, Not Conceding," *AP News*, November 16, 2020, https://apnews.com/article/donald-trump-tweets-he-won-not-conceding-9ce22e9dc90577f7365d150c151a91c7.
2. Martha Joynt Kumar, *Before the Oath: How George W. Bush and Barack Obama Managed a Transfer of Power* (Baltimore, MD: Johns Hopkins University Press, 2015).

3. *Romney Readiness Project 2012: Retrospective & Lessons Learned* (Los Angeles, CA: R2P, Inc., 2013).

4. Michael Lewis, *The Fifth Risk: Undoing Democracy* (New York: Norton, 2018).

5. John P. Burke, *Presidential Transitions: From Politics to Practice* (Boulder, CO: Lynne Rienner, 2000); Carl M. Brauer, *Presidential Transitions: Eisenhower through Reagan* (New York: Oxford University Press, 1986).

6. *Washingtonian* staff, "Guest List," December 2, 2020, https://www.washingtonian.com/2020/12/02/guest-list-2/.

7. Alice Miranda Ollstein, Alex Thompson, and Theodoric Meyer, "How Biden's Covid Bubble Popped," December 18, 2020, https://www.politico.com/newsletters/transition-playbook/2020/12/18/how-bidens-covid-bubble-popped-491200.

PART I

HISTORY

Presidential Transitions in Historical Context

KEN BURNS AND GEOFFREY WARD

> We have had an unbroken succession of presidential administrations. No troops have been alerted. Nobody has fought. They may have gone unhappily, but they've gone.
>
> —Ken Burns, May 22, 2020

> We are in totally unprecedented territory. There has been nothing like this before.
>
> —Ken Burns, November 22, 2020

AT THE height of the COVID-19 pandemic and in the run-up to the 2020 election, I asked historian Geoffrey Ward what history could teach us about the moment in which we found ourselves. "The vital importance of national leadership," he replied. "We need to define where we are and be assured things are going to go well and we have a plan."

What qualities does a president (or president-elect) need in order to lead in times of crisis? Documentarians Ken Burns and Geoffrey Ward—the two are longtime collaborators and no strangers to the crunch points and key personalities in American history—set out at least four.

First, they must be unifiers, able to communicate with equal parts eloquence and empathy.

Second, they must be masters of politics—in other words, command the tools of persuasion and maneuver necessary to achieve a vision in the real world.

Third, they must understand history without being shackled to its precedents; for as Burns puts it, "if you are going to apply strictly all the lessons of the past, you will exacerbate the problem."

Fourth, and above all, they must present their vision with optimism and supreme self-confidence, summed up in Lincoln's absolute conviction, at the outbreak of the Civil War, that the "chorus of Union" would swell once more in America.

Over his four-decade career, Burns has made more than thirty documentaries, ranging from *Baseball* to *The Civil War*, and earned countless awards.

Like millions of Americans, I had been a huge fan of Ken Burns for years. In May 2020, as we realized COVID-19 was creating a leadership crisis in the White House as well as a humanitarian tragedy for our country, we could think of nobody better to help put the moment in historical perspective.

Burns invited Ward to join him in our interview. Like Burns, Ward has enjoyed a spectacular career as an interpreter of history. Besides writing nineteen books, he has served as the sole or principal writer for *The Civil War*, *Baseball*, *Thomas Jefferson*, and almost a dozen other films, earning himself two Writers Guild Awards, seven Christopher Awards, and seven Emmys.

In order to prepare, my team and I decided to rewatch around twenty hours of Burns documentaries, looking for parallels to the current tumult, with our simultaneous crises in public health, the economy, racial injustice, and politics. Several of Burns's films, including *The Civil War*, *Baseball*, *The Roosevelts*, and *The Vietnam War*, provided illuminating historical analogues.

We taped our first interview with Burns and Ward two months after the country shut down for the pandemic, at a time when Americans were still wiping groceries with Clorox and letting mail sit for twenty-four hours before opening it. No vaccine had been developed. Indeed, no one really understood the disease. The moment reminded me of the panics over polio that had swept America during the first half of the twentieth century, as described in the Burns and Ward film *The Roosevelts*. I watched and rewatched one remarkable moment in episode 4 when Burns broke one of his own unspoken filmmaking rules by putting Ward, the writer, on camera. Ward, himself a polio sufferer, broke down in tears as he described how it felt to be suddenly paralyzed by a dreaded illness.

In addition to the obvious parallels to the fear and tragedy in those early days of the COVID-19 pandemic, the footage of Ward spoke to another central theme of our conversation: Franklin Roosevelt's own experience of contracting polio at the age of thirty-nine proved the catalyst for his transformation from patrician playboy to an exceptional politician with seemingly unending humility and empathy—two qualities that Burns and Ward identify as essential for great leaders in times of transition.

Ultimately, while not blind to our divisions, Burns expressed an optimistic view of the future, inspired by Lincoln's famous confidence in the "better angels of our nature." The next time I interviewed Burns, seven months later, he saw things a little differently. By then, in addition to a spike in COVID-19 cases and a national reckoning with racial injustice, we had reached the height of the constitutional crisis over President Trump's refusal to accept the election result. Given all the horrors of history he has documented in his career, I assumed nothing could surprise him anymore. I was wrong. The differences in Burns's tone, as readers will see below, spoke volumes.

Eventually, of course, President-elect Biden, the winner of the election, took office. The chain of transition, unbroken since George Washington, remained intact. Our institutions were strained, not sundered. But as Burns warned in our second conversation, the Civil War never really ended; we just found different ways to fight each other. It still remains to be seen whether "normal" politics can be restored.

"They may have gone unhappily, but they've gone"

DAVID MARCHICK (DM): [With the onset of COVID-19 pandemic and the nation's shutdown,] we're in the biggest crisis our country has faced maybe since World War II today. What can history teach us about the moment we find ourselves in?

GEOFFREY WARD (GW): The vital importance of national leadership.

DM: Just expand upon that, Geoff.

GW: We don't do well without it. We need to define where we are and be assured things are going to go well and have a plan. I think that that was the great gift of Franklin Roosevelt. I think it's essential to our health and survival.

DM: Is there a historical corollary to today? What's the greatest parallel in U.S. history to what we're facing today?

GW: I'm always a little uneasy with parallels, but I suppose 1933 and 1861.

DM: This is the third-biggest crisis our country is facing? That's incredible. We're going to talk about those two presidential transitions, from Buchanan to Lincoln and from Hoover to Roosevelt. But let's talk about presidential transitions in general. Ken, we were talking earlier this week, and I was lamenting how presidential transitions are never perfect. They always have problems. And you had a more optimistic view. So, what's your view on how historical presidential transitions have gone in the United States?

KEN BURNS (KB): First, let me just echo that I agree completely with what Geoff said. This crisis is on the level of the Second World War, but particularly the Depression and the Civil War. As Lincoln predicted in his first inauguration, we would not be attacked by other people. An early speech that he gave actually said that the danger didn't come from without, but from within, and now that's literally, medically, epidemiologically true, but also politically and socially true. So this is as great a crisis as we've had.

Let's step back a little bit and celebrate that since 1797, when George Washington gave up the presidency after two terms and John Adams took over, we have had an unbroken succession of presidential administrations. No troops have been alerted. Nobody has fought. They may have gone unhappily, but they've gone. I'm not sure that it's guaranteed in the future, but at least until this moment, the very fact, unique in human history, is that we've had this unbroken chain of transitions.

When you step back, that's terrific. Human beings, as Thomas Jefferson said, are wont to suffer tyrannies, and we decided not to. We created a government unbelievably imperfect in its scope and understanding, and yet, for more than 230 years, we have been able to hand off the ball without a single fumble. That's amazing. Let's celebrate that.

"One magnificent, poetic sentence"

DM: Let's go to what Geoff said was the last big moment like today. Lincoln wins in 1860. There's a four-month interregnum, and in those four months, seven states secede. That's a pretty big problem that Lincoln faced. What was he doing during those four months to actually prepare to take the presidency?

GW: He had a unique problem. Seven states had seceded. There was another president, Jefferson Davis, and another government. This is when we came as close as we ever did to breaking. It was essential to him that he not make more states secede, that is to say, not make things worse. Buchanan was paralyzed, unable to do anything. He was just living in the White House. It was nothing. Lincoln was accomplishing nothing and really couldn't do anything until he got there. He had no wiggle room. He won a minority of less than 40 percent of the vote. He couldn't compromise at all one way or other on that. So, in one sense, he's the most eloquent man saying very little that we've almost ever had. There's a wonderful new book by Ted Widmer called *Lincoln on the Verge,* which is just about that train trip he took during the transition as he moved to Washington. Anybody who wants to know about that should read that extraordinary book. [The following interview in this volume is with Ted Widmer.]

DM: Jefferson Davis took office in February of that year. It took Lincoln four months to take office. Was Buchanan just doing nothing to ease Lincoln's entrance into office?

KB: Nothing at all; the nonactor here is Buchanan. Up until recently, many historians viewed him as the worst president ever. And what's amazing is that by the time Lincoln is up there getting his inauguration, there are really nine states, soon to be eleven, that are going to join the Confederacy. He's got a job in that first inaugural address to remind people of why they cohere. And one of the greatest things is . . . he looked out on the mostly southerners there and said: "We must not be enemies. Though passion may have strained, it must not break our bonds of affection."

And then he says this unbelievable, stupefying sentence, the most poetic sentence I know that he ever wrote. Realizing that they still share this revolutionary past in common, he said, "The mystic chords of memory, stretching from every battlefield and patriot grave to every living heart and hearthstone all over this broad land, will yet swell the chorus of the Union, when again touched, as surely they will be, by the better angels of our nature."

In one magnificent poetic sentence, he described exactly what was going to happen. He described what good leadership was about, and he showed empathy, which we'll find is a key ingredient. Do I understand how someone else feels? Not just my supporters, not just the dead, but what do the people on the other side understand and do? That's the transition, right there. It is a magnificent job of discipline and attention that saved our country.

GW: In addition to his astonishing eloquence and the empathy that Ken describes, he was a master politician. I contend that whenever we've had a serious crisis, the people who save us are people who understand politics and see it as the honorable profession that it is. Lincoln liked to say, "I don't know much about how things are done in politics," but it was a pose. He had furious ambition and an ingenious way of figuring out how to defang his enemies. Doris Goodwin wrote a very good book, *Team of Rivals,* on Lincoln's cabinet, but no other president has ever had the supreme self-confidence that that man had. To say to these guys, all of whom hate me and whom I beat out at the convention, which they still don't understand, I'm going to make them serve the greater cause of our country. And he persuaded all of them to do it. Those are incredibly rare gifts, and they are essential to being a great president.

DM: What in his youth or his upbringing—he had a lot of suffering and hardship—what do you think gave him both that steely spine and that empathy that made him such a great leader?

KB: I've always said that all of biography—indeed all of history—is failure. Because even those people closest to us in our own lives remain in some degree inscrutable. How do we presume to get into the minds and the hearts of people who lived a hundred, two hundred, three hundred, five hundred, a thousand years ago and accurately bring them back? We can't. But we're still nonetheless obligated to strive. What you feel in Lincoln, the loss of a mother, the steely resolve at education, the masterful early days as a lawyer, the eloquence that comes from Shakespeare and the Bible, and the ability to speak, as someone said, "With the bark on." He understood how ordinary folks on the frontier spoke, and that kind of humor gave him a relationship to the inscrutable ways of life that combined with that ambition.

"He came to this job with this extraordinary optimistic spirit"

DM: Let's move to another great president and another crisis [in our country], the Hoover-to-FDR transition. At that time, the country faced a deep crisis [the Great Depression], political polarization, a debate over the role of the states, and the question was, would Roosevelt rise to the task? Roosevelt is elected in November, but he doesn't take office until March 5. What is he doing during this time to take over and be ready?

GW: I've done four books on him and this film, and I think about him all the time because he's so impenetrable and so fascinating. He, like Lincoln, is mysterious. He's a very different kind of person. He came to this job with this extraordinary optimistic spirit, the quality of empathy, and a supreme self-confidence. He really believed that if he was in charge of whatever he was in charge of, it was going to work out fine. Herbert Hoover was the opposite of that. He was a grim person. It's not fair to say paralyzed, but certainly reluctant to use federal power in this crisis.

Hoover believed that by principle, a lot of things should not be done so that everything could shake out, which ignored the plight of millions of people without jobs and whose bank deposits were threatened and so on.

Hoover was determined to make Roosevelt sign on to his policies. FDR was just as determined not to do so. So FDR prepared a program. He accepted the fact that there was nothing he could do until he took power, and he refused to get lured into signing on to things in which he did not believe. It was an extraordinary performance. There are people who think somehow, and certainly Hoover thought that somehow, it was irresponsible. I don't see how he could have done anything other than what he did.

DM: Do you think that the fact that they didn't work together, that they didn't collaborate, did that extend the depth of the crisis and slow the recovery?

GW: I don't think so, because I don't think there was any way you could compromise the two sets of policies they had. The other element in this is just a personal one. They couldn't stand each other, and that made it more difficult. Roosevelt blamed Hoover for an event which probably wasn't really his fault. In the spring of '32, when Roosevelt was hoping to persuade the Democratic Party to nominate him, there was a gathering of the nation's governors at the White House. The Roosevelts arrived a little early because of the difficulty FDR had in walking. It's a long way to the East Room, and he ended up having to stand up for half an hour. He and Mrs. Roosevelt, probably not publicly, but later in a book, pretty much said that they thought Hoover had done that to him on purpose. I don't think that's true, but there was a lot of personal animus between the two of them. Hoover thought Roosevelt was a lightweight and a second-rate person and insincere, and he called him a comedian in plaid.

DM: Ken, you've done a lot of work on the combination of Roosevelt's upbringing, the fact that he was on top of the world and then, at age thirty-nine, struck with polio. How did that episode and that disease impact who he was and his development of empathy?

KB: I think you've hit the jackpot right there. That's one of the keys. He does remain, as Geoff said, inscrutable and kind of opaque and impossible to understand. But the main question is, how is this to-the-manor-born, pampered, only son—who could do anything, who was handsome and athletic and kind of rather thin and not substantive, suddenly stricken at age thirty-nine with infantile paralysis and never walks unaided again in his life—able somehow to get us through the two great crises?

FDR and Lincoln are tied for number one in terms of the greats. You can disagree with their policies. You can disagree with how they did. Both of them made huge and glaring mistakes, but a sign of their leadership was their willingness to accept those mistakes, to acknowledge them publicly, to take the blame, to have the buck stop with them and to move on and try something else. It's extraordinary. And if you think about the empathy embodied in Lincoln's first inaugural sentence that I cited, and then you've listened to the first "fireside chat" [a format FDR used to address the nation over the radio], people actually got up and put their money back in the banks because some disembodied voice of a patrician who couldn't walk made them think that he knew them as well as anyone knew them.

GW: When you look at them, Lincoln and Roosevelt seem very different. But there are things that are similar. One of them is absolute mastery of politics, of how to persuade people of things, of how to educate people to what they needed to do, what the country needed to do. But they are both truly opaque human beings. They're both undersold by the people who knew them when they were young, who never could quite get used to the fact that they were great men.

The other thing is they both had a great political trait, which was that when people went into their office to try to persuade them of something, they were capable, because they knew what they wanted to do, of making those people think they agreed with them. It is startling to me to read accounts of people who went into Lincoln's office, convinced *they* had convinced Lincoln of something he didn't want to be convinced of. Exactly the same thing happened with Roosevelt. I think it's part of political skill. There's a story about empathy. There's a way of nodding and smiling when people talk which makes the visitor think that the president has been enlisted in their cause. It isn't necessarily true, but he has heard them out. It's great in getting what you want done.

DM: Hoover famously met with Roosevelt after the election, and he thought he had convinced Roosevelt to kind of give up on many of the New Deal policies because Roosevelt nodded and grinned.

GW: That's right. And also because he really thought Roosevelt was a playboy lightweight. He had seen him when he was young, when he was some of those things. And Roosevelt smiled and said, "That's interesting." And Hoover thought he was persuaded. He was not persuaded.

"As much as you want to study history, at some point all great leaders have let it go"

DM: Let's move to another crisis, which was the Vietnam War. Many people say this was one of the most divisive times ever in our country. But looking at your film series on Vietnam, it almost doesn't compare [in severity to the Civil War period]. So how do you compare the two periods in terms of the divisiveness in the country?

KB: Well, I think you're right. Neither of them—that is to say, this moment right now and the Vietnam period—compare to the Civil War.

I think it's really important that Lincoln made the warning as a young lawyer that we would not be attacked by someone else. He understood that the Atlantic and the Pacific Ocean and two relatively benign neighbors to our north and south insulated the United States in ways that no other large and important country has ever been insulated. Unfortunately, the things that it incubates that are positive, like freedom and this kind of curiousness and restlessness and entrepreneurial spirit, have concurrent, darker things.

It is very fashionable to say that history repeats itself. It never, ever, has. Ever. Mark Twain is supposed to have said, and if he said it, it's a great comment, "History doesn't repeat itself, but it rhymes." And I think Geoff and I have been at this long enough that we know that every time we finish a film, whether it's Prohibition, Vietnam, the Roosevelts, the Civil War, every film we made rhymes in the present. And so you begin to realize that human nature isn't changing, and we're dealing with the various good and bad and in-between parts of human nature equally. It's funny: as much as you want to study history, you have to realize that at some point all great leaders have let it go.

Lincoln said in his message to Congress, in what we'd call the State of the Union: "The dogmas of the quiet past are inadequate to the stormy present. As our case is new, we must think anew and act anew. We must disenthrall ourselves and then we shall save our country." Each great crisis requires someone in the highest office of the land curious about history, but also one realizing that if you are going to apply strictly all the lessons of the past, you will exacerbate the problem. It's a funny conundrum, and the greatest leaders have been able to resolve it. The greatest leaders have all been great readers and students of history. That's a pretty interesting fact that we can all, as we think about transitions, come to understand.

DM: Based on everything you've said and how history rhymes but doesn't repeat itself, should we be optimistic, pessimistic, or should we be just downright depressed today?

KB: George Will said about Franklin Roosevelt as he was assuming the mantle, he was armed with "a Christian's faith that the universe is well constituted and an American's faith that history is a rising road." Despite all the facts that show how selfish, how greedy, how divisive we can be, we also have these examples of how generous, how empathetic, how self-sacrificing we can be.

Could there be a profession, anything nobler than being a nurse today? It's not a captain of industry, it's a nurse. The captains of industry are hiding in their mansions. It's a nurse who gets on the subway or the bus and goes into trouble. Just as we ask ourselves, "Why did somebody go off in June 1944 with no conquest or no material reward in mind, only an idea to liberate Europe?" We have got the opportunity here to press a kind of reset button about our values. As a student of history and a storyteller, I feel always optimistic, but I am not Pollyannaish. I know that there are great threats and great difficulties at any moment, and we are filled with opportunity as much as we are filled with threat. And it is my fervent hope that we Americans choose the path toward finding a way to have a reset in a very new and spectacular way. Just as the other crises—the Civil War, the Depression, and World War II—they have to be seen together. Now, I hope this provides us with the opportunity to re-create something.

"We are in totally unprecedented territory"

DM: We are releasing this podcast on November 23, 2020. Polls closed three weeks ago tomorrow. The networks called the race sixteen days ago. Unfortunately, the General Services Administration—typically a highly professional, nonpolitical agency, one which did an overall great job on transition planning before the election—has not "ascertained" the "apparent winner" under the 1963 Presidential Transition Act. The formal launch of handoff is stalled.

Ken Burns, is there an analogy in U.S. history to what we're seeing today in the United States?

KB: Definitely not. We are in totally unprecedented territory. There has been nothing like this before. The extraordinary record of the United States, since its founding—to be able to hand off to each new administration smoothly, more or less, the workings of government—has been one of the signal testaments to the strength of our Republic. All of that is being undermined. All of that is being tested and called into question now.

I'm beginning to see, with the crisis that we've been in for most of the last four years [of the Trump presidency] combined with the overlay of COVID combined with a reckoning with our 401-year-old virus called racial injustice, we are in a kind of perfect storm that in some ways outranks, in terms of the fragility of this machine, the Second World War, the Great Depression, and even the Civil War.

DM: Let's look back on history at both successful handoffs and fumbles and the implications of those successes and failures on the country. How do you see those in the past affecting what you see today?

KB: It begins with George Washington giving up his military commission. It begins with George Washington saying two terms, that's it, I'm gone. The next interesting moment happens when John Adams, after one term, presumes that he'll be like his mentor and be able to have two terms. But Thomas Jefferson, another student and disciple of George Washington, says no. And so, they're at loggerheads. But as it turns out, they end up tied in electoral votes. Adams and another candidate of the Federalists end up distant third and fourth. Tied are Thomas Jefferson and Aaron Burr. Alexander Hamilton, who is diametrically opposed to everything that Jefferson and Burr represent, nonetheless realizes that Jefferson is the true patriot. He urges the Federalists to throw their support toward Jefferson, lest somebody as unqualified as Burr should get it. What you have is somebody subsuming their own self-interests, their own political inclinations, for the greater good.

In the election of 1876, Samuel Tilden, the governor of New York, wins the popular vote, but Rutherford B. Hayes becomes president. He's from Ohio. And the reason is that two electors in Florida—I can't make this up—changed their vote. But they changed their vote from the Democrat Tilden to Hayes, under the quid pro quo that all federal troops that have been enforcing Reconstruction are withdrawn from the South. Republicans made the first of many deals with the devil, meaning that, "We don't really have to care too much about the very reason why we formed as a party, which was the emancipation of the slave; we can be more interested in business and conquering the continent and that sort of thing." What happened is that Reconstruction collapsed; white supremacy was brutally reintroduced across the old Confederacy; Jim Crow was the law of the land; monuments were built for the first time to these southern generals; and the flag of the Ku Klux Klan—which was only one battle flag of the Army of Northern Virginia, not the flag of the Confederacy—starts working its way into state flags, first in Mississippi.

We all know the rest of the history. We postponed any addressing of civil rights for literally decades and decades.

You can think of Gore handing the presidency to Bush, despite the fact that some scholars believe that a recount would have produced a several-thousand-vote advantage to Gore in Florida had a recount actually happened. You have these moments where even though you're upset that you've lost, you've done something that was bigger than yourself for the Republic. I think what we're *not* seeing now is that impulse toward serving something bigger than yourself.

DM: At some point, this crisis will end, and the unbroken chain of smooth handoffs that started 223 years ago will continue. Looking ahead into 2050 or a hundred years, how will history record this moment?

KB: Well, from your lips to God's ears about that actually taking place. It has to happen first before we can then have a perspective back.

Lots of variables are involved. I made a film on the history of the Vietnam War. If I'd made it ten years after the fall of Saigon, in 1985 in the middle of a recession, when Japan was ascendant and America was losing its mojo, you would have thought that Vietnam was the ball and chain, the death knell of the American superpower. If you'd waited twenty years until 1995, in the middle of the greatest peacetime expansion we had had to date, when we were the sole superpower, Vietnam would seem important in terms of an event in the second half of the twentieth century, but just a blip in America's upward progress. If you'd waited thirty years to 2005, you've got wars in Iraq and Afghanistan, we're being bogged down, and there was asymmetrical terrorism that was going on.

Each generation rediscovers and reexamines that part of the past that gives their present meaning. Assuming this Republic survives, however fragile[ly] it is constituted going forward, it will be for those future years to look and find different aspects of this moment to report back.

DM: Let's assume the transition happens smoothly at some point in the next few days, how long will it take for the country to come together after this moment of fracture?

KB: There's one moment at Appomattox when a now defeated Confederate soldier comes up to a Union man and says: "This war is never over. I hate you, sir. I hate you." Clearly that has continued, as Barbara Fields, the Columbia University scholar, said in our film at the very last moment: "The Civil War is still going on. It's still being fought; and regrettably, it can still be lost."

However, I think that symbolism is hugely important, particularly with the office of the president. Just changing the tone, just changing the degree of empathy or listening, can be hugely great. Think of the transfer between the dour Herbert Hoover and Franklin Roosevelt. George Will told me in our Roosevelt series that the best of the Roosevelt New Deal programs was his smile. We think always when we talk about it, even in the most superficial context, that it's the fireside chats—infrequent, even though we think they were constant—that brought people into the intimacy of government.

It's finding a leader who knows how to subsume a lot of that in favor of erring on the side of the tensions of freedom, our number-one theme, right? There's what I want, personal freedom, as opposed to what we need, the kind of collective freedom. We've got to figure out a way to come back and devote ourselves in a spirit of civic engagement to the things bigger than ourselves. For most people, that just means your neighborhood, your town, whether your fire department needs a new pumper or whether you could wait another two years before you replace one. In other cases, it may be who do we let in the G7, what's our stand on the Paris Climate Accord, where are we with the Iran nuclear agreement. All of these are very, very complex things, but they're all essentially the same thing. They require a concerted collective American willpower. And if there are people who are making money and who are promoted by their promotion of divisiveness, then we've got a long road.

Buchanan to Lincoln: The Worst Transition in History

TED WIDMER

> We are so vulnerable at any transition, but we are especially vulnerable during a bad transition. The Founders didn't really tell us how to do a transition very well. Lincoln's transition showed just how fragile our country can be at times.
>
> —Ted Widmer

NO TRANSITION, before or since, has come close to the tribulations of 1860. During the interregnum, seven states seceded. James Buchanan, the outgoing president, was paralyzed by dysfunction and ill-disposed toward his successor. Members of Buchanan's cabinet joined the southern cause; several pressed for recognition of the Confederacy; Buchanan's treasury secretary called Abraham Lincoln "an enemy of the human race." Congress was torn apart by the same fault lines that divided the country.

In the midst of this turmoil, Lincoln embarked on a momentous journey from his home in Springfield, Illinois, to Washington, DC. This thirteen-day train ride was, in a very real sense, Lincoln's transition. Whereas during the campaign, as was customary at the time, Lincoln had given no real speeches, during the trip to Washington he gave more than one hundred. He found his voice—and his resolve to keep the country together. Having been elected with less than 40 percent of the vote—the second-smallest margin in history—he now developed and galvanized a base of support among people and politicians. He even transitioned his appearance, growing a beard.

Lincoln's crowds were among the largest the country had ever seen. Ten thousand people showed up in the small town of Springfield, Illinois, where Lincoln gave his famous farewell address. In tiny Line, Indiana, the *Chicago Tribune* reported that Lincoln's speech drew three times the town's population.[1] The crowds continued to swell over the journey: 75,000 in Buffalo; 150,000 in Cincinnati. In New York City, a quarter million people watched Lincoln's procession.

While he avoided traveling through southern states like Virginia—the sheer number of death threats he received made that impossible—Lincoln stopped in southern-leaning areas of the North. In places like Cincinnati, which lies on the Ohio River, one of the traditional borders between North and South, Lincoln spoke directly to southerners in respectful, conciliatory tones. His words were picked up by southern newspapers and read across the South, helping to convince border states like Kentucky to remain in the Union.

Lincoln also made pilgrimages to various state capitals in the North, knowing that if a war broke out, he would be dependent on the legislatures and governors to raise troops. Here, too, Lincoln used the transition period to anticipate the challenges of the coming months and years. These actions helped ensure that the president-elect who arrived in Washington that March was far stronger than the one who had left Springfield.

More than fifteen thousand books have been written on Lincoln, but the more I spoke to historians on the *Transition Lab* podcast, the more I was told that I had to read one in particular: Ted Widmer's *Lincoln on the Verge: Thirteen Days to Washington.*[2] When I sat down to read it, I understood why.

Ted Widmer is currently a professor of American history at Macaulay Honors College, but he was not always an academic. A few years after receiving a Ph.D. from Harvard in American history, Widmer took a position in the Clinton White House, serving as a foreign policy speechwriter and advisor. He has retained a speechwriter's love of language ever since. Analyzing Lincoln's rhetoric during the transition, Widmer uncovers glimpses of the policy direction the Lincoln presidency would eventually take. For example, Widmer sees Lincoln's discussion of the American Revolution's fundamental ideals in these speeches as presaging Lincoln's soon-to-be-developed argument about the moral necessity of ending slavery.

Widmer's book is an account of an extraordinary transition, taking place when the country was literally being torn apart. As exceptional as it was, however, the 1860–61 transition bears several lessons for the future.

First, personnel choices made during a transition are critical. In Lincoln's case, his appointments reflected the diverse, unruly coalition that had brought him to office. He stopped in Pennsylvania to placate two squabbling political bosses of the state, giving one, Simon Cameron, the position of secretary of war. Other appointments, like that of Secretary of State William Seward, a former rival for the Republican presidential nomination, were also made during the transition. These choices were to have lasting consequences: Cameron would be fired after a tenure marked by damaging corruption and scandal, whereas Seward would become one of Lincoln's closest and most influential advisors.

Second, transitions represent periods of vulnerability. While the United States has never again faced a national security threat comparable to the Civil War, the confusion inherent to transitions creates incentives for adversaries to move against the United States. In Lincoln's case, his personal safety was in just as much jeopardy as that of the country. Several assassination plots surfaced during the transition, leading Lincoln to abandon his presidential express in Harrisburg, Pennsylvania, and hop on the equivalent of a commuter train, entering Washington under cover of darkness, dressed as an average American.

Third, collaboration between outgoing and incoming administrations can help mitigate the vulnerabilities created by transitions. There was little such collaboration during the Buchanan to Lincoln handoff—at least formally. The more responsible senior officials, like Edwin Stanton, Buchanan's attorney general, helped keep the government—and the country—together. The role played by these officials, even as the outgoing president dithered and toyed with disbanding the Union, underlines the stabilizing role senior officials can play during a transition.

For Widmer, the Buchanan-to-Lincoln transition had an impact far beyond the Civil War itself. In fact, Widmer sees Lincoln's choices as having shaped the whole of the twentieth century. Without Lincoln's successful effort to hold the border states in the Union, the North may well have lost the Civil War. And without a strong and unified America, the past 150 years would have played out very differently around the globe.

Counterfactuals inherently resist resolution; but it is inarguable that presidential transitions serve as a critical juncture in history, a moment of flux where political actors are granted an uncommon degree of freedom. Taking stock of these moments can offer deeper insights about our history and arm practitioners with the knowledge needed to take advantage of future opportunities.

"We are especially vulnerable during a bad transition"

DAVID MARCHICK (DM): Let's set the stage for this period. In 1860, Lincoln gets elected, and within days, southern states start seceding. What else is going on in the country at this moment?

TED WIDMER (TW): Well, it's a terrible transition. We are so vulnerable at any transition, but we are especially vulnerable during a bad transition. The Founders didn't really tell us how to do a transition very well. Lincoln's transition showed just how fragile our country can be at times.

He's elected on November 6, 1860, and he has a very small share of the vote: only 39.8 percent. It's the second-smallest plurality ever in our history. The South just goes ballistic. They start threatening to secede, and then they begin to actually secede. South Carolina is the first state to secede in December, and then six other states secede.

Lincoln is way out there in Illinois. He can't really control anything that's happening back in Washington. He certainly can't control anything in the southern states that have seceded. It's not clear what he is even the president of. It's a long wait from November 6 to March 4, which is when inaugurals were in the nineteenth century.

He's also got to put together a cabinet, and his coalition is not that coherent. There are people inside his coalition who don't like each other. Certain states, like Pennsylvania, are very divided. There are different factions in Pennsylvania, both of which want to be in Lincoln's cabinet. He's got to coordinate with people like William Seward, whom he's just defeated for the nomination, but now is a new ally. It's just all very dicey.

He also hasn't given a speech all year, basically. And then he's got to embark on this train trip, a train trip of almost two thousand miles. But as it turned out, the train trip was his deliverance from a lot of his problems. He found that being on the road on this train, he was able to speak a lot to the people, alleviate their concerns, and also give messages to southerners, saying: "Don't worry. I want to be a good president for you too." Even though those first seven states went out and wouldn't come back in, he kept the border states in the country long enough to get to Washington. That was actually a huge achievement.

DM: What was the Buchanan administration doing at this point? Was there any coordination with Buchanan?

TW: Very little. Buchanan is kind of a disaster right at this time. He has not been a very good president anyway. He's a northerner, he's from Pennsylvania, but he's completely allied with the Deep South. I mean, there are factions within the South, too, and he's always with the parts of the South that are the most pro-slavery. As the secession crisis approaches with Lincoln's election, and then the months after, Buchanan falls apart. He has pretty bad cabinet officers, and the most pro-southern ones start resigning. It turns out they've been guilty of a lot of corruption, also of embezzling funds or of secretly leaking U.S. government plans to the southern states that are about to secede or have seceded. They're really a pretty rotten bunch. And then Buchanan can't even make up his mind. He says vaguely pro-northern things when northerners are in the room, and he says very pro-southern things when southerners are in the room, and he basically loses the confidence of everyone. So, in addition to all of his other problems, Lincoln has to deal with the fact that the actual president is falling apart.

"He got off the train a much stronger president-elect"

DM: All hell is breaking loose, and Lincoln decides to take a train to Washington. But it wasn't just a trip directly to Washington. How did he choose the route?

TW: The book opens with a map inside the cover on the endpapers, and you can see right away: the route just goes so far out of its way. It goes all through the Midwest—and not in a straight line through the Midwest, either. And then it veers up into upstate New York and then comes down through New York City and New Jersey and Pennsylvania, Philadelphia, then shoots out to central Pennsylvania, before doubling back.

The first reason for this route is that it felt dangerous to go through the southern states. To go from Springfield to Washington directly, you would have to go through Virginia, and Lincoln didn't feel like that was a great idea. And he didn't feel like going through Kentucky was a great idea either, even though he was born in Kentucky. It just didn't feel safe. It felt unsafe politically because those places are wrestling with whether or not to secede. And it felt unsafe to his person because there are just so many public threats of violence from southerners to him. But, as he goes on this winding route, it turns out to be pretty fortunate that this is the route he chooses.

I talk a lot in the book about how different every state was. The South isn't all one place, and the North isn't either. Even within a state, you get a lot of differences. In Illinois, Indiana, and Ohio there were differences between the southern part of the state and the northern part of the state, as you might expect. The southern parts are much more sympathetic to the South, and Lincoln shrewdly goes into some southern parts of midwestern states. Cincinnati, for instance, is in southern Ohio. It's right on the Ohio River, which is the boundary there between the North and the South. And he has a really good visit in Cincinnati; he has a lot of friends there. He speaks to Kentuckians in a really compelling way about how much he respects them. Those speeches are heard. They're printed in the papers and read by southerners. I think they do a lot of good, actually.

At the same time, he's also going through state capitals. That's important because he needs the support of every governor and legislature. Presidents had much less power then. If there was going to be a war, which we all know there was, he was going to need help from the governors to raise troops. One of the big changes of the Civil War by the end of the war, the federal government is doing that because it's much more effective. And that's one of the many ways Lincoln really kind of reinvents the presidency.

DM: There were several interesting things about the train trip. One is that he really seems to have found his voice. As you mentioned, he really didn't give speeches during the campaign. But on this trip, he gave over a hundred speeches. How did those speeches and his message affect what he would do as president?

TW: Back then, if you were a candidate for the presidency, you were expected to stay at home and not speak. So, he does speak in the beginning of 1860. But then he gets the nomination in May, and he just clams up. He stops speaking.

There's one awkward moment in August where he's sort of dragged out in public and forced to say a few words, and they're not very interesting words. He basically says, "I don't want to give a speech," but technically it was a speech. And then no more speeches until he's elected in November.

But then, once he gets on the train on February 11, 1861, he gives an extraordinary speech, a farewell to his friends and neighbors in Springfield. A very short speech, probably only about one minute long. But it really humanized him for a national audience that did not yet know him. He talked about his sadness about leaving his small town, how much he loves the people he's lived among, how he's raised his children there and has buried one child there. It's just a very moving and nonbombastic speech by a neighbor saying goodbye to his neighbors. It was telegraphed around the country, appeared in all the newspapers the next day, and did him a lot of good because he'd been described inconsistently by some people as a sort of tyrant, and by others as a buffoon, someone who lacked education, and by giving that speech he just appeared like a normal guy. Someone you would want to get to know.

Over the course of the thirteen days of speeches on the train, he just keeps getting better. He gives a lot of them, a lot of impromptu speeches. He can't keep up. He tried to write some speeches out ahead of time, but there's so many stops, he just has to speak impromptu. As he gets closer to Philadelphia, he begins to talk very beautifully about his memories of reading books as a young boy about what America stands for. It's about the brave men who fought in the American Revolution, but even more it's about the idealism of this country and freedom. All of it built up into a very emotional and very persuasive argument that America is better than slavery, that America really stands for a moral principle at home and around the world. By the end of the trip, it's only been thirteen days, but he's really pretty close to the Gettysburg Address, which he'll give in 1863.

DM: Another thing that was extraordinary about this trip was the crowds. Can you just describe the crowds and how large they were and how those crowds affected his public support?

TW: He had absolutely huge crowds in every place he passed through. In the large cities like New York, he had a quarter million people. Even today that would be an extremely large crowd. And in many cities or small towns, fifty thousand or one hundred thousand people would come out. Often two or three times the actual population of the town would be there. Everyone was coming in from the surrounding countryside to see him. People would stand by the track in farmland just for the chance to look at his face or wave to him when he went by. Some of that was fear. Fear about where the country was heading and fear of a war that was imminent. A lot of it was just immense curiosity to see someone who'd gone from near-total nonentity to the biggest celebrity in America.

But he was a strange kind of a celebrity because no one really knew what he thought, or even very well what he looked like. And his appearance is changing. He's growing a beard at exactly this moment. It's the most dramatic change in how a president-elect looked in any transition that I'm aware of. He's in transition as the country is in transition. And everyone's just dying of curiosity to see what he looks like.

DM: One of the things you say is that Lincoln transformed the country with these crowds. He only got 39 percent of the vote, he only won a small number of states, but his trip helped win over the people and converted a lot of the people that voted against him.

TW: I think he got off the train a much stronger president-elect than he was when he got on the train. Part of that is he shored up his own party, which was pretty disorganized. More than 40 percent of the North is behind him by the time he gets to Washington, and a lot of people who didn't vote for Lincoln still want him to have his chance to be president. They believe in fair play. He says over and over again to people, "I'm aware that my election has caused a lot of controversy, but the genius of our system is if for any reason I screw up, you can just vote me out in four years." That's impressive to people, and they form a deeper attachment to him. A lot of people who didn't vote for him wanted him to survive his train trip. They wanted him to survive his first year and ultimately his entire term as president.

"The simple act of his arriving made his presidency possible"

DM: Let's turn to what we would currently call a transition. Had Lincoln already selected most of his cabinet by this time?

TW: He was getting there, but not all of them. He had a big mess in Pennsylvania that he had to sort out, which included two different bosses of the state. They didn't like each other. But the man who had done a lot to deliver Pennsylvania into his column, which was crucial both for his nomination to be the candidate for the Republican Party and then for his election, was a guy named Simon Cameron. One of the reasons Lincoln has to go to Harrisburg at the end of his trip is he's got to placate the two sides of Pennsylvania politics who hate each other. The governor is a guy named Andrew Curtin who hates Simon Cameron, but Lincoln has decided that he's going to offer the position of secretary of war, which is an incredibly important position, to Cameron.

DM: In Washington, things were just frozen, and Buchanan was considering recognizing the Confederacy. How did Lincoln's speeches and building of public support affect what Buchanan was doing in Washington?

TW: That's another kind of a miracle for which we should all be grateful. It's not simply that Lincoln made it. While we usually begin the history of his presidency with the first day being his inauguration, I argue that it was kind of a miracle that he made it to the first day. But it was really important that Buchanan, this pro-southern president from the North, not recognize the Confederacy. It was important for the winning of the Civil War that the South be regarded by Lincoln and by European powers as a kind of renegade group of rebels, or traitors, or anything short of a legitimate government. Fortunately, Buchanan stopped just short of that.

One reason, I think, is that in December, in the middle of this transition, all of the financial corruption of the pro-southern part of his cabinet was revealed. Three of the southerners in his cabinet resigned. That suddenly tilted the balance of that cabinet to being pro-northern. A really important guy at that moment is Edwin Stanton, who's going to be Lincoln's secretary of war [after Simon Cameron]. He's attorney general under Buchanan, and he plays an important role holding it together until Lincoln can get there.

DM: Let's go to the most important plot in this book. Lincoln has a couple of people around him—one's named Pinkerton—doing intelligence gathering around the country. They uncover a plot in Baltimore to kill Lincoln. Tell us about that.

TW: Lots of people wanted to kill Lincoln. You can read southern newspapers from the fall of 1860, the winter of 1861. It's a lot of people issuing taunts about violence to Lincoln, or threats like "he will never make it to Washington."

There is a very interesting woman named Dorothea Dix. She's from New England, but she's accepted in the southern states because she's done a lot of good work in them. She's a mental health advocate, and she's helped northern and southern states build hospitals for mentally handicapped people. She knows people in every state. She gets to Washington at the end of 1860—she actually goes even farther north, to Philadelphia—and she finds the head of a railroad called the Philadelphia, Wilmington, and Baltimore Railroad. And she goes to that executive and says: "There is a serious plot to kill Abraham Lincoln when he comes over your train line into Washington. I have to tell you this, I know all the details. I know where they're going to try to do it." That man, named Samuel Felton, wrote down a record of his conversation with her. And based on that conversation, he sent for a railroad detective, Allan Pinkerton. They began a kind of *Mission: Impossible* sting of the would-be assassins, who are mainly in Baltimore but also a little bit in northern Maryland along the train route. They act like southerners, and they infiltrate the killers. They find out all the details, and they report back to Lincoln's entourage as Lincoln is en route on the train.

So he's giving these beautiful speeches about democracy, but every night he's getting this intelligence that he may not make it to his capital. It's an incredibly dramatic moment. I didn't fully understand it when I started the book, but at the end, I was just like, "Wow, could this have been any more dramatic for a president in transition, with all of these hurdles he's got to get over?" But he does it.

DM: Lincoln has this train, called the Special. It's a presidential train. Then he's in Harrisburg having dinner with the governor at the governor's mansion, and he slips out the back door. What does he do from there, and how does he get to Washington, and how did his plans change?

TW: Only on the last day, they dramatically changed his plan. Pinkerton, with help from a couple of railroad executives, arranged a secret train. Lincoln goes out the back door in Harrisburg, like you said, and he put on a different kind of a hat and a different kind of a coat than his traditional top hat, I guess a sort of a soft hat and a pea jacket, those blue jackets that sailors wear. He was not in disguise, which is important to say because his critics later accused him of going in disguise, maybe as a woman or maybe as a Scottish person with a kilt. He didn't do that; he dressed like an ordinary guy. He was later described as looking like a farmer by someone who saw him get off the train.

He went on a secret, tiny train from Harrisburg to Philadelphia. And he got off that train in the middle of the night in Philadelphia and boarded the last train from Philadelphia to Washington that was going to go through Baltimore. So that was the train that would take him through what was called the "seat of danger" by the reports from the spies. He just sat there with three people. Allan Pinkerton was one, an old friend of his named Ward Lamon was another, and a female spy called Kate Warne, who was incredibly brave throughout the story. The four of them sat in an ordinary compartment on the late-night train from Philadelphia through Baltimore to Washington. Warne got off at Baltimore, but the others went all the way to the end. Lincoln got off at dawn in Washington. That's where an old friend named Elihu Washburn was waiting for him and said he just looked like a well-to-do Illinois farmer, sort of coming into Washington for the first time. The simple act of his arriving made his presidency possible.

"Everyone is included, and that is the core of Lincoln's message"

DM: You make the point in your book that this train trip and his sneaking into Washington is one of the most important events in all of American history. Not just in Lincoln's presidency, not just compared to the Civil War, but in all of American history. Why do you say that?

TW: The simple answer is: if he doesn't make it, his presidency doesn't happen, and the North probably loses the Civil War, in my opinion. But also, these thirteen days were so important for him developing a moral argument for America's greatness. That we're not just a large country and a power-ful country; we are a great country for our moral standards. That we have dared to declare human rights for all people, not only in our country, but all people on earth. That is what is claimed in the Declaration of Independence. Lincoln is remembering the Declaration and defending it with greater and greater eloquence on every day of this trip, and that culminates in his visit to Independence Hall, where the Declaration was signed, on the last full day of the trip. He gives an incredible speech there, talking about how he has never had a political sentiment that did not derive in some way from the Decla-ration of Independence. The obvious implication is African Americans are included, and in the fullness of time, women are included, and immigrants are included. Everyone is included, and that is the core of Lincoln's message.

Without him getting off the train, I don't think the North wins the Civil War. What does the twentieth century look like if America doesn't stand for human rights and democracy and the potential of women and the po-tential of all people from all racial and religious backgrounds to work out government together? What does the end of World War I look like? We tried for a League of Nations. We didn't succeed, but that effort was important. What does World War II look like, when the defense of democracy was one of the major resources in the arsenal of democracy that Franklin Roosevelt defined? The UN, even with all of its flaws, borrows a lot of American ideal-ism, and that idealism is still important. Maybe even more important in a world that has grown rather cynical.

Notes

1. Cited in Ted Widmer, *Lincoln on the Verge: Thirteen Days to Washington* (New York: Simon and Schuster, 2020), 261.
2. Widmer, *Lincoln on the Verge*.

Hoover to FDR: The Second-Worst Transition (before 2020-2021)

ERIC RAUCHWAY

> I became persuaded that the hundred or so days before Roosevelt took the oath of office for the first time were actually as important as the much more famous Hundred Days that came after.
>
> —Eric Rauchway

No STATES seceded in 1932 or 1933, but the four-month interregnum between Herbert Hoover and Franklin Delano Roosevelt was tumultuous nonetheless. At home, unemployment peaked. Banks failed. Across the Atlantic, Hitler came to power in Germany. Wartime allies defaulted on their debts. Farther afield, Imperial Japan quit the League of Nations, signaling a redoubling of belligerence in Asia.

Held in the long shadow of the Great Depression, the election of 1932 was a contest between the small-government policies pursued by Herbert Hoover and a "New Deal" being offered by the then governor of New York State, Franklin Delano Roosevelt. While its specific policy contours had not yet been defined, during the campaign Roosevelt had set out a basic agenda that would include new financial regulations, an aggressive public works program, support for farmers and unions, and legislation to create unemployment insurance and social security.[1]

Hoover had created—or acquiesced to—various government interventions in the economy, like the creation of the Reconstruction Finance Corporation, which doled out loans in support of banks and corporations. But he viewed FDR's New Deal as radical and dangerous.[2] In campaign speeches, Hoover argued that the centralized power created by FDR's proposed New Deal would endanger American liberty and do little to help the economy. Later, he would suggest that the New Deal would send the country "on a march to Moscow."[3]

After three long years of economic pain, however, the American people were ready for something different. On Election Day, more than forty million voters went to the polls, a new record. They came out overwhelmingly for Roosevelt; he won forty-two of the forty-eight states and beat Hoover by seven million ballots in the popular vote. As Rauchway notes in the introduction of *Winter War*, however, "The election did not decide the outcome of this contest, but only began it."[4]

In the spring of 2020, as the COVID-19 pandemic spread and unemployment numbers skyrocketed, the Center for Presidential Transition began to study what a transition in a crisis would look like. One of the first scholars from whom we sought advice was Eric Rauchway, a professor of history at the University of California, Davis. Rauchway's last three books have focused on the Great Depression. His latest, *Winter War: Hoover, Roosevelt, and the First Clash over the New Deal*, specifically covered the Hoover-to-Roosevelt transition.

What we did not realize when hosting Rauchway on the podcast was how much history would repeat itself in 2020 and 2021. Like the 1932 transition, when the already disastrous Great Depression came to a head, the COVID crisis peaked during the Trump-Biden transition, killing 172,000 Americans. Both outgoing presidents sought to minimize the federal government's involvement in their respective crises. Both incoming presidents saw the federal government as the indispensable solution. As with Hoover, Trump personally was of no help to the incoming president. And Trump and Biden demonstrated the same mutual disdain as did Hoover and Roosevelt. At least Hoover had the courtesy to meet with Roosevelt—even though the meetings were frosty. Donald Trump and Joe Biden never met privately, never spoke outside of the presidential debates.

Over the course of 2020, we brought Professor Rauchway on *Transition Lab* twice. The first time was in June. In November, in the immediate aftermath of the 2020 election, as President Trump refused to cooperate with the Biden transition, Rauchway appeared on Transition Lab. Each time, he emphasized the need for cooperation between incoming and outgoing administrations and the importance of respecting the choices made by the American people.

Although Roosevelt was elected in November 1932, his inauguration would not occur until March 1933. As a result, his transition into office, like those of his predecessors, took four months. Congress had ratified, and the states had approved, the Twentieth Amendment, moving

Inauguration Day to January 20, but it would not come into effect until the following presidential cycle.

In the face of mounting crises, Hoover became fixated not on helping the new administration prepare but on inducing FDR to recant the promises he had made during the election. FDR held firm. He was also inclined to avoid any affiliation with an increasingly unpopular president whose actions had failed to revitalize the economy.

FDR would stay committed to his New Deal agenda throughout the transition, working together with academics, labor leaders, and figures from both parties to develop a set of concrete policies.[5] The famous Hundred Days, when Roosevelt successfully submitted legislation on issues ranging from public works to banking regulations, were born out of these initial preparations.

For Rauchway, the hundred days before Roosevelt took the oath of office were as important as the Hundred Days after. The stakes were literally life and death. Roosevelt's experience underlines both the importance of prepresidential planning, particularly during a crisis, and the degree to which a smooth transition depends on cooperation from the outgoing president.

"Things have gotten quite dire"

DAVID MARCHICK (DM): You've written three books on the Depression, the New Deal, and FDR. But why did you write about this transition period, this four-month period before Roosevelt took the oath of office?

ERIC RAUCHWAY (ER): As you say, this is the third of the three books that I've written. Over the course of researching the other two, I became persuaded that the hundred or so days before Roosevelt took the oath of office for the first time were actually as important as the much more famous Hundred Days that came after. In fact, the previous hundred days really paved the way for that burst of legislative activity that happened upon his coming into office.

DM: On Election Day in 1932, the country was in a crisis, but the wheels came off even more in those four months before Roosevelt took office. Could you summarize what happened during those four months?

ER: The Depression has been going for three years at this point, since the 1929 crash. Unemployment rates are probably up to around 25 percent. There's not a terrifically accurate way of measuring that, but that's what our best guess is. Farm prices have plummeted, so people in the agricultural sector—which accounts for maybe 20 percent of the economy—can't generate income. Their crops are rotting in their fields, even as unemployed people are going hungry. The economy is basically already broken by the time you get to the 1932 election. And then, as you say, things start to get really bad.

You first have, immediately after the election, the nations in western Europe that owe the United States money since the Great War defaulting on their debts or at least declining to pay them momentarily. That creates a crisis of international economic affairs. You have international crises, with Hitler coming to power in Germany in January 1933 and with Japan leaving the League of Nations over the Manchuria crisis. Meantime, beginning just before the election, but extending right through to Roosevelt's inauguration, you have the last of the great waves of banking panics that occurred throughout the Depression. This one is by far the worst and most catastrophic, and it accompanies a currency panic where people lose faith in the dollar. The Federal Reserve is teetering on the brink of default. Many banks have shuttered their doors. And as you say, things have gotten quite dire by the time Roosevelt takes the oath of office.

"The mistrust started at the very beginning"

DM: Typically, after an election, the loser shows some graciousness and deference to the American people and to the winner. But in this case, that didn't happen. Did Hoover not think that FDR had a mandate to lead?

ER: No, he didn't. He thought that the American people had made a poor choice in a moment of desperation, that they would shortly come to their senses, and that when they did, they would regret having supported this candidate whose proposals Hoover regarded as radical and far outside the mainstream. Hoover firmly believed that the New Deal, if enacted, would fail and that, when it did, the grateful American people would rush back to him and vote him into office again in 1936.

DM: There were some meetings between Hoover and FDR and some correspondence. Let's talk about those and just drill down on the lack of cooperation. A little after the election, Roosevelt called Hoover, and, in your book, Hoover says, "I don't even want to talk to this guy alone because I don't trust him, so I want to make sure there's someone on the phone taking notes." Was the mistrust really that bad?

ER: The mistrust started at the very beginning. Hoover made sure that the conversation was recorded, and then he said he wouldn't meet with Roosevelt personally unless they had other people there, presumably to serve as witnesses. He was very much afraid that Roosevelt would mischaracterize what they said or say something manipulative or evasive and then spin it around on him. So Hoover wanted from the beginning to have a kind of architecture of surveillance around their meetings.

DM: Hoover and Roosevelt actually met on November 22, 1932, which is about two weeks after the election. What happened there? Did they try to reach an agreement on what they might do together?

ER: The occasion for this meeting was the debt defaults by European nations, which owed the United States money from war financing from the Great War. The question was, what to do about that? Hoover wanted to use the meeting to try to bind Roosevelt's hands. He wanted Roosevelt to accept his policies for negotiating or renegotiating any debts. He wanted Roosevelt to agree to go along with whatever the outgoing administration was going to do, and he wanted to be allowed to appoint a debt commission which would carry over into Roosevelt's administration.

Roosevelt wanted to avoid agreeing to anything. Roosevelt didn't even want to signal what he might do. So he didn't ask any of the more financially literate prominent Democrats to go with them. Instead, he asked Raymond Moley, a Columbia political scientist who really had no views whatsoever on international finance, just to have somebody to go along with him. Hoover had his secretary of the treasury, who was Ogden Mills—not only a cabinet officer but also a childhood frenemy of Franklin Roosevelt's who bore responsibility for some of the unattractive rhetoric used in the campaign. So they were already on bad terms.

Hoover used the occasion, by both sides' account, to dominate the conversation and explain to a person whom he regarded as ill-informed just how international finance worked, to insist that these were business obligations and had to be dealt with in a business manner, that politics didn't enter into it, and that Roosevelt should therefore accept Hoover's appointees as people to negotiate how to deal with these debts. Roosevelt, of course, took the opposite view; he didn't want to be bound by any decisions that Hoover might make, and moreover that he shouldn't be anything more than informed at that point because he was still governor of New York State and had no authority at the federal level and certainly none for foreign policy.

DM: Then they had some letters back and forth, and Hoover got so frustrated with Roosevelt's responses, which were kind of noncommittal, that he leaked them all to the press. That certainly didn't help either, I assume.

ER: If Roosevelt had retained his formerly good opinion of Hoover up through December 1932, certainly by around Christmas and the leak of those telegrams, I think he must have given it up because that was not very friendly. Roosevelt continued to say: "I am willing to cooperate. We will discuss how to deal with these things, but I will have my own policy when I become president." Hoover continued to insist that really Roosevelt had to accept his policies. This issue, of course, seemed very pressing in November, December 1932. This was before it was overtaken by the banking panic as the main subject for noncooperation between the two of them.

DM: To make matters worse, in February 1933, Roosevelt is in Miami with some other officials, including the mayor of Chicago, and an Italian immigrant tries to assassinate him. Obviously, he wasn't assassinated, but Hoover then wrote Roosevelt a nine-page letter. Presumably that letter said, "I'm glad you're not hurt, and thank God for the country"?

ER: You might think that that would be what it would say. That is, in fact, not what it said. I think there's about one sentence of, "I am relieved at your escape." [Hoover used] the rest of the nine pages—which Hoover, as he usually did, very carefully drafted, hand-wrote it out and edited over and over again, so he was very clear about what he was saying—to say the ongoing financial crisis is your fault; that you are the only one who can do anything to stop it. The only way, he said, that Roosevelt could stop the ongoing financial crisis would be to disavow the New Deal. Specifically, to assure the country that he would keep the dollar on the gold standard and not adopt a policy of inflation; that he would balance the federal budget; and that he would not undertake debt-financed public works. Only by making these three promises could Roosevelt stop the financial panic.

Now, privately, Hoover said to a friend that he was doing this because he hoped it would get Roosevelt to abandon, as he wrote, "90 percent of the so-called New Deal." Roosevelt obviously didn't do these things because he had run on the New Deal, and he wasn't about to abandon it two and a half weeks before taking office.

DM: Let's talk about how much of this was politics or just a clash of ideas and how much of it was personal between the two, Hoover and Roosevelt. In your book, you talk about how they've known each other for fifteen years. They weren't that far off in age, even though they were far off in demeanor. They didn't like each other very much at this point in their life, right?

ER: It's fair to say certainly that Hoover probably never really liked Franklin Roosevelt—or anyway, that's what he said. He said, "I had no use for that man after 15 years of acquaintance." They'd been moving in similar circles for a long time, going back really to the Great War, when Hoover had been food administrator for the Wilson administration and Franklin Roosevelt was assistant secretary of the navy in the same administration. And although they weren't that far off in age—Hoover was seven and a half years or so older than Roosevelt—Roosevelt's youthful demeanor made him seem a lot younger than he was. Hoover thought of him as callow and immature, and frankly, Herbert Hoover wasn't the only one; Roosevelt had a definite sense of humor.

Over time, Hoover continued to have this view of Roosevelt as sort of a lightweight, a view that was then reinforced in Hoover's mind when Roosevelt contracted polio and became physically disabled. Hoover, like a lot of people at that time, had a prejudice about physically disabled people and regarded them as mentally disabled as well.

DM: In modern days, ex-presidents tend to fade into the sunset. They don't criticize their successor. They don't comment on the successor's policies outside of maybe the Democratic or Republican conventions when they obviously have to support their party's nominee. But Hoover, how did he behave toward Roosevelt throughout his lifetime?

ER: Hoover decided almost immediately after the election in 1932 that the best use of his time was going to be to stage a public relations effort to remind people how successful his presidency had been so that when the New Deal failed, Hoover would be able to step in as the Republican nominee in 1936. So he employed writers who were former aides to his administration to write up favorable reviews of various aspects of his presidency. He also articulated an ideological opposition to the New Deal as fundamentally anti-American, making steps toward Moscow, as he would have put it at the time. He devoted himself immediately to a program of opposition to the New Deal and, indeed, really [continued that] for the rest of his very long life.

"He begins to take advice from experts and politicians and industry leaders"

DM: Let's talk about what Roosevelt is doing positively during the transition. He is certainly preparing to lead and putting his cabinet together. What does he do over this four-month period?

ER: Well, the first things he begins to do are associated with the promises he made in the campaign, so he begins to take advice. He goes to his vacation house in Warm Springs, Georgia, where he meets a whole bunch of various Democrats and liberal Republicans and starts to marshal ways of putting through the kinds of legislation that he had promised during the campaign: legislation to relieve farmers, particularly; legislation to build dams at public expense and operate them to produce hydroelectric power at public expense; legislation that's friendly to unions; legislation that's going to push forward what we would now call a sort of proto-welfare state; legislation like unemployment insurance and social security. He begins to take advice from experts and politicians and industry leaders on how best to do those things. As the banking and currency panics gathered steam in the latter part of 1932 and the early part of 1933, he begins increasingly to consult with bankers about what to do and how to do it.

He sends up trial balloons. He tries to get legislation through Congress. He tries to get people in his party and sympathetic members of the Republican Party onside. He begins to put together a cabinet that is shaped with those policies in mind and in deference to the kinds of constituencies that he thinks will support him.

Maybe most notably for the latter part of his transition, he confers extensively with Hoover's secretary of state, Henry Stimson, to discuss how to handle the aggressor powers, as they then refer to them, which are beginning to gain strength overseas. He also confers with the French ambassador in the United States to talk about possibly putting together some kind of alliance among France, Britain, and the United States to keep Germany at bay. He does a lot of work during these times to try to prepare for the many crises that are going to beset his presidency.

"People actually died"

DM: What was the cost to the country of the lack of cooperation between Hoover and Roosevelt? What was the impact on the country, and our recovery, of that lack of cooperation?

ER: Well, if you could let me take a second here to remind folks where the country is in 1932, 1933. You have an unemployment rate that is up near, if not quite at, 25 percent. You have people actually going hungry while commodity prices are so low that farmers are declining even to harvest their crops and letting them rot in the fields because they can't make any money bringing them to market. The economy is effectively broken at this point in 1932, 1933, in large measure because people have stopped making their debt payments, particularly their mortgage payments. Banks are starting to go under at a truly fearsome rate. They had failed throughout Hoover's term, and there had been sort of waves of bank failures, but when you get into 1932 and 1933, there is a much larger wave, and it accelerates to really quite dramatic levels. It looks like the entire financial system, possibly even the Federal Reserve system, will have to shut down.

Roosevelt ran on a campaign of government intervention, right? That's what the New Deal is about. They're going to subsidize crop prices. They're going to relieve unemployment. They're going to get people to start buying things, and they're going to regulate the financial sector and kind of put it back together.

Roosevelt begins to acquire advice through the transition that he needs to take aggressive action. Which is to say, shut down the banking system, audit the banks, make sure that the ones that appear sound are in fact sound, and let them reopen again. He says he is going to do this as soon as he takes office. And in fact, of course, we now know that is what he does.

As soon as he takes office, he shuts down the banks. He uses that same mechanism to induce inflation, that is to say, to help bring prices up by going off the gold standard. Many economists believe that this is the reason that you see a recovery right there in March 1933, when Roosevelt takes office. The idea is that the government is now behind the banks, the banks have been stabilized, and there is an expectation of inflation, which means that you want to start spending your money if you have it. That's what gets the economy going again.

Now, if you understand that to be what happened, you should also understand that that could have happened a week earlier, two weeks earlier, three or four weeks earlier. Recovery was available to the country a little bit before it actually occurred, had Hoover been willing to do it.

As you know, Hoover refused to declare a bank holiday. Roosevelt advised Hoover that Roosevelt would be declaring a bank holiday immediately on taking office, and that Hoover should go ahead and declare one that would expire at noon on March 4. Hoover declined to do that. Hoover was, of course, in principle against inflationary policies.

So Hoover delayed the recovery. That means that a lot more people lost their jobs. A lot more mortgage payments went unpaid. Banks collapsed. A lot more people lost their savings. And given that we're talking about a time when people are actually starving, some people actually died as a result of this delayed recovery. So there's quite a considerable cost.

Notes

1. Eric Rauchway, "The New Deal Was on the Ballot in 1932," *Modern American History* 2, no. 2 (February 2019).
2. For more on Hoover's complex relationship with the New Deal and progressivism, see Kenneth Whyte, *Hoover: An Extraordinary Life in Extraordinary Times* (New York: Vintage, 2018).
3. Eric Rauchway, *Winter War: Hoover, Roosevelt, and the First Clash over the New Deal* (New York: Basic, 2018), 11.
4. Rauchway, *Winter War,* 14.
5. Eric Rauchway has also written a wonderful introduction to the history of the New Deal (see Rauchway, *The Great Depression & the New Deal: A Very Short Introduction* [Oxford: Oxford University Press, 2008]). For other accounts, see Arthur Meier Schlesinger, *The Coming of the New Deal: 1933–1935* (Boston: Houghton Mifflin, 2003); and Ira Katznelson, *Fear Itself: The New Deal and the Origins of Our Time* (New York: Liveright, 2014).

Evolution of the Modern Presidential Transition

MARTHA KUMAR

> Especially after 9/11, the feeling of vulnerability meant that you needed to start [the transition] early. So you [now] have presidential transition legislation that provides resources for candidates after the conventions but before the election. Ultimately, the legislation is responsive to what candidates have found and what the government thought was wise.
>
> —Martha Kumar

A SCHOLAR of presidential transitions, Towson University professor Martha Kumar has studied it all: the good, the bad, and the ugly. She brought to life the gold standard of transitions in *Before the Oath: How George W. Bush and Barack Obama Managed a Transfer of Power,* a book I read twice and referred to nonstop during my time as director of the Center for Presidential Transition.

For Kumar, the bad and ugly varieties are perhaps best typified by President Truman's transitions into and out of office. Truman was only vice president for eighty-two days, about the length of a modern transition, but for Truman, elevated to the presidency by Franklin Roosevelt's death in office, there would be no transition. Roosevelt had kept his vice president in the dark on key issues—Truman only learned of the existence of the atomic bomb after assuming the presidency. Just 116 days later, the *Enola Gay* dropped the bomb on Hiroshima.

Professor Kumar's research identifies a sequential set of reforms that shaped the modern presidential transitions. In 1933 Congress and the states ratified the Twentieth Amendment to the Constitution, shortening the lame-duck period from four months to two. Presidents no longer needed lengthy periods of time to get themselves to Washington, and an overlong interregnum carried risks of its own.

Three decades later, a bipartisan committee established by President Kennedy called for the first substantive transition reforms. Although President Kennedy publicly lauded his transition into office following the 1960 election as one of the most effective in U.S. history, he also had concerns about the lack of federal support.[1] Kennedy's effort resulted in the Presidential Transition Act of 1963, which requires that the General Services Administration (GSA), which manages federal properties and provides operational support to federal agencies, supply services and facilities to the president-elect. For twenty-five years, no significant changes were made in the legislation, but the federal government continued to grow. In 1988, Congress passed the Presidential Transitions Effectiveness Act, which attempted to address the lessons learned from the Johnson, Nixon, Ford, Carter, and Reagan transitions. Perhaps most importantly, more public funds were allocated, and transparency requirements were imposed on private contributions.

A new set of reforms were driven by lessons learned from 9/11, when transitions came to be seen as an inherent national security threat. George W. Bush's transition was reduced to thirty-five days because of the election dispute in Florida. Partly as a result, on September 11, 2001, many key national security positions stood vacant.[2] The 9/11 Commission called for a number of reforms, including the processing of security clearances for candidates' teams before the election.[3]

Growing appreciation for the challenges associated with the modern presidency led Congress to pass the Pre-Election Presidential Transition Act of 2010. This bill enabled presidential candidates to receive GSA funding and office support after the nominating conventions, instead of having to wait until after the election. In doing so, Congress sent an important signal: candidates should begin their transition planning long before the election. In doing so, Congress helped break some of the taboos that had previously surrounded early planning. Though no formal transition to a new administration occurred between 2010 and 2015, this period was marked by an intensified focus on preelection preparations. In 2012, Mitt Romney's transition team, led by Governor Mike Leavitt and Chris Liddell, became the first to benefit from the 2010 Pre-Election Presidential Transition Act. When I interviewed Leavitt for the podcast, he noted that this statutory mandate for early planning allowed his team to be proactive without seeming presumptuous.

The Presidential Transitions Improvements Act of 2015 enumerated the responsibilities of an outgoing administration in the transfer of power. The law, named after two of the nation's finest transition practitioners, Ted Kaufman and Mike Leavitt (this book includes interviews with each of them), sought to codify some of the important actions taken by the outgoing George W. Bush administration in particular and make it politically easier for a sitting president to prepare for a potential loss by requiring the incumbent to make reasonable transition-planning efforts.

Professor Kumar's scholarship represents one of the most thorough sources of historical knowledge on transitions. As the director of the White House Transition Project, Professor Kumar provides nonpartisan expertise to incoming administrations, in addition to her academic pursuits. Several transition teams, including the Biden team in 2020, have drawn on her expertise, and the Partnership for Public Service has collaborated with her for more than a decade. Throughout the 2020 cycle, she was a constant source of advice and history for me. Her diligent analysis of past transitions enables forward-looking reform and helps flatten the dramatic learning curve between campaigning and governing.

"Transitions grew in importance"

DAVID MARCHICK (DM): The transition used to be much longer; the election was held in November, and presidents used to be inaugurated in March. In 1933, that law was changed, and Eisenhower was the first president who actually had the shorter transition in January. Now it's about seventy-four days. Why was that transition period shortened?

MARTHA KUMAR (MK): It is important to have a shortened transition period because travel and information are moving much faster now than they were. With the kind of vulnerabilities that you have in the period between presidents, it's important to have a period that's long enough to get your policy and personnel in order, but not too long. In fact, if you look at President George W. Bush, his transition was only thirty-seven days, but they had done so much work beforehand preparing for it that they were able to come in and have a very smooth beginning.

DM: In 1963, Congress passed transition legislation which has then evolved over time. What did that legislation do, and how has it evolved?

MK: In President Kennedy's case, it was the political party that provided all transition funding, but he knew that you needed something more than that and that the government should be involved in a transition. So one of his last initiatives was transition legislation, which then passed in 1964 [the year after Kennedy's assassination]. It laid out a basic framework, and it was called the Presidential Transition Act of 1963. The law provided for the General Services Administration [GSA] to give some services and facilities to the [incoming] president and vice president.

After the first period, from 1963 to 1987, transitions grew in importance. From 1988 to 1999 you have legislation that deals with problems that are coming up and the ways in which candidates are dealing with transitions. One problem is that there's not enough public money, so they increased the amount of government funding and allowed for private contributions, which have to be noted publicly and limited to five thousand dollars.

The third period goes from 2000 to 2009. That is a period during which 9/11 occurs, and transition becomes a different set of issues because national security is so important. People in and out of government realize the vulnerability of an administration during that time period. In 2000, President Clinton created an executive order that called for a transition coordinating committee that came out of the White House. Also in 2000, [Congress adopted a new version of the] Presidential Transition Act which requires GSA to provide computer and communications information prior to the election. Another piece that's important and touches on transition is *The 9/11 [Commission] Report*. The 9/11 Commission called for security clearances prior to the election so that when a candidate won, he or she could bring in people quickly that have preelection clearance.

DM: Because Bush didn't have all his people in place on 9/11, the 9/11 Commission said that could have compromised our country.

MK: Right. Bush, as he was going out, had an executive order similar to Clinton's that called for a White House transition council which sets policy for transition. From 2010 to 2015 there was the thought that you really need to prepare even earlier, so legislation called for the candidates to get funding once they had been nominated by the major parties before the elections. They get some travel funds, they get office space that GSA provides. In fact, they provided a space in the same building during the last transition, which was near the White House, but they had the Clinton and Trump teams on different floors. Romney used preelection funding for the first time in 2012, but Obama was running for reelection so didn't get it as the incumbent president.

From 2015 to 2020, you have the Presidential Transitions Improvements Act of 2015, which requires the president to create two councils. One is the White House Transition Coordinating Council, and then there's an Agency Transition Directors Council. Congress provided in law that the president shall create these two councils after Obama did not do so in 2012, because they recognized that a president running for reelection does not want to signal that he might lose. The White House sets the policy in its transition council, and then the Agency Transition Directors Council brings together representatives of the fifteen departments and largest agencies. Then they carry out the policies dealing with the departments and agencies, what information they should prepare, and when they should have it ready.

The latest piece of legislation, the Presidential Transition Enhancement Act of 2019, was recently passed and is now sitting on the president's desk.[4] The law deals with the memorandums of understanding that govern ethics rules and enforcement and the ways in which congressional staff can be involved in transitions.

"To reduce suspicions, to reduce overlap, to reduce conflict"

DM: You've written a lot about presidents hitting the ground running quickly. One of the things that you've found is that presidents usually get a big bounce in favorability postelection—on average about 15 percent—from where they were at the time of the election. Why is that? How does that affect their agenda?

MK: People have goodwill for a new administration, and they want to support them. Even though George W. Bush did not win the plurality of the votes, when he came in he had strong support. Part of that is the natural tendency to support a new president, but he also took steps that I think sent signals that he wanted to come in as a person who was going to work with Democrats, not just with Republicans. The first issue he tackled was one that he and his team picked because they knew they could get bipartisan support, and that was the issue of education. They had Ted Kennedy involved in it from the Senate and George Miller from the House, who was also a Democrat.

DM: Do presidents typically get a second-term bounce?

MK: The second term is very different than the first, because the first term you have a new agenda lined up as you come in. In a second term, you're basically left with leftovers from the first administration of things that you couldn't get through. Presidents have tended to focus on foreign policy and taking executive action in their second term because they run up against the limits of getting a strong coalition.

DM: One of the other things you've written about is the clashes that occur between a campaign operation and a transition team after the election. Why does that happen, and what can be done to avoid that?

MK: One of the factors here that's very practical is that people who are working on the campaign are usually working without a great salary. Some are even working for free. Their idea is that they're going to come into the administration, but you have a transition group that's working on planning, and campaign workers fear that they're going to take all the best jobs. In order to handle this suspicion that naturally arises, the best way of doing it is to have people meet occasionally and just let the campaign people know what the transition people are doing. In 2000, Clay Johnson, who was doing the transition work for George W. Bush, met with Karen Hughes, who was doing communications, and Karl Rove and Joe Allbaugh, who were running the campaign. Johnson would meet with them informally and just tell them what he was finding to reduce suspicions, to reduce overlap, to reduce conflict. It also depends on the person you appoint to head the transition, the executive director. In Clay Johnson's case, people knew him as a friend of Bush's who was not politically inclined, so they didn't see him as any kind of threat.

"The White House staff is your decision-making system"

DM: One of the other things you've written about is prioritization. Presidents Carter and Clinton famously made mistakes by focusing too much on cabinet selection. You've written that history shows that it's much more important for presidents to focus on the White House staff. Why is that?

MK: Clinton talked about that later, that he should have paid [more] attention to the White House staff. The reason is that the White House staff is your decision-making system. Before you go out and start picking cabinet members, you want to have your system in place where you set out what information you want, what kind of a cabinet you want, what your priorities are, and how all of that is going to fit with the legislation that you're prioritizing.

If you don't do that, if you're just picking cabinet members first, one of the things that you can end up doing is using White House positions as rewards for campaign workers, rather than thinking that the people you hire in a White House need to be ready for governing, which is very different than campaigning. You can see some of that in the Trump administration, where he picked a person from *The Apprentice* to be an assistant at the presidential level, which is one of the top twenty-five people in the administration.

DM: One of the things you've written about extensively is the design of the White House. You have organizational charts from every White House going back to Kennedy. What are the critical issues that a candidate for president or a president-elect needs to decide in terms of organizing his or her White House?

MK: One of the things they need to do is think of whether that organization is going to be hierarchical or flat. Does everybody at the top level get access to the president on a regular basis or do they have to go through the chief of staff? The White Houses that have been best able to deliver a president's goals tend to be hierarchical. An example would be in the Clinton administration. Leon Panetta was the chief of staff, and he pulled together people who were involved in policy, politics, and publicity. Those three are important to have in the room at the same time, because if you want to put forward a policy, you have to know whether the politics are there: Can you get it through the Congress? You need to know if the politics are going to work with the policy. And then: Can you communicate it? Do you know enough about how the policy is going to work that you can explain it?

Mike McCurry, who was the press secretary for Clinton, has talked about that. When they would talk through the selling of a particular piece of legislation or policy, Clinton would ask him what the publicity should be. If he couldn't explain it in a simple, straightforward way, it shouldn't be introduced. The George W. Bush White House had these three parts as well, and it makes for a much smoother-running operation.

"Make them think about what the presidency means"

DM: Let's do a history lightning round. I'd like you to share one-word answers to the following questions. What was the worst transition in U.S. history?

MK: Roosevelt to Truman because of the enormous importance of the development of an atomic bomb that Truman was not told about.

DM: What about Harrison? He had thirty some days in office and then he died; that was a pretty bad transition.

MK: And you could also say John Quincy Adams to Andrew Jackson because Adams went horseback riding instead of attending the inauguration.

Another one of the worst transitions was Nixon to Ford because Ford, when he came in, had three staffs to deal with. He had a lot of competing interests. He had the Nixon staff, he had the staff that he brought with him to the vice presidency from the Hill, then he also had some vice-presidential staff, and he was bringing on new people for presidential staff. People don't actually think about that being a transition from Nixon to Ford, but it was a challenging one for Ford, and it was a challenging time for the country.

DM: How about the worst relationship between an incoming and an outgoing president?

MK: Truman and Eisenhower is up there.

DM: President Truman, you wrote, was the first president to really think about transition planning, in part because he was held in the dark by President Roosevelt. He actually reached out to both candidates for the presidency in 1952. What ended up happening there?

MK: In Truman's case, he decided that he wasn't going to run and announced it in the winter. Then, he had his head of the Bureau of the Budget prepare information for the new people coming in because he thought that it would be good to have both sides come to the White House. During the summer of 1952—in August—he invited Adlai Stevenson and General Eisenhower to come to the White House and get briefed by the CIA, individual cabinet members, and White House staff. Stevenson did come, but Eisenhower was not in favor of doing it, so he wrote Truman back turning down the invitation: "I believe our communication should be only those which are known to all American people. Consequently, I think it would be unwise and result in confusion in the public mind if I were to attend the meeting in the White House to which you have invited me." Truman was very unhappy, and in a characteristic Truman response, he wrote: "I am extremely sorry that you have allowed a bunch of screwballs to come between us. You have made a big mistake and I'm hoping it won't endanger this great Republic." Eisenhower did eventually come and see Truman after the election, but he wrote in his memoirs that he didn't really learn anything from him.

DM: And I understand also at that meeting that Eisenhower wouldn't even talk to Truman, he would talk to one of Truman's aides. Truman would ask him a question, and Ike would respond to an aide. What's the modern president who had the best transition in?

MK: Barack Obama. The outgoing administration, the administration of George W. Bush, took the transition so seriously. In Bush's case, he talked to his chief of staff, Josh Bolten, in December 2007 and told him that he wanted to have the best transition in history because there were two wars underway. Bolten took that very seriously. In the summer, he brought in the representatives of Obama and McCain and had them agree on a memorandum of understanding on how the transition would unfold between the transition team and the government so that whoever won, that memorandum of understanding would be ready.

DM: Who would you say has had the best transition out of the presidency?

MK: George W. Bush had the best one in the modern period. And of course, he was the first one after 9/11 to be considering a transition and the vulnerabilities that could be associated with it. The financial collapse was also occurring at the very end, so the incoming and outgoing—the Obama and Bush people—worked together on that, too.

DM: Who would you say is the senior official in the modern era, so the last forty years, with the most White House experience?

MK: There are people who work in a White House that the public doesn't see. Joe Hagin, who worked for both Bushes and served as the deputy chief of staff for operations, he was important. Andy Card was very important as well; he served in the first and the second Bush administrations and also for Reagan. And then there's a woman, Katja Bullock, who has worked in all of the Republican personnel operations, so she is very much [a person with] an institutional memory.

DM: Who is the senior official that's done more to advance the cause of transition planning than any other?

MK: I think Josh Bolten would be that person. What he did during that final year in 2008 preparing for the transition was not called for in any legislation; it was just the president wanting him to have the best transition. He thought about bringing in the two candidates and working on tabletop exercises so that whoever came in would be aware of the severity of what could happen, the problems that could happen, and really make them think about what the presidency means. What he did found its way into legislation.

DM: Who's the person in Congress who's had the biggest impact on transition issues?

MK: Ted Kaufman was very important in the 2015 legislation. He was a senator from Delaware who took Joseph Biden's place when Biden became vice president. He really focused on transition planning and what needed to be done to bring it up to date. That legislation is named after Ted Kaufman and Mike Leavitt, who was a former governor and member of the George W. Bush administration who was very involved in transition planning and handled Romney's transition planning.

Notes

1. John Shaw, *Rising Star, Setting Sun: Dwight D. Eisenhower, John F. Kennedy, and the Presidential Transition That Changed America* (New York: Pegasus, 2018), xv.

2. In an interview with the University of Virginia's Miller Center, Stephen Hadley, Bush's deputy national security advisor at the time, suggested the slow pace of nominations undermined the administration's ability to develop a response to the threat posed by al-Qaeda: "When people say, 'Well, you had nine months to get an alternative strategy on al-Qaeda,' no, you didn't. Once people got up and got in their jobs you had about four months" ("Stephen J. Hadley Oral History," interview, University of Virginia Miller Center, https://millercenter.org/the-presidency/presidential-oral-histories/stephen-j-hadley-oral-history).

3. For a more detailed summary of the evolution of presidential transition law, see Henry B. Hogue, "Presidential Transition Act: Provisions and Funding," Congressional Research Service, November 13, 2020.

4. It was signed into law by President Trump on March 3, 2020.

PART II

MEMORY

Jimmy Carter's Farsighted but Flawed Transition

STUART EIZENSTAT AND DAVID RUBENSTEIN

> You have to be very careful about the kinds of decisions you make in a transition.
>
> —Stuart Eizenstat

JIMMY CARTER was the first modern president to devote significant campaign resources to transition planning—something that former Carter advisors Stuart Eizenstat and David Rubenstein ascribe to his background as an engineer. As Stu Eizenstat put it in our interview, Carter "believes in advance planning." But Carter also made serious mistakes, particularly in failing to coordinate between the campaign and transition teams, prioritizing cabinet over White House appointments, and not articulating clear legislative priorities. These errors went on to hamper at least his first year and, arguably, elements of his entire presidency.

In the spring of 1976—impressively early, even by contemporary standards—Jimmy Carter asked Jack Watson, a former law partner of Carter advisor Charles Kirbo, to begin developing policies and an organizational structure for a potential Carter White House. Although the campaign was dominated by Carter loyalists from Georgia, the transition team drew on seasoned Washington operators like Tony Lake, who would later serve as Bill Clinton's national security advisor.

Despite this early start, the Carter transition ultimately misfired. Several mistakes led his transition effort astray. First, the transition team's existence was kept secret from the campaign, meaning that no communication flowed between the two groups. With just a few weeks to go before the election, plans for Carter's early days emerged in the press, befuddling his campaign staff. This set the two parallel organizations up for a showdown that delayed the effective launch of the transition itself. As the *New*

York Times reported on December 10, 1976, more than five weeks after Election Day, "The Carter people are finding it more difficult to exercise power than to seek it [and] harder to keep peace among themselves."[1]

Second, Carter made missteps when it came to appointments. The Nixon administration had become notorious for its corruption, and one of the symbols of that corruption was Nixon's all-powerful chief of staff, H. R. Haldeman. Having presented himself to the American public as the opposite of Nixon in every way, Carter chose not to appoint a chief of staff at all, a decision that led to a dysfunctional West Wing.

Third, and for similar reasons, White House staff were not a priority for Carter. Instead, he focused first on appointing his cabinet and then allowed cabinet nominees to pick their own senior staff. Only later did he turn to the White House, where in place of seasoned Washington hands he appointed mainly loyalists from Georgia who lacked experience at the federal level. In some cases, the senior leaders chosen by Carter did not gel as a team, most notably in the foreign policy space, where National Security Advisor Zbigniew Brzezinski and Secretary of State Cyrus Vance were frequently at odds.[2] These personnel decisions produced an administration in which the competing priorities of individual agencies often threatened to drown out the president's own agenda.

Finally, Carter failed to place the items on his legislative agenda in priority order. He ordered his staff to publish a list of hundreds of campaign pledges and sent so much legislation to Congress all at once that even Democratic House Speaker Thomas "Tip" O'Neill repeatedly asked him to slow down. Again, the result was confusion that likely did more to arrest the president's agenda than to further it.

Stu Eizenstat and David Rubenstein were young staffers—thirty-three and twenty-seven years old respectively—on Carter's long-shot bid for president in 1976. Less than a year later, they assumed high-ranking positions in the Carter White House: Stu as chief of domestic policy and David as his indefatigable deputy. From that vantage point, they helped usher in many of the administration's major achievements, from energy deregulation to doubling the size of the National Park system.[3]

Stu Eizenstat was raised in Atlanta. After a brief stint working in the White House under Lyndon B. Johnson, he served as a policy advisor to Johnson's vice president, Hubert Humphrey, during the latter's unsuccessful 1968 election campaign. In 1974, he met Jimmy Carter—then governor of Stu's home state of Georgia—and told him that if he played his cards right and won a couple of southern primaries, he might have a shot at the vice-presidential slot on the Democratic ticket. Carter told Stu he was not interested—he wanted to be president.

Shortly thereafter, Stu joined the Carter campaign. He quickly made himself a master of policy, known for taking assiduous notes and working himself so hard he would sometimes fall asleep in meetings. Following Carter's departure from office in 1981, Stu served in a number of senior government roles, including ambassador to the European Union and deputy secretary of the treasury, as well as becoming a partner at the law firm of Covington and Burling.

Perhaps the only person in the White House who worked harder than Stu Eizenstat was his deputy, David Rubenstein. David grew up in modest circumstances in a Jewish neighborhood of Baltimore. Neither of his parents graduated high school, but David won scholarships first to Duke University and then to the University of Chicago Law School. He practiced law and worked briefly for Senator Birch Bayh of Indiana before joining the Carter campaign.

Around the White House, David's work ethic became legendary. Not wanting to waste time on lunch, he got most of his meals from a White House vending machine. In the evenings, he would be the last staffer to leave the West Wing, in order to make sure that Stu's domestic policy memos would be at the top of Carter's inbox the next morning. After Carter left office, David went on to found the Carlyle Group investment firm, amass one of the largest fortunes in the country, and become one of the nation's most important philanthropists.

Despite its challenges, the Carter transition was a foundational effort. Government scholar John P. Burke sums up its contribution to the art of presidential transition: "Although Carter's successors in office would sometimes do less, sometimes more, and often with different emphases, the Carter transition set out the basic formula each would follow. It is difficult, if not impossible, to imagine a future president-elect turning back to the transitions undertaken by Carter's predecessors."[4]

Students of transition planning will draw clear lessons from my interview with Stu and David. On the positive side, the Carter transition makes clear the value of early, systematic, well-resourced efforts by a team staffed with experienced Washington operators. Equally, future campaigns will want to avoid Carter's mistakes. They should facilitate continuous, high-level communication between the campaign itself and the transition-planning staff, as George W. Bush, Romney, and Biden did. They should prioritize appointments of senior White House staff, with an early announcement of chief of staff–designate, as George W. Bush, Obama, and Biden each did. Finally, unlike Carter, the most effective transitions have prioritized creating a strong, centralized White House with clear legislative priorities.

"There had to be a collision"

DAVID MARCHICK (DM): In one sense, Carter modernized transition planning because he was really the first president in the history of the United States that actually diverted significant resources, both personnel and campaign funding, to transition planning. Why did he think that was important?

STUART EIZENSTAT (SE): I think the reason was that Jimmy Carter is an engineer. He believes in advance planning. And he felt that if he could get a running head start by having a transition team begin to put together the kinds of policies that we would implement, that this would help his presidency.

Actually, the reverse happened. David and I were heading the policy staff of the campaign, and unbeknownst to us until about a month before the election, Jimmy Carter had a parallel policy planning group for the transition headed by Jack Watson, who was a young partner of his closest friend, Charlie Kirbo. Jack had literally fifty people working on policy issues, parallel to us but without any vetting.

DM: You were running the campaign policy team, and you knew nothing about this?

SE: I knew only at the very end, and I went to see Jack twice. But we were so totally consumed with trying to win the election, with putting out policy papers, with answering press questions, no one had the opportunity to even think about what Jack was doing.

After the election, Jack took three black, huge binders full of policy recommendations, not one of which had been vetted politically, not one of which had been shared with us, and went down to Plains [Carter's campaign headquarters in Georgia] and gave it to Carter. Carter, remarkably, appointed Jack to head transition planning instead of the campaign manager and his really brilliant campaign strategist, Ham [Hamilton] Jordan. So here we had two parallel groups: Jack's, working very much in secret because that's the way Carter wanted it, and our policy group.

There had to be a collision. And there was.

DM: A little before the election, there were some leaks from the Watson group, or maybe he talked to the press, and there were news stories about what Carter would do after he's elected. You didn't know anything about this, and that caused tension. It also didn't look that good for the campaign since it looked uncoordinated.

SE: They were leaking some of the more provocative suggestions which had not, again, been politically vetted. This exposed the fact that there was this parallel group. It's those leaks that led me to finally go to Jack's office and say, "What's happening here?"

DAVID RUBENSTEIN (DR): [The year] 1976 was the first time that a Democratic president had been elected to succeed a Republican president since 1960. If you go back, what John Kennedy did [during the transition] was very modest. There was no money allocated from the federal government for the transition postelection. No money was allocated preelection. All he did was ask Richard Neustadt [a political science professor and former Truman advisor] and Clark Clifford [a lawyer and former Truman advisor] to write a memo. The transition was run out of Kennedy's townhouse in Georgetown and a little bit out of his father's house in Palm Beach.[5]

I think President-elect Carter wanted to do something different and have a more systematic view of things. He was, as Stuart said, an engineer, and always wanted to have everything be very systematic. He just had an ability to bifurcate. Sometimes your brain can have two lobes to it, and they don't necessarily have to work together. So, he had a lobe for the campaign and a lobe working on the transition, and he didn't really see that they had to interact. I think that was a part of the problem.

DM: Did either of you go to then-candidate Carter and say, "What's going on?" Or you just dealt with Jack Watson?

SE: About a month before the election, when the leaks started to occur, I did go to see Jack. But afterward I went to see Ham Jordan, because Ham was in the same uncomfortable position I was. I think Jack wanted the position I ended up getting—domestic advisor—or perhaps chief of staff.

[Carter] was cutting out the person who had planned the entire campaign. Ham and I were very much together on this, as were Jody Powell [Carter's press secretary as governor and later as president] and Frank Moore [the Carter campaign's finance director and later assistant to the president for congressional liaison] and all of the major campaign people. We left it to Ham to go to see President-elect Carter. And what Carter did, is he said to Jack and to me and to all the other people, "Write out a job description of how you see your job." Well, mine and Jack's were quite similar, right? Finally, he realized that there wasn't room for the two of us. So he said, "Why don't you try to work it out?" So the way we worked it out was that I would be a policy advisor, we would develop policy, we would develop legislation, and Jack would help work with state and local governments to implement it. Mine was a much more senior position, but that's the way it finally worked out. And it only worked out that way, I think, because Ham insisted that I have the top policy position.

DR: Remember, Hamilton Jordan and Jody Powell basically gave several years of their life to help get Carter elected. I think Carter looked at politics as being a bit dirty and therefore: "You guys are the political people. You've got me elected, now I have to govern, and the guys who have all the fancy degrees and who have all the credentials in Washington, that's who should govern. But thank you very much for getting me elected." I think Hamilton and Jody went to President-elect Carter and said, "Hey, we got you here, and we know a lot about politics, and you owe us something." Carter in the end went in their direction.

DM: Perhaps one of the lessons learned that Presidents Bush and Obama implemented was to have an effective transition planning apparatus, but one that has to be subservient to the campaign, and then they need to merge peacefully after the election. So do you have some thoughts on lessons learned from the problems that you experienced?

DR: It was a problem clearly in the transition because you had people fighting over positions, and you couldn't really prepare that well for the new administration because people didn't really know who's going to get what jobs. I think Stuart didn't firmly get his position until two or three weeks before the swearing in.

DM: Which is incredible, because you had basically given two years of your life to then governor Carter.

SE: Yes. And Frank Moore, who was the congressional liaison, didn't learn until a week before that that was going to be his job. So because you had these parallel structures, because you had this clash, it took up an enormous amount of time.

DR: It was stressful because we had to put out the fires of everybody coming to Washington looking for jobs. Everybody who worked in the campaign all over the country wanted a job. We didn't have authority. We didn't know whether we had jobs ourselves. There wasn't a lot of security in those days. People could just walk in and look for jobs. It was a little strange.

"Carter was obsessed with getting the cabinet done"

DR: Governor Carter was always the smartest person in the room in his view—and he probably was when he was governor. He didn't really feel he had to have very powerful people on the White House staff because in his view, everything was going to be in the cabinet. And because he was running against a strong White House staff that Nixon had had, he didn't want to have everybody think it's going to be a White House staff just like Nixon.

DM: He wanted to do the opposite of Watergate.

DR: He kept talking about cabinet government. So with the meetings that Stuart helped organize down in the Pond House, Miss Lillian's house [a building on the Carter estate in Plains, Georgia, informally named for Jimmy Carter's mother, Lillian], they were really de facto interviews for people who would be cabinet officers. Carter was obsessed with getting the cabinet done. The White House staff people were not that significant: "Who cares about staff people? We'll deal with that later."

So rather than most people in Washington today saying, "Figure out who your top White House staff will be and then deal with the cabinet," he did it a different way, and it didn't work out that well.

DM: Stu, you were thirty or thirty-one, and David, you were twenty-six or twenty-seven, and you both were perhaps two of the more experienced and accomplished White House staff. Were you actually qualified for these positions when you got them?

DR: I wasn't. Stuart was qualified; he'd worked in the White House before. I wasn't qualified because I was relatively young and didn't have that much experience, but no White House staff is completely fully qualified. You have a few people qualified. But remember, White House staffs are generally filled with relatively younger people who've given their time to a campaign. Fifty-year-old people who were at the top of their career in Wall Street or in a corporate setting don't usually give that up and go work in a campaign. You get twenty-year-olds working in campaigns, thirty-year-olds working campaigns, and therefore they often work as White House staff. Occasionally you'll get a Jim Baker, but that's a rare situation.

SE: You had with Johnson the Texas mafia; you had with Nixon the California mafia. Each president brings the young people who are willing to drop everything, have almost no income for two years, and kill themselves on the campaign trail. No one can imagine the brutality of the hours and demands. Even working in a White House is better because at least you have a place to go home to and you know there'll be a tomorrow. You make one mistake in a campaign, and it can be fatal. But what happened here was the following: Carter decided for the reasons David very aptly said to be the opposite of Nixon.

Nixon had Haldeman as the all-powerful chief of staff who blocked everyone from seeing him. So Carter decided he was going to be his own chief of staff. Dick Cheney, who was chief of staff for President Ford, warned Ham— very visibly. He took a bicycle wheel that had been given to him by his staff because they had initially in the Ford White House done the so-called "spokes of the wheel," where five or six aides had equal access to the president, and there was no chief of staff saying, "This is broken, don't do this." But Carter insisted on doing it, and that meant no one to combine policy and politics. It meant no one to set priorities. What goes first? Who has to wait? He was for cabinet government. He cut the White House staff by a third, and it was already very small.

The president basically gave the cabinet secretaries free rein to name their own top deputies, deputy secretaries, undersecretaries, assistant secretaries, who therefore were more loyal to them than they were to the president. Not a good idea.

In addition, one really seminal personnel decision was made after one of the CIA briefings in Plains. I was the only staff person there, and there was a break in the briefing. Carter took me by the side door of his house, and he said: "You've managed both foreign and domestic policy. I'm thinking of naming Cy Vance as secretary of state and Zbigniew Brzezinski as national security advisor. What do you think?"

I said, "Each individually would be great, but putting them together would be a serious mistake." And he said, "Why?" And I said: "Because I've seen during the campaign they have diametrically opposite views on the most crucial issue you'll be facing, which is the Soviet Union. One is a dove and the other's a hawk." And the president-elect said: "Well, I like different opinions. I can handle it." This caused a dissonance in our foreign policy that went throughout the administration.

DM: He adjusted later and actually appointed a chief of staff.

SE: Only after two years. He appointed Ham as chief of staff.

DM: But administrations typically accomplish the most in their first year—because they have the mandate and there's energy.

DR: Jimmy Carter became president of the United States when he was fifty-two years old. His senior staff people were by and large in their thirties, and it was hard for them to tell him no, because he would say, "Look, I'm twenty years older, I'm smarter, I'm whatever." It's very good to have a chief of staff who is maybe older than you or at least your age who can say no to you and get away with it, which was what Jim Baker [chief of staff to Presidents Reagan and George H. W. Bush] effectively did. And it worked much better. When you have young people, it's hard for them to convince the president.

DM: Carter didn't want a lot of Washington hands in the White House because it was a kind of an anti-establishment, post-Watergate, anti-Nixon campaign. What was the impact of that?

SE: The impact was devastating because he was inexperienced, and the White House staff was inexperienced because they were all Georgia people, the so-called Georgia mafia. Had we had one or two people that had that kind of experience and the age factor that David mentioned, they could have gone to the president and said: "The emperor has no clothes. You can't do this, Mr. President."

"They just bombarded Congress"

DM: No chief of staff, a flawed personnel process, and this dissonance between the campaign and the transition. What was the impact on governing for either of you?

DR: Jimmy Carter really wanted to honor his campaign promises. Many of those promises were put together by people who were no longer really in positions of power. In other words, we had a small policy staff, but the people who were running the cabinet departments, they hadn't bought into some of those promises. We had conflicts from time to time in that regard. It was a complicated situation.

Carter is a very, very smart person, but he wanted to engineer everything, and he didn't prioritize. He wanted to do so many things. He did a lot of things, but he might've gotten more done if he had prioritized things a little bit better.

SE: We threw so much up at the Congress that Tip O'Neill at leadership breakfasts would say week after week: "You've got to tell us your priorities. We can't absorb all of this." We had the economic stimulus package; a comprehensive energy bill within ninety days of inauguration when energy wasn't even a campaign issue; water projects; welfare reform; tax reform; SALT-II; Panama Canal. All of these things came into Congress in the first year or so, and they just bombarded Congress. We actually accomplished an enormous amount, but it always paled in comparison to what we threw up.

SE: After about nine months, when it was clear that the absence of priorities was really hurting us, he had Vice President Mondale, he had a small group, David now worked on the domestic side, Brzezinski and [deputy national security advisor] David Aaron on the national security side. And we set the following priorities: those things that would be key presidential priorities requiring presidential time and personal effort, those things that were White House decisions but would take less of the president's time, those things that could be handled at the cabinet level. That really helped in that we did that every one of the succeeding years, but it was that first crucial year where that wasn't done.

"There was really a disdain for anything that Carter and his staff had to offer"

DM: Let's fast-forward to year four: You're running for reelection. David, I've heard you describe this many times, that you were convinced Carter was going to win right up until the last moment.

DR: Our view was that Carter was very smart; Reagan, not as smart. Carter was experienced; Reagan was not experienced. Carter was a moderate; Reagan was too conservative. So how could a very conservative former governor of California, a former movie actor, sixty-nine years old—then the oldest person ever who had run for president—how could he possibly beat a very smart Carter? It wasn't his fault we had hostages [at the U.S. embassy in Iran]; it wasn't his fault we had gas lines [owing to the collapse in oil production]. So we thought the polling was inaccurate because people were not going to tell a pollster, "I'm really going to vote for Carter." Because they wanted to say, "Well, I might vote for Reagan because I want to show Carter that I really want him on his toes more."

SE: The fact is that going into the first and only debate, which was held eight days before the election (which was a horrible mistake), Reagan was a great debater. It took away a lot of the fear factor that this guy was trigger happy, he was too conservative, he was an "aw shucks" kind of guy.

And then what happened was on the Sunday before the Tuesday vote, we were at the Hilton hotel in the Chicago airport, and I got a call about two or three o'clock in the morning to be on Air Force One in forty-five minutes; the president's going back, he's gotten a new offer from Iran. I begged him not to go back. I said: "Just look at the offer. Don't go back. It'll bring the whole issue back." And then when he was on the plane, Gerald Rafshoon [Carter campaign media advisor], Ham, and I said: "Okay, if you've got to do it, this is obviously not enough to break the hostage crisis open. Blast the hell out of them for interfering in our election." Instead, he gave a sort of moderate state-ment saying: "Well, you know, it's a step forward. Not enough." The whole floor collapsed at that point because it brought the whole hostage crisis back and what had been an even race turned into a landslide loss.

DM: Let's talk about the transition out of office. Did you or did President Carter and his team have any planning or any work to effectively hand off the reins to President Reagan?

SE: Yes. Let me tell you frankly, the Reagan people, at least the ones I met, cared nothing about what we had to say. They felt they had wiped us out, we were a spent force, this was a new ideology, a new Republican majority, and they met us with a real disdain. Reagan did learn lessons from our transition. He appointed Jim Baker his chief of staff, for example. But there was really a disdain for anything that Carter and his staff had to offer.

DM: When you're in government, everything's, "You're smart, you're funny, you're handsome, you're good-looking, you've had a very successful career." When you left the Carter administration, were people banging down the doors to hire you?

DR: They were banging down the doors to keep me away from being hired by them. Stuart had been a partner in a law firm, and his former law firm was happy to have him back, and he had other offers as well. I had only practiced law two years, and selling access to the Carter White House wasn't that pro-ductive when Carter wasn't president, so it was more difficult for me. You have to remember when people come in and tell you how great you are, you have to take that with a grain of salt because in the end, if you're out of power, they don't really care about you anymore.

"Any transition is going to have its flaws"

SE: Even the best-laid plans of a transition have a huge disadvantage. You don't have a formal interagency process; you can't draw on the expertise of the budget office or of most of the departments. And so putting together, for ex-ample, the economic stimulus package which Carter wanted to do from day one when he came into office ended up with flaws. The fifty-dollar stimulus [a package of measures that included a fifty-dollar tax rebate to every citizen] ended up biting the dust because it hadn't been well thought through. You have to be very careful about the kinds of decisions you make in a transition.

DR: There is a Chinese curse that says, "May you be condemned to live in a time of transition." Which is to say, transition is difficult, and getting through a transition is never going to be easy. Any transition is going to have its flaws. You can look at the lessons of the past, but just remember all transitions are difficult because people are grabbing for power, for positions. It's a complicated thing for people to think about it and study the history of it. I think we'll do better than people who ignore it, though.

Notes

1. Hendrick Special, "Strains in Carter Transition," *New York Times*, December 10, 1976, https://www.nytimes.com/1976/12/10/archives/strains-in-carter-transition.html.
2. For a discussion of these clashes, see Daniel Sargent, *A Superpower Transformed: The Remaking of American Foreign Relations in the 1970s* (Oxford: Oxford University Press, 2017), chap. 9.
3. For Eizenstat's account of the Carter presidency, see Stuart Eizenstat, *President Carter: The White House Years* (New York: Thomas Dunne/St. Martin's, 2020).
4. John P. Burke, *Presidential Transitions: From Politics to Practice* (Boulder, CO: Lynne Rienner, 2000), 180.
5. In addition to these memos, the Kennedy team developed task forces focused on key issues. Their work was, however, limited in scope when compared to the Carter team's transition efforts. For a discussion of these task forces, see John Shaw, *Rising Star, Setting Sun: Dwight D. Eisenhower, John F. Kennedy, and the Presidential Transition That Changed America* (New York: Pegasus, 2018), 171–72.

Reagan's Prior Preparation Prevents Poor Performance

JAMES BAKER

> I don't think it will ever happen again in American politics where a president-elect will go, "You're someone who has run at least two campaigns against me and beaten me in one of them," but ask them to be their White House chief of staff. I think it's something about the broad-gauge nature of the Gipper.
>
> —James Baker

IN DORIS Kearns Goodwin's masterpiece on Lincoln's cabinet, *Team of Rivals,* the author wrote that Lincoln's "political genius [was] revealed through his extraordinary array of personal qualities that enabled him to form friendships with men who had previously opposed him."[1] In that sense, Ronald Reagan demonstrated his own uncanny self-confidence in picking James Addison Baker III to serve as his White House chief of staff. After all, Baker had run not one but two campaigns against Reagan, first as chair of President Ford's reelection campaign in 1976, when Reagan ran to unseat him, and later as chair of George H. W. Bush's campaign in the 1980 Republican primaries, which Reagan won handily.

In the previous interview on Jimmy Carter's transition, Stu Eizenstat and David Rubenstein recalled their astonishment that Carter could lose to Reagan, whom the Carter team regarded as a cowboy of inferior intellect. But by announcing Baker as his chief of staff the day after his landslide election victory, Reagan showed his smarts and avoided one of Carter's cardinal errors. Nor was this the only Carter mistake that Reagan rectified. In addition to having a strong chief of staff, he focused on staffing the White House before the cabinet; he drew on experienced Washington players; and he carefully selected and sequenced his priorities before Congress. Along the way, Reagan created an additional best-practice precedent: he gave Baker control over staffing the White House, while Edwin Meese, the head of his transition team, supported the president in picking the cabinet and subcabinet.

It was Michael Deaver and Stuart Spencer, two of Reagan's longtime advisors, who hatched the plan to announce Baker as chief of staff the day after the election. In the fall of 1980, Deaver invited Baker to sit with Reagan on the campaign plane so the two could get to know each other. As Peter Baker and Susan Glasser wrote in *The Man Who Ran Washington*, their tour de force on Baker, "it was more than a little presumptuous, of course, to begin handing out West Wing offices before anyone had cast a ballot."[2] Perhaps, but we will see time and again that candidates who are "presumptuous"—who plan a transition as if they will win—have the leg up in launching an effective presidency. To this, Baker adds his own pithy admonition, based on a favorite dictum of his father's: "prior preparation prevents poor performance."[3]

Reagan gave Baker carte blanche to staff the White House, with one request: "make it right" with the man Reagan had passed over, Ed Meese. Baker met with Meese and, on one piece of paper, outlined their respective responsibilities. Meese's name went first. Meese would have cabinet rank. Meese would serve on or chair the policy councils. Meese would chair meetings in Reagan's absence. Meese left that breakfast at the Century Plaza Hotel feeling empowered. His allies told the *New York Times* the next day, "There is one Number One and that is Ed Meese."[4]

What did this division of labor leave for Baker? Only tasks that, from the outside, seemed less influential and more ministerial: Managing the flow of paper in and out of the Oval Office. Controlling the president's schedule. Supervising legislative and press operations. Chairing meetings of White House staff. In addition, Baker would have the chief of staff's office—the largest in the West Wing and the only one with a fireplace. In other words, Baker had reserved for himself all the real levers of power. "In the White House," Baker once said, "Cabinet rank doesn't mean a thing."[5] Not for nothing did *Time* magazine once call him the "Velvet Hammer."[6]

Baker went on to set the gold standard as chief of staff. He filled the White House with capable, nonideological doers—highly competent officials like Bob Kimmitt, Richard Darman, Bob Zoellick, and Margaret Tutweiler, who later became known as Baker's "plug-in unit" because they took on senior roles with Baker as secretary of the treasury and secretary of state. From this position of strength, Baker managed Reagan's first-term agenda, including landmark tax cuts, a buildup in defense spending, and deregulation of the economy.

On March 30, 1981, less than seventy-five days after Reagan took office, Baker faced an event for which, he admitted, he was not ready—Reagan was shot. Throughout the administration, chaos ensued. As spokesperson Larry Speakes unsuccessfully pleaded for calm, Secretary of State Al Haig rushed to the press briefing room, sweat pouring down his forehead after running up the stairs, telling the assembled media, "I am in control"—upending the order of succession that started with the vice president before passing to the Speaker of the House, followed by the Senate leader pro tempore and then the secretary of state. A few hours later, Baker returned from Reagan's hospital bedside to the White House, "suit creased and tie firmly in place," and calmly and effectively took control of the situation.[7]

Baker went on to serve as secretary of the treasury and secretary of state. In each position, he orchestrated monumental achievements. At Treasury, he managed the most significant tax reform in decades and negotiated the five-party Plaza Accord, easing a currency crisis. As secretary of state to George H. W. Bush, he helped facilitate the end of the Cold War, usher in the reunification of Germany, and create the international coalition to secure the liberation of Kuwait. I remember watching enraptured—on CNN in my college cafeteria—when Baker concluded his negotiations with Iraqi foreign minister Tarik Aziz, announcing that "regrettably" they did not have an agreement. A few days later, with five hundred thousand coalition troops already positioned in the Middle East, the bombs fell on Baghdad, and the liberation began.

Later, as the economy slowed and Bush's popularity waned, Bush called on Baker one last time, to return to the White House as chief of staff and help coordinate Bush's flagging reelection campaign. But it was too late to transform the president's fortunes. Bill Clinton won the election, and Baker, as chief of staff, presided over one more transition—Bush's departure from office.

Baker's legacy is unique in our history. Former national security advisor Tom Donilon called Baker "the most important unelected official since World War II," while biographers Peter Baker and Susan Glasser dubbed him "Washington's indispensable man."[8]

When I initially approached Baker about being on the podcast, he demurred. He wrote me a formal letter, thanking me for the invitation but suggesting that I interview his old rival Ed Meese, since it was Meese who ran the Reagan transition. I reached out to Meese's son, General Mike Meese, who reported that his father was unwell and could not participate. Only then did Baker agree to come on our podcast.

Three months after our interview, I was worried to learn that Baker, at age ninety, had contracted COVID-19. But true to form, Baker beat the odds and the disease. In September 2020, David Rubenstein, Michael Abramowitz, and I hosted a book event for Peter Baker and Susan Glasser with more than seven hundred prominent Washingtonians. We invited Baker, but he declined—he was hunting elk in Wyoming.

"The five *P*s"

DAVID MARCHICK (DM): Your grandfather, James Addison Baker, had a piece of advice to lawyers joining his firm, which was work hard, study hard, and stay out of politics. You've worked hard and studied hard, but you didn't listen to that last piece. What happened there?

JAMES BAKER (JB): I tell people that in baseball, 66 percent is not a bad batting average. My grandfather told me to be a little bit less facetious about it. I lost a wife to cancer when she was only thirty-eight years of age, but I had a really good friend here in Houston, Texas, who had just gone into politics. His name was George [H. W.] Bush. He was my tennis doubles partner, and he came to me after my wife died and said, "You need to get your mind off your grief and help me run for the Senate." I said: "That's great, George, except for two things. Number one, I don't know anything about politics; and number two, I'm a Democrat." He said, "We can change that latter thing." So, I helped him.

That was 1970. I helped him run for Senate against Lloyd Bentsen, who beat him, but we ran a good race. So that's how I happened to get into politics. My good friend saw it as a way for me to assuage my grief, and he got me in it. I was his Harris County campaign manager on that Senate race in 1970, and from there I did a lot more things in politics.

DM: One of the things you're famous for is preparation, focus, and never being at a loss for words. Your father had an important saying about five *P*s. What were those five *P*s?

JB: My dad used to call it the Mantra of the Five *P*s: "prior preparation prevents poor performance." He drilled that into me from the time I was a young man, and it's really stood me in very good stead throughout all the politics and public service I have participated in. It also stood me in very good stead in the United States Marine Corps, in law school, and in the practice of law because I was never one who would try to wing it. A lot of times you try to wing it, and it doesn't fly. By observing the five *P*s, I was always prepared.

"I think it's something about the broad-gauge nature of the Gipper"

DM: Let's fast-forward to the Reagan election. There was a very unusual thing that happened in that election: you spent five years trying to keep Ronald Reagan out of office. First when you were running Gerald Ford's effort and then later running George Bush's efforts. Then Reagan approached you to be chief of staff after you tried to defeat him twice. Why would he approach you as chief of staff, and will that ever happen again?

JB: I tell people when they talk to me about this that I don't think it will ever happen again in American politics where a president-elect will go, "You're someone who has run at least two campaigns against me and beaten me in one of them," but ask them to be their White House chief of staff. I think it's something about the broad-gauge nature of the Gipper. He was looking for someone who knew and understood how Washington works. He was coming in right after Jimmy Carter, who was an extraordinarily bright person and didn't think he needed anybody in the District of Columbia to tell him how to do things. They didn't do a really good job of massaging the interest groups in the city or working with Congress. In fact, right off the bat, they got crossways with the Democratic Speaker of the House, Tip O'Neill, who referred to Hamilton Jordan, Carter's [eventual] chief of staff, as Hannibal Jerkin.

Reagan was determined that he wasn't going to suffer that same fate, so he looked for somebody who knew how Washington worked. I was that person. He was persuaded to give that a try by Stuart Spencer, who was his political strategist, and Mike Deaver, who was his very close aide, almost his closest family. They talked to Nancy Reagan about it and convinced her. And then the three of them spoke to the president. That's how it happened.

DM: According to Peter Baker and Susan Glasser's book, Spencer and Deaver had you go on a plane trip with then-governor Reagan to test you out and establish a relationship between Reagan and you. That went pretty well, and then he turned to you.

JB: That's correct. They put me on the campaign plane for two weeks. I was working in the campaign, and I was the only Republican at that point in time who had run a campaign for president of the United States and not gone to jail. They put me on the plane so that I would become acquainted. The president had to measure me, see if he really wanted to try to bring in as his chief of staff someone who'd been running campaigns against him.

"My job was to make sure the trains ran on time"

DM: Ed Meese had been working on the transition, but as chief of staff your job was to put together the White House staff. One thing that you had to do was negotiate an arrangement with Ed Meese, because he was a longtime aide to Reagan, his chief of staff [as governor of California]. Tell us about that.

JB: The night of election, President Reagan said, "Jim, before you go back to Texas, I want to see you." I said, "Fine, Mr. President-elect." I went home, and I told my wife, Susan, about that. She started crying because she figured out what was coming. The next morning, I met with the president. He said, "Jim, I want you to be my White House chief of staff." After I picked myself up off the floor, he looked at me, and he said, "But I want you to make it right with Ed Meese," who had been his chief of staff [as governor] and who was counting on being his chief of staff after he became president. In fact, he already had the organization tables drawn up.

I called Ed, and I said, "Let's go to breakfast and talk about this." We went down there, and I said, "Let's figure out a workable way to divide up the responsibilities in the White House." I had been in the Ford White House, not full-time, but I worked closely with him as Ford's campaign chairman, and I knew a little bit about how it worked. So, we sat down, and we drew up a one-pager, just one page with two columns, JB on one side and EM on the other, delineating what we would agree would be our respective areas of authority and responsibility. We each agreed that the other would have walk-in rights to the Oval Office, and we agreed on those kinds of things and just jotted them down. That was kind of our Bible going forward.

DM: And you did that with classic Jim Baker skill and grace. You gave him cabinet status, and you didn't reserve that for yourself; you gave him authority over policy. But you did maintain the core levers of power for yourself in terms of the scheduling, the operation, and the time of the president, which you often said is the most valuable asset.

JB: You have to remember that while Ed had been Reagan's chief of staff as governor of California, Ed was interested in policy. He was a wonderful policy synthesizer for the president. So, we agreed that he would have a responsibility for the domestic policy council. The national security advisor would report to the president through him. He would have cabinet rank, and my job was to make sure the trains ran on time. Making the trains run on time meant I had to have authority over congressional relations, press relations, political relations, and operate from the chief of staff's office, which is the biggest office in the West Wing and the only office that's big enough to have large meetings. It really worked out well for the president-elect, it worked out well for me obviously, and I think it worked out okay for Ed, although he was extremely disappointed at the time not to be named chief of staff.

"People who could get the job done"

DM: How did you and President Reagan, as you pulled together the staff, bal-ance between California loyalists and people that had worked on his cam-paign and Washington insiders and people that you were comfortable with?

JB: We didn't have to balance it. President Reagan said, "I want you to be my chief of staff." I asked if I could staff the White House because, as I said, "I know the people that you're going to want around you who can get things done." That was the only real function I had in that transition. I didn't deal with transition-ing the cabinet departments or anything else. Ed Meese ran that.

I ran the transition in the White House, and President Reagan gave me a carte blanche to hire the White House staff. I hired a number of people, who some of the more hard-line members of the administration thought were inappropriate because they weren't "Reaganites." But they were people who were pragmatic, just like I was, and just frankly like Ronald Reagan was, and people who could get the job done and got the job done for you.

By the way, when I took the job of secretary of state for my longtime friend George H. W. Bush, I had a carte blanche to staff the State Depart-ment. I never had to go over hat in hand to get the approval of presidential personnel because I'd run all of his campaigns, so if anybody knew who was politically okay, it would be me.

"You can't be ready for assassination"

DM: Talking about "prior preparation prevents poor performance," just over two months after Reagan took office he was shot. Were you ready for that? Was the administration ready? How does a chief of staff get ready for some-thing so unexpected, especially so soon after you're in office?

JB: Well, you can't be ready for assassination, and we were not any more ready than any other administration would be. You never know when it's going to happen. The contingency plans were plans that the Secret Service quickly implemented on the spot there. Plan number one was to move the president quickly to a hospital. But first, they were going to head back to the White House because they didn't know he'd been shot. Whether or not we would have done anything differently? My answer to that would be, "No." Everything seemed to work out pretty well. The president did go to the hospital. He fully recovered, and by the next day, he was signing a piece of legislation that I took over to [the hospital in order to] show the world that he was functional and everything was okay.

"Realize that you're staff and not chief"

DM: In 1984, Reagan gets reelected, and an unusual transition occurs. You swap jobs with the treasury secretary, Don Regan. He became chief of staff, and you became secretary of the treasury. How did that happen? And whose idea was it?

JB: It was Don Regan's. It may never happen again either, but if it does, I think the suggestion or the idea will originate with the president. In this case, it originated with Regan, who had been the closest cabinet officer to the president. They were both Irishmen; they were both roughly the same age. Regan had been chairman of Merrill Lynch, and he and Reagan were very close. Regan did a good job as treasury secretary, but he was very ambitious and wanted more power.

The chief of staff job is the second-most-powerful job in Washington, provided you realize that you're staff and not chief. I'm not sure Don ever realized that because he'd been a principal. I've always said you should not ever put someone who's been a principal in that job, because the title is chief of staff.

So, it was his idea. He was mad about a leak in the *Washington Post*. He sent me a letter saying: "I hereby resign as treasury secretary. Please give this letter to the president." I said: "Come on, Don. Take a deep breath. I'm going to come over there and see you." And I went over to the Treasury and got him to withdraw his letter, and I patched it up with him.

He looked at me and said, "You're tired, aren't you?"

I said, "Damn right, I'm tired of this. I've held this job longer than anybody in history that hasn't gone to jail."

He said, "You and I ought to exchange jobs."

I said, "You better not say that again because if the president is willing, I might take you up on that."

I went back and forgot it, but he called me again about a week or so later. I said I would consider it if he was really serious and went back and talked to Deaver about it. I talked to Dick Darman, my assistant, a very good right-hand man and friend. I talked to Susan, my wife, about it. They all thought if it's something the president wants to see done, you ought to do it.

Deaver first took it to Nancy. She was the director of personnel, really, of the Reagan administration. She was his guardian, his protector. And she said she thought it was a good idea since she knew how close Reagan and Regan were to each other. We talked to the president about it, and he agreed. That's how that happened.

"People are policy"

DM: Let's move to another transition, when George H. W. Bush gets elected. I think he's the third sitting vice president ever to be elected, but it was the first time in over a hundred years. You moved to become secretary of state. In your book, you called that transition a "hostile takeover." Andy Card [a key figure in George H. W. Bush's transition and the subject of the following interview in this volume] similarly said that transition from one party to another is much easier than a transition between members of the same party. Why is this so?

JB: It's hard because you've got all these people you've been serving with who are all good Republicans and expect to serve in another Republican administration. But the new president needs to put his imprimatur on the government, which means you need new people. People are policy. They're not going to be too quick to want change. That's why I say it was a hostile takeover because everybody expects to be reappointed. Therefore, it's a little difficult, because you have to go through and say, "Alright, we're going to change you out." So I agree with Andy.

DM: You pretty much brought all new people into the State Department at the senior levels, really quite capable people like Bob Kimmitt, Bob Zoellick, and Dennis Ross, and people that have gone on after working for you to have distinguished careers as well.

JB: I brought what the press referred to as my "plug-in unit," people that went from working with me on campaigns to the White House, to Treasury, and then to State. I took them with me everywhere I went. Most of the model I followed was the same model that Henry Kissinger used, where he staffed some of the upper echelons on the seventh floor of the State Department with people he knew and people he had constancy with, as opposed to career employees that he might not know. But having said that, I had a lot of really good career public servants and foreign service officers who occupied very senior positions in the State Department.

I had the first foreign service officer who ever became deputy secretary of state, Lawrence Eagleburger. I had also had career people in many of the assistant secretary slots. It was only there at the top where I put Bob Kimmitt in as undersecretary for political affairs, but I had Larry Eagleburger or career officials over him. I brought Bob Kimmitt in as counselor. I had Margaret Tutwiler. I had John Rogers as assistant secretary for management. I did bring in my plug-in unit, but I would argue that I didn't foreclose important positions for careers.

There's always a little bit of suspicion and hostility toward a new secretary of state, particularly because 80 percent of the people in the State Department are career officials. They know that the political people are there for a short period of time, so there's a tendency to suspect that they may not have the best interests of the building in mind. That was the rap on me when I first went in there. But after they found out about my seamless relationship with President Bush, and that because of that the State Department was going to be the lead in formulating and implementing foreign policy, they loved it. It turned out very well, primarily because of my relationship with the president, which put the State Department in the lead on all foreign policy matters.

DM: One of the things that you dealt with when you were chief of staff in the Reagan administration was that the first national security team didn't really work together very well. They had Richard Allen at the NSC [National Security Council], General Haig at State, and Cap Weinberger at the Pentagon. In the Bush administration, they had perhaps the best foreign policy team of any modern president, including Brent Scowcroft and Dick Cheney. Did your Reagan experience and the dysfunction of the Reagan national security team affect the way that you and President Bush put together your team?

JB: Yes, it did. Very much so. And it affected the president, who put the team together with my help. One of the things we made sure of was we went with people who were all friends and who had served with each other in other government jobs. That was one of the reasons we worked well together. I've often said that I think 41's national security team was the way the national security team ought to work, but we were the exception to the rule. If you go down every other administration, you'll see all sorts of backstabbing and inciting and leaking on each other on the part of the national security apparatus.

George Bush knew how his national security apparatus was intended to work, and he saw to it that it worked that way. Part of that was getting people whose competence was unquestionable, but who were friends and who had been known to work together in past iterations. That's one reason I think we were so successful: we had great leadership, and we were all friends.

Notes

1. Doris Kearns Goodwin, *Team of Rivals: The Political Genius of Abraham Lincoln* (New York: Simon and Schuster, 2005), xvii.
2. Peter Baker and Susan Glasser, *The Man Who Ran Washington: The Life and Times of James A. Baker III* (New York: Doubleday, 2020), 129.
3. On the origins of this adage, and its application throughout James Baker's career, see James A. Baker and Steve Fiffer, *"Work Hard, Study—and Keep out of Politics!"* (Evanston, IL: Northwestern University Press, 2008).
4. Baker and Glasser, *The Man Who Ran Washington*, 134.
5. Deborah Hart Strober and Gerald S. Strober, *Reagan: The Man and His Presidency* (Boston: Houghton Mifflin, 1998), 63.
6. *Time*, February 13, 1989, cover.
7. Baker and Glasser, *The Man Who Ran Washington*, 155.
8. Both quotes from Baker and Glasser, *The Man Who Ran Washington*, 15, 22.

Bush 41's "Friendly" Takeover

ANDY CARD

> This was a friendly takeover, so we had the added burden of managing the expectations of people who are working for President Reagan who just assumed they would stay in their jobs if George Bush was elected.
>
> —Andy Card

ONE MIGHT think that the transition from Reagan to Bush would prove seamless. After all, not only was this a same-party transfer of power; Bush had served for eight years as his predecessor's vice president—making him the first sitting VP to be elected president since Martin Van Buren in 1836. What I learned from Andy Card, who served as deputy chief of staff for President George H. W. Bush and helped drive his transition, was that "friendly" transitions may, in fact, be more difficult than "hostile" ones.

Until Joe Biden's victory in 2020, George H. W. Bush had perhaps the most experience of any person to be elected president. In addition to his two terms as vice president, he had been a congressman, the Republican Party chief, an envoy to China, and the head of the CIA. Early in 1988, Bush asked longtime aide Chase Untermeyer to quietly begin transition planning. Bush instructed him to keep it small and focus on organization, not personnel. Bush himself spent little time on the transition, preferring to focus on his role as VP and on campaigning.[1]

President Reagan helped ease Bush's transition in many respects, including by asking Bush to join him in a critical summit with Soviet leader Mikhail Gorbachev. Several cabinet officers obligingly resigned, enabling Reagan to appoint officials more acceptable to Bush, like Nick Brady, Bush's longtime friend, at Treasury; Dick Thornburgh, the governor of Pennsylvania, at Justice; Lauro Cavazos at the Department of Education; and William Webster at the CIA. Each of them would continue to serve under Bush. Nevertheless, Bush faced two major challenges in his transition to power: personnel and symbolism.

With respect to personnel, Bush wanted to put his imprint on the presidency. This was where the "friendly takeover" turned less than friendly. Many Reagan appointees simply assumed they would stay on board. Reagan's fourth and final chief of staff, Ken Duberstein, had to send not one but two letters to Reagan political appointees asking them to tender their resignation to clear the deck for Bush—most officials simply disregarded the initial missive.[2] Ironically for a man with perhaps the best network of any president-elect up to that point, Bush's appointment process was rocky and slow—possibly because he had the luxury of relying on Reagan holdovers. Only three of his cabinet nominees received pre-inaugural hearings, and only six new nominees were confirmed by the end of January 1989. Ultimately, however, Bush made several important choices, including appointing John Sununu as White House chief of staff and putting together perhaps the most effective national security team of any president in the modern era.

In terms of symbolism, Bush needed to distinguish himself from his predecessor, burying the narrative that his presidency would simply be the equivalent of Reagan's third term. Accordingly, he used his transition and first year to signal important differences from the Reagan administration. Whereas Reagan had dealt in high-level thematics, Bush would be an activist president, engaged in policy details. He signaled a softer edge on race relations by meeting with Black leaders on Martin Luther King, Jr. Day. And he held more news conferences in his first three months than Reagan had in his last two years.[3]

Andy Card, a pivotal figure in this transition, was the ultimate Bush family loyalist: he ran Bush's 1980 campaign in Massachusetts, served for eight years in the Reagan administration, for four years under George H. W. Bush, and an astonishing six years—the longest tenure ever for that role—as chief of staff to Bush 41's son, George W. Bush. Card is also one of the most experienced transition veterans in the United States, having worked on transitions into office for both Bushes, as well as leading H. W.'s transition out of office. My interview with Card was therefore focused not just on the George H. W. Bush transition but also on his experience at the top levels of government for more than twenty-two years.

Andy also played an influential role in the 2020 transition. When GSA administrator Emily Murphy declined to ascertain the apparent winner, citing the decision by the Clinton White House not to ascertain a winner during the 2000 election dispute as precedent, Andy teamed up with

former Clinton White House chief of staff John Podesta to write a persuasive *Washington Post* op-ed arguing that election of 2020 was in no way
like the election of 2000.[4] He also worked with his successor as chief of
staff, Josh Bolten, as well as numerous Republican governors to ensure
that Biden's electoral victory was recognized and accepted by Republican
leaders.

What I will always remember about Andy is not his significant role
in government over twenty-plus years, nor the fact that he was the man
who whispered "America is under attack" in President Bush's ear on 9/11.
It was how we met. I was a young staffer at the Office of the United States
Trade Representative; Andy headed the automotive trade association. We
worked together for several years on auto trade negotiations with Japan.
He was a former senior White House official and cabinet officer, yet he
took the time to engage with me, a twenty-five-year-old kid who knew
nothing. In my mind, Andy was proof that, even in politics, nice guys
finish first, not last.

"It was kind of left to Chase the day after the election"

DAVID MARCHICK (DM): The 1988 transition was unusual because George H. W.
  Bush was the first vice president to be elected president since Martin Van
  Buren in 1836. When did then–vice president Bush actually start to think
  about transition planning?
ANDY CARD (AC): Because he had served in so many different positions under so many different presidents, including vice president to Ronald Reagan, he had a pretty good understanding of how government worked. So I
  don't think that his expectation on transition was to learn how government
  worked and then decide how to do it. Instead, it was, "I've been doing it for
  a long time, and I want to show everyone how well I can do it." I think that
  he spoke to Chase Untermeyer very early on in 1988, which was the election
  year, and assigned Chase the responsibility to put together a plan for a transition. That would've been January or February 1988, and Chase did it all by
  himself. He didn't call a lot of attention—he's never been one to look for the
  limelight—but he did a lot of quiet work and wrote papers and stimulated
  discussions. There weren't many people that even knew he was doing it until
  the summer after the primary process had almost come to an end and we
  were getting ready to get to the Republican National Convention. I think it

was David Broder [of the *Washington Post*] who wrote a story and kind of outed Chase Untermeyer for planning for a transition.

DM: How did that leak out?

AC: Well, I seriously doubt that it came from Chase Untermeyer. I think it was actually the candidate, George H. W. Bush, who had great respect for David Broder and maybe had somehow got the word to Broder that he was ready to be president and had somebody working on the transition. I also think that it might've been done to calm people down before the Republican convention if they were all going to start looking for jobs. It kind of outed Chase Untermeyer as the person that was going to help people find jobs in the administration if they were successful.

DM: Chase's work was run outside of the White House. It was supported by the RNC. Why wasn't it part of the vice president's office?

AC: Chase was given this task without a lot of consultation. I don't think Vice President Bush talked to many people about doing it. Chase had probably stimulated some interest; I think he sent a memo to Vice President Bush saying he ought to think about how to transition in. President Bush's relationship with Chase was so close that I'm sure he just made this decision on his own and kind of tasked Chase with doing it. I think it was smart how they funded it and did it. Chase worked under the Republican National Committee's budget. He didn't spend a lot of money doing it anyway, but he was smart to do it under the Republican National Committee's budget because there was no provision for the federal government's tax money to be used on a transition. Now the laws have been changed, and they do allow federal money to be spent preparing candidates to be ready to be president. But at that time, they did not, and it wouldn't have made sense to use money that was donated to the campaign to elect George Bush president to fund a transition. So I think it was prudent and the right person. He also kept his mouth shut. Chase is not one who stands on the mountaintop yelling and screaming for attention.

DM: Bush was vice president. He was a candidate for president. How much time did he actually spend on transition, and how often did the transition team brief him or meet with him?

AC: In the early days of the campaign, he did not spend much time with it. He left Chase to his work, and Chase wrote memos, and those memos would be reviewed. They really anticipated a problem that not many people thought about. This would be a friendly transition. It wasn't a hostile takeover. Most of American history has had transitions that were centered around hostile takeovers. This was a friendly takeover, so we had the added burden of managing the expectations of people who are working for President Reagan who just assumed they would stay in their jobs if George Bush was elected. Chase anticipated that and actually started working on that with some of his memos early on, so we paid a little bit more attention. But candidly, the campaign was so focused on the campaign, they were not spending a lot of time thinking about the transition. It was kind of left to Chase the day after the election.

DM: One of President-elect Bush's first decisions was to pick his chief of staff. There was a big battle then between his longtime aide, Craig Fuller, and John Sununu, who was the governor of New Hampshire. How did that play out? And what do you remember about that decision?

AC: I remember this process very, very well. President Bush and I had a candid relationship that went back years. I was the volunteer chairman of his campaign when he first ran for president and ran the Massachusetts part of the campaign in 1979 and '80. He would occasionally talk to me and ask what I thought about different people, including Craig Fuller, John Sununu, and others. I was not surprised that most of the Washington community was in the "Craig Fuller is going to be the chief of staff" camp. There were others that thought that Jim Baker was going to have a disproportionate role in picking who the chief of staff would be, and there was even talk of a troika similar to what President Reagan had with [James] Baker, [Ed] Meese, and [Michael] Deaver.

I had worked at the White House when the troika was three chiefs of staff, one person with the title—James A. Baker III—and two others who didn't have the title but functioned as chiefs of staff. I found it very awkward, so I was someone who counseled the vice president against the troika system. I'm not sure that John Sununu's name came up an awful lot, even in the political community. But I knew that President Bush was very grateful for the work that Governor Sununu had done in New Hampshire to help them overcome defeats in the Iowa caucuses and in the Michigan experience. New Hampshire put Vice President Bush's campaign back on track to success and created a climate that allowed them to win, so I was not surprised when John Sununu's name was mentioned. I'm going to guess it was after the election, it was probably around November 10, 11, or 12 when I had a sense that Vice President Bush was giving some very serious thought to having John Sununu be his chief of staff.

DM: You were going to be deputy chief of staff, which you knew, so you were essentially involved in picking your boss. That's a pretty good job.

AC: Well, that's kind of an overstatement. I'm blessed to have known John Sununu in politics. I was a member of the planning board in the town of Holbrook, Massachusetts. I got elected to that position in 1971, and John Sununu was on the planning board in the city of Salem, New Hampshire, so I was a big John Sununu fan and still am. He's one of the most intelligent people I've ever met. Sometimes he's not that smart, but he's really, really intelligent, so I was pleased that President Bush was thinking about John Sununu as a chief of staff. I was told that that's who it would be, but not to tell anybody except for Ed Rogers [a veteran of the Reagan White House who would go on to serve in the Bush administration]. Ed Rogers and I were brought in the loop, and we took good care of John Sununu as he was transitioning from being the governor of New Hampshire to be announced as the chief of staff. I don't think he was announced until November 17, but I'm pretty sure I knew about it on November 12, 13, or 14.

"It's really two transitions that a president makes"

AC: Ken Duberstein helped later on in the transition by sending letters to all of the appointees, saying: "A new president is coming in, we want to make sure the new president has the right to put people in positions that he wants to put in. So think about sending in your letter of resignation." That letter I don't think generated any response.

DM: I guess he had to send that twice because people ignored that piece of mail.

AC: Yes. This was the challenge of having a friendly takeover where people who are working for President Reagan presumed that they would of course just stay on the job and continue to do what they were doing. But Ken Duberstein understood the real responsibility of a president, and that's to put people around them that they want to put in there, to build a team. Ken tried to help, and eventually it did make a difference, but it did take some time to catch on, and it was much later in the process than what Josh Bolten did helping with the transition from George W. Bush to Barack Obama.

DM: How did the Bush 41 team decide which Reagan appointees could stay in and which should go?

AC: That was kind of Chase's job: first to understand the lay of the land and then, when the transition was formalized, it was collecting names, assessing abilities, and trying to make people fit. But I do want to call attention to a reality that has been missed in a lot of the books I've read about transitions.

We tend to think of the transition as one transition. It's really two transitions that a president makes: one is the White House staff itself, and the other is the transition of the executive branch of government. I feel strongly that Presidents George H. W. Bush and George W. Bush both recognized that transition at the White House has to be done, I think, under the tutelage of a chief of staff because the chief of staff is responsible for running that staff.

Transitioning the cabinet agencies is very different. In the transition even from Ronald Reagan to George H. W. Bush there was a separate transition from the White House staff vis-à-vis the rest of the executive branch, and where the responsibility overlaps is in the Office of Presidential Personnel. Chase was brought in to run the Office of Presidential Personnel right after the transition had been completed. His job was building the departments and agencies, Schedule Cs [junior political appointees], the cabinet secretaries, the deputy secretaries, assistant secretaries, and the commissions and the ambassadorships. The White House staff transition is really run more by the chief of staff. And just to put things in context, I had the privilege of working under every chief of staff that served Ronald Reagan and eventually George H. W. Bush before I became chief of staff. But every time there was a change in chief of staff, especially under the Reagan administration, I would tender my resignation.

I started off as a special assistant to the president for intergovernmental affairs, a very heady title and a great responsibility. And when chiefs of staff would change, I would tender my resignation, expecting that the new chief of staff should decide who the staff should be. I don't know why, but fortunately I was told each time that they wanted me to stay. I do feel that the chief of staff should have a disproportionate say in who the White House staffers are since the chief of staff is held accountable for how the staff is doing its job. I would say that history would show that the two Bush administrations and the Obama administration did a good job of that, focusing on the White House staff first and letting the chief of staff pick the staff.

DM: Whereas the Clinton administration and the Carter administration really focused on the cabinet more and not the White House staff. That probably hurt both of their presidencies at least in the first year.

AC: Oh, I think it did. For example, Mack McLarty, who was a dear friend, he's a wonderful guy, was first chief of staff to President Clinton, but he was about the last person named. So the White House staff was all built before he became the chief of staff, and the cabinet was built without his input. I don't think that was the best model. I think George H. W. Bush had a very good model, and Ronald Reagan had a good model. Remember, he kind of surprised people when he picked Jim Baker to be his chief of staff. James A. Baker III had been very, very involved in Vice President Bush's campaign against Ronald Reagan. So when Jim Baker became chief of staff, that sent a big signal as well, which was very positive.

"Everybody understands that there's a new sheriff in town"

DM: One of the books that I read preparing for this interview had a quote from you that said that hostile takeovers in a transition are easier. Why did you say that, and why was the Reagan-to-Bush transition so difficult?

AC: Well, again, the friendly takeover has the expectation from people who are working on the "same" team that they're going to continue to work on the same team. In a hostile takeover, everybody understands that there's a new sheriff in town; there's a credible expectation that things are going to change, including people. But even then, I ran the transition out when there was a hostile takeover when Bill Clinton came in and George H. W. Bush was leaving office. I remember President Bush asking me to call the Clinton people and say: "The president will do whatever you want; if you want him to clear the decks so that you can just put people in, we'll do that. Or we'll leave people in there and you can clear the decks, which would you like?" They said: "Oh, that's very nice of you to do that. It'd be wonderful if you'd clear the decks, with the exception of a few people." We said, "Well, tell us the names of the people that you want to not have resign and we'll suggest that they should stay on." Well, obviously the vast majority of people, according to the Clinton incoming team, would need to resign. I was given the task to call those people and say, "President Bush will accept your resignation effective the day that he leaves office."

It was surprising how many people, including cabinet members, said: "No, I'll just wait until they remove me. I'm not planning to leave." President Bush said, "No, I promised I would clear the decks, we'll clear the decks." It was much easier to do that in the context of a hostile takeover than a friendly one where the conversations were very different. You know: "I always supported the president when he was Ronald Reagan's vice president. I've been doing a good job. I'd like to stay on the job, so I think I'll stay."

DM: Who was the hardest person to actually get out of their office in your recollection?

AC: Under George H. W. Bush, it would have been [Secretary of Housing and Urban Development] Jack Kemp. He just did not want to leave. He said, "I'm

going to stay here as secretary of HUD, and I won't leave until my successor is confirmed." I said, "The president would like to accept your letter of
resignation effective at noontime on January 20." He said, "I'm going to stay
on until my successor is confirmed." But yes, there were several; that was just
one of several. In fact, he basically told me that he was ignoring me, that I
did not have the authority. I said I was calling at the president's request. He
said, "I don't believe that." It was a very awkward thing for me to do.

DM: How did you help Bush put his own stamp on the presidency after Reagan? And what are the key things that President Bush did early on to show
that his presidency would be different?

AC: It started with George H. W. Bush, who recognized that he didn't have the
same personality as Ronald Reagan. He wasn't the same kind of communicator as Ronald Reagan, and the world was also different. George H. W. Bush
has the greatest résumé of anyone who's ever been president. But it's a résumé
grounded in relationships developed through his years at the UN or as envoy
to China or director of the CIA, or chairman of the Republican Party, or vice
president, whereas Ronald Reagan's was built by a celebrity status and great
communications and the ability to translate political jargon into common,
everyday language. George H. W. Bush recognized he wasn't Ronald Reagan.
He agreed with Ronald Reagan on most of the policy aspects, but he wasn't
Ronald Reagan. He was going to have a different style to his government,
and he was adjusting to his style. I think that it ended up proving to be that
George H. W. Bush was the most successful one-term president in the history of our country. He had unbelievable success stories during his four-year
presidency, starting with the fall of the Berlin Wall. We went from a Cold
War to transition to a unified Germany without a war, and the relationship
with the Soviet Union changed dramatically. So from a foreign policy point
of view, unbelievable successes, but he did not have a Congress controlled by
his party. The Democrats controlled the Senate and the House, and he was
still able to get the Americans with Disabilities Act passed. He was able to
get the Clean Air Act passed. He had tremendous successes, and we tend to
forget that, but it was a difference in style, not so much a difference in policy.

"He's our president, and we want him to succeed"

DM: So my last question for you is about the crisis we're currently experiencing. We're taping this in late March [2020], in the middle of a shutdown
nationwide because of the coronavirus. It's the biggest crisis in my lifetime;

I'm fifty-three years old. The second-biggest crisis in my lifetime happened on 9/11, and I remember perhaps one of the most poignant pictures of the [George W.] Bush presidency is when he's reading to a bunch of kids, and you came in and whispered in his ear, "The country's under attack." Having lived through that crisis, what advice would you have for the Trump administration on how to manage and how to improve their management of this crisis?

AC: A steady hand is critically important. When the president arrived at the Emma E. Booker School in Sarasota, Florida, there had been a buzz in the air, and I remember two people raising it. Karl Rove and Dan Bartlett both asked a question: "Anybody hear about a plane crash in New York?" When we arrived at the school, the president went to a secure phone and called Condoleezza Rice, who was national security advisor. I did not hear that conversation, but as we were getting ready for the president to go into a classroom with second-graders, I had already gone into the classroom and checked it out and saw the second-graders lined up. They were all excited to be going into this classroom. I saw the press pools starting to gather with [White House press secretary] Ari Fleischer, and I came into the holding room with the president. I'm standing at the door beside the principal of the school, and a White House advisor who was the acting national security advisor on the trip came up to the president and said, "Sir, it appears a small twin-engine prop plane crashed into one of the towers at the World Trade Center in New York City."

The president, the principal, and I all had the same reaction: "Oh, what a horrible accident. The pilot must have had a heart attack or something." Then the principal opened the door to the classroom, and she and the president walked into the class. The door shut, and I'm left inside the holding room, and the director of the White House Situation Room came up to me and said: "Sir, it appears that was not a small training prop plane. It was a commercial jetliner." My mind flashed to the fear that the passengers on the plane must have had. They had to know it wasn't gaining altitude. I don't know why that's where my mind went, but that's where it went, but that was only a nanosecond because Captain Loewer came up to me and said, "Oh my God, another plane hit the other tower at the World Trade Center."

My mind then flashed to three initials, UBL: Usama bin Laden. I knew who he was. I knew about the attacks on the World Trade Center in early '93, late '92, and I knew about the al-Qaeda network. That thought didn't last very long because I then said, "I've got to tell the president." One of the toughest jobs chiefs of staff have is to ask, "Does the president need to know?" This was an easy test to pass. Yes, he needs to know. What do I tell him? I made a conscious decision to pass on two facts, make one editorial comment, and to do nothing to invite a conversation because I assumed that he was sitting under a boom microphone. I knew that he was sitting in front of a second-grade class and a press pool, and I didn't want to have a dialogue with them about it.

I opened the door to the classroom, and, long story short, I whispered into his ear: "A second plane hit the second tower. America is under attack."

He did not turn around and talk to me, which I was pleased about. I then stepped back from him, I could tell he was thinking and thinking, and then I went back to the door. I looked at him again. He was still, his head was kind of bobbing up and down. The students were so attentive to their books, taking out books to read with the president. The press pool was all turned around talking to Ari Fleischer, and I saw the principal of the school and the secretary of education, Rod Paige, mouthing, "What's up?" I walked into the holding room, and the first thing I said was: "Get the FBI director on the phone, get a line open to the vice president. Get a line open to the White House Situation Room. Get the crew back on Air Force One. Secret Service, get ready to turn the motorcade around. We're going to have to leave." Dan Bartlett gets some remarks written for the president—he's going to have to say something, too. We have six hundred people in a gymnasium. He's going to say something, but we can't say anything we do not know to be the truth. That was 9/11.

The goal should be today that the president doesn't say anything he doesn't know to be the truth, that he doesn't practice hyperbole, and he doesn't overly state the nature of the problem. But lift people up, too, so that they understand that we can solve these problems, we can work together, we can make it through. What would I recommend today is to take COVID-19 seriously, practice social distancing, keep those people who are most vulnerable from being infected with the disease, and rally as a country to follow the president's lead. He's our president. Whether you like him or not, he's our president, and we want him to succeed and help us get through this. That's what I would tell people.

Notes

1. John Patrick Burke, *Presidential Transitions: From Politics to Practice* (Boulder, CO: Lynne Rienner, 2000), 192–96.
2. Don Regan was eventually replaced by Senator Howard Baker, in a bid to repair Reagan's relationship with Congress. Duberstein served as Baker's deputy and help the position during Reagan's final months in office.

3. Gerhard Peters, "Presidential News Conferences," The American Presidency Project, https://www.presidency.ucsb.edu/node/323900.

4. Andy Card and John Podesta, "Opinion: The Life-Threatening Costs of a Delayed Transition," *Washington Post,* November 10, 2020, https://www.washingtonpost.com/opinions/podesta-card-bush-gore-transition-trump/2020/11/10/ae1a960a-239f-11eb-8672-c281c7a2c96e_story.html.

Clinton's Bumpy Transition

MACK MCLARTY

> It was really a matter of not enough work being done before the election.
> And once you get behind, it just does not leave you any room to catch up.
> —Mack McLarty

BILL CLINTON finished his second term as one of the most successful two-term presidents of the twentieth century, but his transition was one of the choppiest of the modern era. Looking back after leaving the presidency, Clinton showed disarming candor in criticizing his own transition into office. "I spent hardly any time on the White House staff," he wrote in his autobiography. "And I gave almost no thought to how to keep the public's focus on the most important priorities, which was obviously the economy."[1]

Prior to the election, his transition effort was neither robust nor tightly coordinated with the campaign—something Thomas "Mack" McLarty ascribes to Clinton's desire to avoid being seen as presumptuous. Post-election, Clinton didn't fully use the work of his existing transition team, preferring to empower an entirely new team with responsibility for planning his government. Martha Kumar quotes a Clinton aide: "They didn't know who they were going to be working for. . . . They didn't know what they were supposed to be doing and, frankly, they were not even clear on the common agenda for the White House and the administration."[2] The result was a slow start, injurious jockeying for primacy among key advisors, and the absence of clear policy priorities.

Clinton's process for selecting cabinet officers resembled a graduate school seminar. Holed up in the governor's mansion in Little Rock with five or six key advisors—Mack McLarty, Hillary Clinton, Vice President–elect Gore, transition chair Warren Christopher, Clinton confidant Bruce Lindsey, and longtime Gore aide Roy Neel—the president-elect would start with a deep dive on the agency concerned, followed by a debate over priorities and hour after hour of debating candidates. Clinton did not make his first cabinet announcement until December 10, more than five weeks after the election. (By contrast, even with his delayed start, Joe Biden had made eight cabinet secretary announcements by that date.)

White House appointments had to wait even longer, with certain senior officeholders not named until a couple of days before inauguration. The fact that Mack McLarty was not named White House chief of staff until December 12, approximately six weeks after Election Day, should in itself have signaled a bumpy start. Best practice for transitions would be to name a chief of staff first, ideally a day or two after the election, as with Reagan's appointment of James Baker. Instead, McLarty was named in mid-December on the same day as Clinton's commerce secretary—an important role, but hardly the center of government.

Intuitively, one would expect a high degree of correlation between the quality of a transition and the success of a new administration. That was certainly the case for Clinton, who got off to a bumpy start to his presidency after a less-than-smooth transition. Instead of focusing on the slumping economy, in the early days of his presidency Clinton allowed himself to be drawn into a "culture war" debate over whether members of the LGBTQ community should be allowed to serve in the military.

Despite this and other speed bumps, Clinton enjoyed one of the most consequential first years of any modern president. In the end, he made more presidential appointments in the first one hundred days than Reagan or Bush, including a world-class economic team—Lloyd Bentsen at Treasury; Robert Rubin at the newly established National Economic Council; Leon Panetta and Alice Rivlin at the Office of Management and Budget; Ron Brown at Commerce; and Mickey Kantor as U.S. trade representative.[3] He named Ruth Bader Ginsburg to the United States Supreme Court; brought Palestinian leader Yasser Arafat and Israeli prime minister Ehud Barak together on the South Lawn of the White House; secured congressional approval for NAFTA; established a new national service program; shepherded gun control legislation through Congress; and, most importantly, passed a landmark economic package that laid the foundation for years of economic growth. His chief of staff, Mack McLarty, played a key role in all of these achievements.

I treasure every moment I have spent with Mack McLarty, ever since I first met him when I was a twenty-six-year-old kid working at the White House. I remember pinching myself when I was in an anteroom to the East Room, standing in a circle with Mack and Presidents Clinton, Bush, Carter, and Ford before a NAFTA event. I told Mack there and then I would carry his bag anywhere, any day. It was thus a challenge for me to talk to McLarty diplomatically and respectfully about one of the most difficult times in his storied career: the Clinton transition and the start of the Clinton presidency.

Thomas "Mack" McLarty and William Jefferson Clinton met as classmates in Miss Mary's kindergarten in Hope, Arkansas, in 1951. Miss Mary must have been a spectacular teacher, because one of her students wound up as president of the United States and another as the thirty-nine-year-old CEO of a Fortune 500 company.

After serving one term in the Arkansas legislature when he was twenty-three years old—making him the youngest representative in the state's history—McLarty took over his family's truck-leasing business and helped build the company. He later joined the board of Arkla, a regional natural gas company, and became its CEO. McLarty was only peripherally involved in Clinton's roller-coaster bid for president in 1992, but when his friend clinched the top job, McLarty was thrown into the hot seat as his first chief of staff—or "chief javelin catcher," as McLarty himself put it. After a rocky start, McLarty changed tack around four months into the presidency, restructuring the White House, imposing greater discipline, and bringing in experienced Washington hands like David Gergen, a veteran of the Nixon, Ford, and Reagan administrations. Thankfully, as historian and Clinton biographer Michael Nelson noted on another episode of the podcast, Clinton possessed two vital traits for any successful president: an aptitude for learning and an interest in doing so.[4]

McLarty prepared more intensely for his appearance than any other guest I had on the podcast. Typically for him, he was determined to get it right. Likewise, he jealously defended Clinton's reputation. From my own time as a junior aide in the Clinton White House, I still remember the press corps' brutal treatment of Clinton in those early days. Because of Mack McLarty and more than twenty-five years of hindsight, history will be much kinder, and appropriately so.

"Hindsight is a great substitute for wisdom"

DAVID MARCHICK (DM): Mack, let me ask you, when you and Bill Clinton were five-year-olds in Miss Mary's kindergarten class, who do you think your teacher thought would be more successful?

MACK MCLARTY (MM): Well, I think Mrs. Mary Perkins pulled for all of us and hoped there would be a lot of success from her class. I still have relatively vivid memories about that kindergarten setting, even though I was five or six years old. I have stayed in touch with a lot of those classmates, including, of course, President Clinton. I think we were all pulling for each other; there were certainly dreams that we all had, but not a sense of competition. I think she hoped for successes from a lot of us, and knowing our class, I think that was largely achieved.

DM: It certainly was. Let's fast-forward to 1992: Could you remind us of the primary election issues?

MM: It was a very unique political landscape, which most presidential elections are. President George H. W. Bush had been enormously popular after a successful Desert Storm [the military campaign to end the Iraqi occupation of Kuwait]. His approval ratings approached 90 percent. But the economy had started to stall. There was increasing unemployment and there was a sense in the country that people were wanting a change or at least wanting to consider a change of direction. You'd had President Reagan for eight years, President George H. W. Bush for four; that's twelve years. There was the sense that we can do better.

Governor Clinton captured that feeling with his New Democrat approach to governing and his record as governor of Arkansas, as he had been active in establishing relationships around the country. As the economy continued to get a bit weaker, Governor Clinton really made an effort to hone in on that, and he used that momentum to get elected. Meanwhile, Ross Perot got 19 percent. It's unusual for a third-party candidate to get that much of the vote, which suggested to me that over 60 percent of the country wanted change, but they didn't want radical change. They wanted thoughtful, measured, real change, but done in a careful manner. And I think that was the tenor of the election in 1992.

DM: Clinton's transition was not the best transition ever. In fact, in his own book, he was pretty critical of himself in the transition. He said, "I spent hardly any time on the White House staff, and I gave almost no thought to how to keep the public's focus on the most important priority, which was obviously the economy." Can you talk about what type of transition work was done before the election in 1992?

MM: I think Governor Clinton had a strong feeling, and it's understandable even with the benefit of history that he did not want to be seen as an underdog candidate who was already beginning to measure the drapes in the

Oval Office. At that time, I was chairman and chief executive of a New York Stock Exchange natural gas company. While I was part of the campaign in terms of economic policy and trying to be supportive of a lifelong friend and governor of our home state, I was certainly not active in the day-to-day campaign. I think really that that was the essence of it.

DM: One of the things that President Clinton reflected on in his memoirs, and he said he could have done it better, was that he spent most of his time focused on the cabinet and not the White House. Transition experts would all say today that best practice would be to focus on the White House staff first and then the cabinet. Why do you think he did the opposite?

MM: Again, I think this was really a matter of, like the song, "Time Won't Let Me." There was just a real crunch after the election. There is such a limited time between November 5 and raising your hand on January 20 to get all the apparatus of government in place, as well as respond to so many well-wishers and meet with members of Congress. There are so many stakeholders, including world leaders. And, of course, he had the economic summit in there [a conference of industrialists, union leaders, and economists that Clinton organized in Little Rock in December 1992].

So I think he felt that the cabinet was critically important. He had been a governor and had seen the importance of having people that could lead certain initiatives. But I think you make a very fair point. You either have to do them simultaneously, or perhaps even better, focus on the White House staff first and then quickly move to the cabinet. But it was really a matter of not enough work being done before the election. And once you get behind, it just does not leave you any room to catch up.

DM: You mentioned the economic summit. Our friend, and one of the most successful trade negotiators in U.S. history, Mickey Kantor, was asked to pull together 150 or so businesspeople, labor leaders, and others, to a summit in Arkansas to focus on the economy. It was a big success, but some critics said afterward that the summit was a mistake because it took President-elect Clinton's attention away from selecting his team and pulling together the government. In hindsight, do you think having that summit was the right thing to do? Or maybe he should have just focused on building the government?

MM: Hindsight is a great substitute for wisdom, as we all know. More fundamentally, the real answer is to begin the transition planning process much earlier in a very formal way. The candidate has to really feel that it's a primary responsibility several months before the election. Inevitably, Dave, it goes back to your earlier point about the message. Here's a president-elect who has only received 43 percent of the vote. He was not well known to much of the country. A lot of the country decided to take a chance on him because they wanted change. So it's important that he continues to engage in a public manner. And again, he had so many demands during that time period.

I think the economic summit did put forward that President-elect Clinton and Vice President–elect Gore were reaching out to a broad range of leaders in the country and really getting their best views and opinions and thoughts about how to get this economy going. So I don't really fault the economic summit. I think it was a good messaging event, and I think it was a good substantive event. Where the complication was, is there's only so much time, and it did take away from a critically needed time to choose a White House staff, to choose the cabinet, and to continue to discharge so many other responsibilities, including personal ones. You've got to remember that President-elect Clinton and Hillary and Chelsea were moving from Little Rock to Washington. There's a lot of saying goodbye to friends and a time of reflection. It's just one of those periods that is very, very demanding.

"Transitions are inevitably challenging, difficult, complicated, and messy"

DM: Professor John Burke [a scholar on the presidency at the University of Vermont] has described the postelection meetings in which you participated in the governor's mansion. There were just six people in the room: you, President Clinton, Mrs. Clinton, Al Gore, our friend Bruce Lindsey [Clinton's national campaign director], and Roy Neel [manager of Gore's vice-presidential campaign]. Basically, you all sat there for hours and hours, day after day, going through the cabinet and selecting officials. What were those meetings like?

MM: They were pretty stimulating. They were long, and they were important. When Governor Clinton was elected, on election night I was sitting by his mother at the old statehouse, and he pointed to me and said, "I need to see you tomorrow." I really did not think too much about that because I had been named to the transition committee—Mickey Kantor was chairman of that. As I recall, there were about eight of us in that group, and we'd had a couple of meetings but not in any serious or focused manner. The next day I did go by the governor's mansion to see President-elect Clinton one-on-one.

I conveyed my congratulations and just my heartfelt feelings about what he had accomplished. It was a big moment for our state, and he was a lifelong friend. It was a special and meaningful moment.

DM: President Clinton wrote in his book that you tried to persuade him not to appoint you as his chief of staff. You told him he should appoint someone that had more Washington experience, and that you wanted to focus on economic issues. You're a persuasive guy, but I guess you couldn't persuade him not to pick you.

MM: I tried to be very honest with the president-elect and, again, a lifelong friend. We did have a serious exchange about why he thought I was the best person under the circumstances, and the pros and cons of that as we were thinking through it. What it really boiled down to in his mind was that he wanted someone that, at least at the beginning, he knew and trusted. Someone that he felt would give him very honest and direct advice and counsel and be a reality check that was consistent with his political philosophy, which was the New Democrat philosophy. He knew in my activities as a member of the Democratic National Committee during President Carter's years, and then the natural gas business, that I had been very active with the Senate and the House. I had good relations on both sides of the aisle in Congress. He just really felt that to get his presidential effort launched, he wanted someone that he was comfortable with, knew, and trusted. He felt like I could provide him with not only support but really serious and direct advice. But also, to give that in the right way and to have a level of trust. I think that was the essence of it, and he's a persuasive fellow himself.

DM: One of the things about transitions is just how difficult they are for the people involved. People have anxiety, they want to know what they're going to do. Overall, there is a lot of uncertainty. Is that type of stress and anxiety inevitable in any transition, or are there things that transition leaders and the president-elect can do to make that period a little easier on the people that put their hearts and souls into a campaign?

MM: Listening to some of your other interviews with some very knowledgeable and capable people whom I know and like and respect greatly, I think you've got it right. Transitions are inevitably challenging, difficult, complicated, and messy. I think a lot of that can be mitigated with a much longer planning cycle, which I think now is accepted. That is absolutely key to avoiding some of the missteps, mistakes, and challenges that we had in the Clinton administration. It's a different time and place. I think now people expect a very thoughtful, serious transition effort. That's number one.

Number two, you make an excellent point. There's just no question: you are dramatically shifting from campaigning to governing, which you want to happen smoothly. That's a big challenge. It's much easier said than done, but I think to manage it takes a recognition of it, which is one of the reasons I think the Partnership for Public Service is so important. It takes a commitment on the part of the candidate to speak thoughtfully and directly to the campaign. People are involved in this campaign, not just senior level but throughout the campaign, young people who have given their lives and set expectations properly.

"An all-star team"

DM: President Clinton made his first cabinet appointment on December 10, a little over a month after the election. Senator Lloyd Bentsen, who was chairman of the Finance Committee, became secretary of the treasury. Leon Panetta, who was chairman of the House Budget Committee, became director of the Office of Management and Budget. Bob Rubin, who was head of Goldman Sachs, became director of the [newly created] National Economic Council. That's really an all-star team. Why did Governor Clinton choose to announce his economic team first? Second, can you imagine today a Democratic president-elect talking about the importance of Wall Street before talking about Main Street?

MM: It was a different time and place. The announcement of the economic team, given the campaign and its focus, was logical and proper, and I think played well both politically and substantively. I was certainly proud of those people that you just named, who are very distinguished, capable leaders, and I had recommended all of them in our cabinet discussions. I knew them well, with the exception of Leon Panetta and Alice Rivlin, who served as Leon's deputy, but I knew Leon by reputation. I think that was a logical and strong statement to make and was very well received both in the United States but also around the world. And that was critical because President Clinton had a formulation to be strong abroad. And I think history will judge that he fulfilled that promise.

DM: Two other things are notable about his transition. One is that he was very focused on selecting the most diverse cabinet ever, which he did. Second is that he created the National Economic Council, which put economic issues on par with foreign policy and national security issues. That was perhaps the most significant change in the White House structure since 1947, when the NSC [National Security Council] was created. Why were those two things such a big priority for President Clinton?

MM: Neither were a surprise to me, number one. He had discussed the National Economic Council concept with me. We had actually discussed it during the campaign, and I was strongly for it. He felt like international economic issues had become foreign policy issues, and traditional foreign policy issues had become economic issues. There was an intertwining; I think he was absolutely right in that regard. We got a lot of criticism for establishing the NEC. It's kind of hard to remember after all these years, but it was another level of bureaucracy. There was a change, but I think it really worked out superbly. I think as far as the diversity, you know, Bill Clinton and I grew up at the same time, went to Boys State together, had worked together in Arkansas and in national politics, and we were very much committed to the New South. An inclusive administration reflected his values and how he had run his campaign. So, I think that was, to me, a kind of a foregone conclusion. I was not the least bit surprised by that; I would have been surprised otherwise.

"It's natural to have a touch of hubris"

DM: Let's shift to the early parts of the administration, which you know were a little bumpy. During the campaign he was laser-focused on the economy. But in the first two weeks of the administration, another issue bubbled up, and it took over everything else. That was the issue of [what was then referred to as] "gays in the military." Can you tell us how that happened?

MM: Well, it certainly got us off track, and you make the exact right point. Campaigns by nature are much more freewheeling. There were a lot of young people on Governor Clinton's campaign. Frankly, it's pretty natural to have a touch—or maybe more than a touch—of hubris when someone is elected president of the United States and those around him that have helped him do that. We beat the opposition. We're now in charge, and we're going to do it our way.

I think a bit more modesty is called for in transitions and in governing, particularly the first year. And I think that was an element in some of these mistakes, you know, getting off-message. President Clinton quickly realized he had to be much more measured in his comments as president than he was as a candidate. President Clinton is a great communicator, but sometimes he likes to think out loud a bit more than he should, and he recognized that. So that's really how the "gays in the military" [issue] began. Instead of tamping that down, he made a response, and it took off as an issue. I do think there was a feeling that this was an administration that came from the outside. It's a governor from a southern state, not quite an insurgent campaign, but certainly not a Washington establishment candidate. That created some natural and pretty serious tension with the press. That led to some of these other mistakes, and we paid a price for that.

DM: On the other hand, you have the economic package, which was a huge success. It cut the deficit by $500 billion, it sent a signal to the bond market, which lowered interest rates. That package won by one vote in the House, and the congresswoman who cast that deciding vote ended up losing her election in the next midterm. What would have happened to the Clinton presidency if you had lost that vote?

MM: As I have said before, it was a life-and-death matter. That may be a bit overstated, but there's no question that President Clinton's economic plan was the foundation of his first year in the presidency. That's what the campaign had been about, and that's what he had been so focused on both in the campaign and when we got to the White House. Had we not been successful in passing that and then it had not resulted, not only in the deficit reduction but also a tremendous lift in job creation and wage gains at all levels and all aspects of society. . . . That, to me, was the real foundation of the [Clinton] presidency.

DM: Also, despite the challenging transition, when you look back on that first year, Clinton had more appointments in the first hundred days than Reagan or Bush. He appointed Ruth Bader Ginsburg to the Supreme Court. He brought Yasser Arafat and Ehud Barak together. NAFTA, national service, the Brady bill, the economic package. Which of these do you think had the biggest impact on the perceptions of President Clinton in that first year?

MM: That's an insightful question, and I think an important one. I would answer it in two ways. One, I think the economic plan had to be the most important. That was the pillar. I really was not persuaded we could balance the budget, nor was Bob Rubin [assistant to the president for economic policy]. We felt like we could slow the growth of the deficit, but we were not convinced that we could balance the budget. That was almost beyond reach. What happened is, once people got confidence in the economy, we were very fortunate that we had moderate energy prices and an increase in productivity that helped us to achieve growth in the economy without inflation. You got the momentum going in a positive way with job creation, low unemployment, rising wages, and all of a sudden we really had forward momentum. I think the other point that was so important the first year was for President Clinton to step on the world stage in a confident, statesmanlike manner. We really worked on that, if you go back to the first year, and almost through his entire presidency, he made very few missteps on the world stage and established enduring deep relationships with leaders around the world. And that served him well.

"Try to remember the mission"

DM: Rhodes College professor Michael Nelson said that President Clinton had one of the worst transitions of any modern president but that he also had the most important trait for any successful president, which is the interest and ability to learn.[5] That trait made him one of the best two-term presidents in the modern presidency. Let me ask you a personal question, which is, how did you deal with the pressure of the moment at that time?

MM: It was a demanding period. I was reasonably prepared for that kind of pressure and stress, although there's nothing like working in the White House. And particularly in the chief of staff position, you really have to keep a sense of perspective about what you're trying to accomplish, why you came to Washington to do a job that you were asked to do, and all you can do is your very best to keep your eye truly on the prize. Are we making progress toward getting our economic plan passed, or the Family Medical Leave Act? Whatever the legislative issue of the day was, are we positioning the president correctly to meet these world leaders? Are we engaging with governors?

You just have to do your job and just focus on the task at hand. I tried to not take some of the criticism either of the administration or of me personally. That's hard to do. I won't say I always succeeded, but I certainly made an effort. I was realistic about that when we entered the White House. But it is demanding, and you also have to take physical care of yourself. My wife was such a great supportive partner. She has been for fifty-plus years now. That was a great help. You try to deal with it as best you can, but you really try to remember the mission: why you went there to serve the American people.

DM: Knowing what you know now, what do you wish you knew when you became chief of staff?

MM: A couple of things. One, I reemphasize my core point: I think transitions, which you're working so thoughtfully and seriously on, have changed in terms of expectations and understanding. A formal transition planning effort well in advance of the election is just absolutely imperative, both from a national security standpoint and from an economic security standpoint. Secondly, there's no question that in politics, and particularly in the first year of any presidency, perception is reality. You've got to be focused in a serious, thoughtful way about how you keep your message in front of the American people and the world more broadly. Now, that's not always possible to do because you're going to have what Tom Brokaw referred to as UFOs: those unforeseen occurrences—hurricanes and international conflicts or whatever. But I think those are the two things in retrospect that I would note to any incoming president and chief of staff and White House team.

Notes

1. William Jefferson Clinton, *My Life* (New York: Knopf, 2004), 467.
2. Martha Joynt Kumar, *The White House World: Transitions, Organization, and Office Operations* (College Station: Texas A&M Press, 2003), 6.
3. The economic appointments made by President-elect Clinton were tremendously important, defining the trajectory of U.S. economic policy during both Clinton's term and for years afterward. These personnel decisions also represented the culmination of a long-running ideological struggle within the Democratic Party about their relationship to the market—underscoring the importance of the choices made during a transition. For a sympathetic account of the Democratic Party's transformation, see Brent Cebul, "Supply-Side Liberalism: Fiscal Crisis, Post-Industrial Policy, and the Rise of the New Democrats," *Modern American History* 2, no. 2 (2019): 139–64, doi:10.1017/mah.2019.9. For a more critical account, see Stephanie L. Mudge, *Leftism Reinvented: Western Parties from Socialism to Neoliberalism,* (Cambridge, MA: Harvard University Press, 2018), chap. 7.
4. *Transition Lab,* "Episode 15: Planning for a President's Second Term," podcast, May 18, 2020, https://presidentialtransition.org/blog/planning-for-a-presidents-second-term/.
5. *Transition Lab,* "Episode 15."

Bush 43's Delayed but Smooth Ride into Office

CLAY JOHNSON

> Whether you had been around the governor, or whether you had DC experience, it all tied back to the president's charge to me: find the best people to do the work.
>
> —Clay Johnson

ONLY FOUR presidential elections in American history have been too close to call: 1800, 1836, 1876, and 2000.[1] In 2000, candidates George W. Bush and Al Gore became locked in a clash over Florida's electoral college votes. Following a 5–4 Supreme Court ruling, Bush was found to have won Florida by a margin of just 537 votes. The dispute, however, cut the time available for the postelection transition—tight even in the aftermath of a "normal" election—to just thirty-five days.

Only eight months later, al-Qaeda attacked America. The 9/11 Commission later found that the truncated transition period had "hampered the new administration in identifying, recruiting, clearing, and obtaining Senate confirmation of key appointees."[2] By George W. Bush's hundredth day in office, the Senate had confirmed only two major national security leadership positions at the Department of Defense—the secretary and his deputy. Four and a half months later, on September 11, just 57 percent of the top Senate-confirmed positions at the Pentagon, Department of State, and Department of Justice were filled. Of those in their seats, almost half had been on the job for less than two months.[3] Congress took note of these challenges and the dangers they posed, and, in the form of the Pre-Election Presidential Transition Act of 2010, passed the amendments to the Presidential Transition Act described in Martha Kumar's interview in this volume—changes that were intended to limit the nation's vulnerability during the start of a presidential term.[4]

Despite its delayed start, the scholar John P. Burke would identify this transition as "the best example to date of an effort that was aware of the experiences of its predecessors, recognized the value of the lessons to be learned, and generally was prepared to reap the positive benefits of its predecessors' experiences but avoid the pitfalls."[5] (Burke was writing in 2002, before the still-better handoff from Bush to Obama.) The Bush personnel operation eventually hit its stride. By the end of his first year in office, Bush had made more nominations (856) and had more Senate-confirmed nominees in place (521) than any president before him. A large part of the credit must go to Clay Johnson III.

A childhood friend and college classmate of George W. Bush, Johnson served as head of appointments to Governor Bush at the Texas state house in Austin before being promoted to gubernatorial chief of staff after Joe Allbaugh left to run Bush's presidential campaign. As chief of staff, Clay budgeted a substantial portion of his time to managing the gubernatorial personnel process. Texas is one of a handful of states that relies on numerous gubernatorial appointees—some 1,500 to be exact—to carry out the governor's policies by running a variety of boards, commissions, councils, and task forces. In that sense, Texas's large number of appointments approximates the task at the federal level.

Given this expertise in the appointments process and his long-term relationship of trust with the then governor, it is not surprising that Bush approached Johnson to head his transition planning. Johnson's response— "I'm honored, but . . . I know nothing about transitions"—is common among those tapped to lead transitions.

The preelection phase of the Bush transition began incredibly early— even before the first primary votes were cast. In sharp contrast to the "no-measuring-the-drapes" attitude of previous campaigns, Johnson says the Bush team "wanted to be able to communicate that we were working hard to prepare to govern." Johnson learned key lessons from previous transitions: setting clear goals; keeping the transition and the campaign separate but in constant communication with each other; selecting a chief of staff early; and making a plan for communicating with the press and the public postelection.

Johnson ultimately became director of the Office of Presidential Personnel at the White House. Martha Kumar has described the Bush White House as a deft balance of five different types of knowledge: knowledge of the president (especially his preferred work style); campaign memory; policy experience; White House experience; and Washington experience.[6]

For his part, Johnson puts this success down to his self-described chilly demeanor, matter-of-fact attitude, and singular focus on the success of his longtime friend—a group of characteristics that earned him the nickname "the ice box: tall, white, and cold." Contrary to this reputation, however, I have always found him warm, open, and eager to share his considerable expertise. A case in point: he set out his detailed advice for future presidential transitions in a June 2001 open memo, later expanded into an essay published in *Public Administration Review* the summer before the 2008 election.[7]

After serving in the Bush administration for all of its eight years, Johnson became a key player in Bush's transition out of office, widely seen as the gold standard. Many of the practices he helped implement have since been enshrined in law. Today, Johnson is a go-to resource for transition teams and has served in senior advisory roles at the Partnership for Public Service's Center for Presidential Transition over three successive presidential cycles.

"How do you suggest I proceed?"

DAVID MARCHICK (DM): Let's start with your background. Before you joined the transition, you were Governor Bush's chief of staff and appointments director. Texas has a lot of appointments, so you had experience doing that. How did that experience help you start the transition planning process?

CLAY JOHNSON (CJ): It was superimportant. There are six or seven states that are set up like Texas, where the government is very citizen-centric. There are boards of people that run the university systems and the different agencies and so forth. Texas had about as many appointees for the governor to make as the federal government did. [In proportion to population, the Texas governor actually makes significantly more appointments: around 1,500 in Texas compared to around 4,000 at the federal level.] We had to deal with the same kind of volume of appointments that Bush was going to have to do if and when he was elected president.

It turned out that Bush's goal for us in his appointments office in Austin was to find the best people to do the work. I said, "Okay, that's fine, Sir, but I don't really know about politics." He said, "No, no, no. I want you to find the best people, and I'll use the political affairs office to deal with the politics." That turned out exactly the way he wanted it approached at the federal level.

DM: When did you start working on his presidential transition?

CJ: His chief of staff in Texas, Joe Allbaugh, was leaving to go run the campaign. And so, he asked me to come down and be his chief of staff. I'm not a political person, but he thought I could do it because the legislature wasn't going to be meeting for the next year. I went down, and he said, "The other thing I want you to do is, I want you to prepare a plan for what I do when I win the presidency."

This was in June 1999. So it's sixteen months or so before the presidential election. I don't think anybody's started that early ever, before or after. I said: "Well, that's great, I'm honored that you're asking me, but I'm just overwhelmed. I know nothing about transitions. How do you suggest I proceed?"

He said: "There's a lot that has been written about it in the last couple of years, so there's a lot to read. I can set up meetings with you and the people that have been integrally involved at the federal level. Your challenge is to take all that and develop a plan."

DM: So you started talking to people, you talked to Jim Baker, Dick Cheney, George Shultz, and then you read a bunch of articles and papers. What was the most important advice you got from these various people and the resources?

CJ: There was a lot of it. Baker and Shultz were just invaluable people, and they were so welcoming. The general direction that I got from them was to be sure you have clear definitions of success that you want to try to accomplish from the transition. Don't go in looking for general things you want to work hard at doing, but develop the list of things that you want to be accomplished by specific dates.

Separately, there was a campaign staff that was different from the transition staff. There'll be a lot of people you'll want to talk to who are on the campaign, but the people that are actively working with you on the transition should not be involved in the campaign. The campaign people are working full-time. The transition people will need to be working full-time as well, and the teams should meet on a regular basis.

The White House staff was very important, and they ought to be in place before Christmastime because the White House staff has to be in place to be able to give the cabinet secretaries direction about what the president wants them to do. The other reason for having the White House staff available as early as possible is, as Andy Card used to say, the most valuable asset in the world is the U.S. president's time and voice, and the president needs to have senior White House staff around him to maximize how he spends his time and what he says.

They also made the point that the public is going to be very interested in how the president-elect is going to act. And so the public affairs people, communication people, need to be focused on that, and they need to be challenged with that. You will also be deluged by office-seekers and advice-givers. Be prepared to have them descend upon you but not take away from what you're trying to accomplish. Be organized enough to be proactive about how you take their input and be very, very clear about what it is you're trying to accomplish. Be very, very good about communicating to the people that we're going to be helping to go forward in the transition, and make sure that they know that all of you are going to be held accountable for getting your president off to the best start possible.

"The goals were still the goals"

DM: So you've planned for sixteen months, you have a great team, you've taken wisdom from people like Secretary of State James Baker, you are organized, and then Election Day arrives. Here's what happened: the country goes into this monthlong limbo. Nobody knows who the next president is going to be until the Supreme Court rules. What did you do the day after the election, and how did this uncertainty affect what you did as the lead of the transition?

CJ: On the day after the election, nobody knew how long it would take to resolve. We were just all standing at parade rest, shuffling papers, remembering what our goals were, and continuing to work on it privately. Maybe ten days into it, Dick [Cheney] decided—and I'm sure he talked to the president about this—that we have to assume we're going to win this thing. We have to prepare as if we know we're going to win it.

The decision was that we would meet up right after Thanksgiving and form a privately funded transition office to start doing the things that a transition would do—before George W. Bush was officially elected. I remember sitting on a plane—somebody had secured a private plane for us to fly up there on—and I remember sitting with my cohorts there, waiting to take off from Austin. I looked at [another staffer], and I said, "You know what we're getting ready to do?"

He said, "No, what, Clay?"

I said: "We're on our way to Washington to try to do what has never been done in American history. This has never happened before. We are off on a history-making venture, and I know we are extremely well-prepared to do this."

[The other staffers] looked at each other and said, "We agree." So we went at it with some kind of serious gusto.

DM: The typical transition is seventy-seven or seventy-eight days, which is not a long period of time. You had thirty-seven days. So how did that shortened period affect your ability to get people appointed, get people selected, and do all the things that you would plan to do in the seventy-seven or seventy-eight days?

CJ: The goals were still the goals. We didn't say, "We'll lower our expectations here on what we're trying to accomplish." We set out as if everything were possible. Andy [Card; Bush's chief of staff–designate] set off working long and hard to think through who the senior people in the White House staff would be, and we had some names. We sat down with the president-elect and started talking to him about people that we casually visited, about who might be good to consider for this cabinet position or that position. We started talking more specifically with Vice President–elect Cheney and policy people about getting agreement on who ought to be the key cabinet department heads.

Besides the fact that we have to assume we won, besides bringing that mind-set to it, Cheney also had the foresight of bringing in a guy named Fred Fielding [White House counsel to Ronald Reagan and later George W. Bush]. Nobody knows more about the functioning of the White House, the ins and outs of Washington, and legal or ethical matters than Fred Fielding. Besides that, he's a fabulous human being. He shows up, and he adds that we don't want to think about somebody seriously for a cabinet position or senior White House position if we are not reasonably certain that they're going to be clearance-checkable and not have conflicts.

He would have conversations with people that we were initially interested in considering for a finance position or for a senior cabinet position. It's what we call humorously the "sex, drugs, and rock 'n' roll" interview that Fred would have with them. He said: "I'm going to ask you some half a dozen questions about what your business interests are, what your investment interests are, any background issues, and so forth. I'm expecting total honesty from you. If and when we are actually elected and we do in fact nominate you, if it turns out you have problems or conflicts [that we didn't know about], you have to know that we're going to drop you like a hundred-pound weight."

So that's why we were able to cut a lot of corners with this, because we had senior people who could do what the clearance process would do more extensively later on, but he had to do it in a hurry. That's why we made good progress. We didn't get to 150, 165 people by April 1 because we didn't get [a quick] start. But before the year was over and done with, we had done as well in the first year as any prior administration had done.

"I had one client, and that was the governor"

DM: One of the big challenges is the control between the White House and the cabinet. You had very strong cabinet officers, including Colin Powell and Mike Leavitt, who has worked with the Partnership. How did you balance who picked the subcabinet and who had control over those selections?

CJ: One of the things that everybody we talked to had advised us was not to delegate to the cabinet secretaries the picking of all of their subcabinet members, because it's never been successful. But don't give them zero say in who their people are going to be because that's also never been successful. The way we structured it—and it was very clear with every cabinet secretary— was that this would be collaborative. We had to both agree on who the sub-cabinet was going to be: the people confirmed by the Senate. It was going to be quick and easily done. And that worked fabulously.

I remember my first meeting with Colin Powell, who I was so proud to get to meet for the first time, and I was explaining how we were going to do this. I said: "Colin, I expect that 92 percent of the people you bring into the State Department are going to be people that you have worked with before, and that'll be fine, but there are a lot of people we will identify for you to consider. And there'll maybe be people you don't know who should be in positions, and we're able to find people for that as well."

DM: How did you balance between choosing loyalists and people that had been around the governor in Texas with people that had DC experience?

CJ: Whether you had been around the governor, or whether you had had DC experience, it all tied back to the president's charge to me: find the best people to do the work. We spent a lot of time thinking about this. A question we asked ourselves when we were looking at a new position we wanted to fill was: What kind of person were you looking for? Do we want this person to be a management person or a policy person? Do we want somebody to be a change agent or somebody to manage what's already well-regarded? Or do we want somebody to be politically savvy? Do we want somebody who has credibility in Congress? Or is it not important? Do we want somebody who has to be a public person, who has made a lot of public speeches? Do we want somebody who's got prior association with an issue? Or maybe somebody that's never been associated with this issue because it's very controversial? You're not looking for a warm body. You're not looking for somebody who helped the candidate get elected or had known him a long time. You're looking for somebody who has the kind of background experience to do what needs to be done.

In Texas, somebody told me about halfway through the governor's first year in office that I had a nickname among the senators there, that my nickname was "The Ice Box" or "The Refrigerator." I asked him, "Why is that my nickname?" He said, "Because when it comes to appointments, you're known to be tall, white, and cold." I was not somebody that was going to be trying to gladhand people and curry favor with people. I had one client, and that was the governor. They came to understand that. That spread up to people in Washington, and it was actually in the paper one time that this was my nickname in Texas, and it was put in the paper as a derogatory statement about me. Well, actually, it's the highest compliment you can pay to somebody who is a presidential appointments person.

"It begins with a realistic, aggressive picture of success"

DM: Clay, you've become an elder statesman, something of a wise man on transition issues. You've worked with the Partnership. You have advised subsequent transition teams like the Romney team. If there's one piece of advice that you'd make sure that every transition team internalized, what would that be?

CJ: Decide what your picture of success is. What do you want to accomplish in a transition? On January 20, what do you want to be prepared to do? What do you have to do by December 15 and December 20 and so forth to be that prepared by January 20? And then go do it. It begins with a realistic, aggressive picture of success. And then you work backward from there to figure out what you have to do tomorrow and the next day and so forth. That's the key to having a successful transition into office.

Notes

1. William Antholis, "It Is Not That Close: This Does Not Have to Be a Political Crisis," UVA Miller Center, November 8, 2020, https://millercenter.org/it-not-close-does-not-have-be-political-crisis.

2. 9/11 Commission, *Final Report*, 198, 422–23.

3. Alexander Tippett, "What the 9/11 Commission Found: Slow Confirmations Imperil U.S. National Security," Center for Presidential Transition, January 5, 2021, https://presidentialtransition.org/blog/what-the-9-11-commission-found/.

4. For a discussion of these issues during the 2008 election cycle, see U.S. Library of Congress, Congressional Research Service, 2008–2009 Presidential Transition: National Security Considerations and Options, by John Rollins, RL34456 (2008).

5. John P. Burke, "The Bush Transition in Historical Context," *PS: Political Science & Politics* 35, no. 1 (March 2002): 23.

6. Martha Joynt Kumar, "Recruiting and Organizing the White House Staff," *PS: Political Science & Politics* 35, no. 1 (March 2002).

7. Clay Johnson, "Recommendations for an Effective 2008 Transition," *Public Administration Review*, July/August 2008, 624.

Obama Navigates the First Post-9/11 Transition

JOHN PODESTA AND CHRIS LU

> You can plan all you want, and if the weather is bad at one of the beaches and you have to come up with an alternate landing site, that's what you have to be prepared to do. We prepared, we were flexible, but we also had people who were smart and experienced and who had served in government before.
>
> —Chris Lu

As DESCRIBED in Martha Kumar's book *Before the Oath,* George W. Bush's experience with a shortened transition in 2000–2001 had made him sensitive to the importance of a smooth handover out of office, especially in light of the national security challenges that came to the fore so soon after he took office. By the summer of 2008, the country was in the midst of two wars, and a financial crisis was looming. Bush was determined to ensure that the handover to his successor went smoothly. Accordingly, Bush committed his administration to a robust, well-organized process, no matter the winner of the 2008 election.[1]

While the combination of preparedness and creativity displayed by the Bush administration was critical, the success of the transition also depended on the incomers. The Obama team was clear-eyed about the gravity of the situation they were walking into and planned accordingly. Led by chair John Podesta, cochairs Pete Rouse and Valerie Jarrett, and executive director Chris Lu, the transition developed several innovations that would become best practice. They built a large agency review team, with more than five hundred people covering sixty-two agencies postelection, as well as a sophisticated personnel and vetting operation.

They also reached out to Congress early in order to smooth the way for nominations. The legislative team, led by the savvy congressional liaison

Phil Schiliro, briefed Senate Majority Leader Harry Reid on priority positions before the election, enabling the Senate to hold twenty-five pre-inaugural hearings for Obama's nominees, a record that still stands. They also established policy councils during the transition to force future appointees to work together and learn how to cooperate on policy development. After the election, the transition encouraged Obama to pick his chief of staff early and give him or her free range to staff the White House—which Obama did, announcing Rahm Emanuel as his chief of staff just days after the election.

When you ask presidential scholars and transition veterans about the best modern presidential transition, they invariably point to the Bush-Obama handover.[2] To understand exactly why it was so successful, we spoke to John Podesta and Chris Lu. My interviews with them bookended the 2020 election cycle; my interview with Chris Lu was one of the first we recorded for *Transition Lab*, while John Podesta appeared on the show the day before Election Day.

Chris Lu has long been a confidant of Obama. They were classmates at Harvard Law, and when Obama was in the Senate, Lu served as his legislative director and acting chief of staff. As Chris told the podcast, one day in the spring of 2008, he and Obama were sitting together in the Senate chamber. Lu was bored—with the presidential campaign raging, all the action was outside of Washington—but Obama said that he needed Lu in DC. Like any good staffer, Lu improvised on the spot, blurting out, "How about I plan your transition?" That was the start of Chris Lu's transition work. Lu went on to serve as executive director of the Obama-Biden Transition Project. After the election, Lu entered the administration, eventually serving as deputy secretary of labor.

After a long career as a congressional staffer, John Podesta joined the Clinton administration, rising to becoming White House chief of staff in 1998. After Clinton left office, John founded the Center for American Progress, a think tank that has become a driving force for progressive politics in Washington. He went on to serve in the Obama administration and as chair of Hillary Clinton's 2016 presidential campaign. John is—along with Dick Cheney and Andy Card—one of the three living Americans with the most senior-level experience in presidential transitions. By my count, he has assisted in four different such efforts: Bill Clinton's transitions in and out of the White House, Obama's transition into office, and Hillary Clinton's transition preparations in 2016.

Working for candidate Obama in 2008, Podesta and Lu made a formidable leadership team. Together, they and others engineered a transition effort that allowed Obama to move aggressively to implement his agenda. For example, the American Recovery Act, the administration's response to the 2008 financial crisis, was signed on February 17, 2009—less than thirty days after his inauguration. Without the smooth transition of power, artfully facilitated by Podesta and Lu, this would have been impossible.

Obama remained grateful for President Bush's support and pledged the same level of cooperation to his successor—whether after four years or eight. In the run-up to the 2012 election, Obama instructed Lu to prepare an outgoing transition should Obama lose his reelection bid—an eventuality few presidents are prepared to face. Lu said it best when he called the presidential transition "literally one of the most important things that can happen in government."

"Now what do we do?"

David Marchick (DM): President Bush talked eloquently about transition planning when he left office. Why did Obama think that transition planning was important?

Chris Lu (CL): It was the first post-9/11 transition. Senator Obama and I shared a love of *The Candidate*, the 1972 movie. It features Robert Redford playing an environmentalist who runs a long-shot campaign for the U.S. Senate. He wins. In the final scene of the movie, he's backstage, about to declare victory, and he says to one of his staffers, "Now what do we do?" Barack Obama did not want to be standing there declaring victory in Grant Park in Chicago and then turning to one of his aides and saying, "Now what do we do?" The transition period is seventy-seven days, or it was for us, between Election Day and Inauguration Day. When you're planning the biggest takeover of any operation in the entire world, seventy to seventy-seven days is not enough.

DM: Josh Bolten and Denis McDonough on another podcast (see their interview in this volume) said that the model for a good transition is for its leadership to be someone like you or Clay Johnson or Mack McLarty, whom the candidate trusts instinctively.

CL: During my time with Obama and as a legislative director, I helped edit his book, I helped deal with his finances and his taxes, I did all kinds of things for him where over the course of that period of time, I essentially had earned his trust.

DM: So you knew nothing about transitions, but he trusts you. He asked you to do this. How did you actually become an expert on transitions?

CL: The first thing I did is, I went to talk to Jim Johnson, who had run John Kerry's transition planning effort in 2004. When I got to Jim's office, he said, "I've been expecting you." He went into his closet. He pulled out all of his transition boxes from 2004, which also contained all of Al Gore's materials from 2000. So that was a fantastic start. I always say with transition planning, it's a little bit like planning the D-Day invasion. You can map the best plans, but unless you actually land the boats on the beach, it really doesn't matter.

"They don't like yes-people around them"

DM: John, why did then candidate Obama choose you to run a transition when you weren't that close to him and had in fact opposed him in the primary?

JOHN PODESTA (JP): The best presidents like strong people around them. They don't like yes-people around them, and they don't try to terrorize and intimidate their staff. They accept that they're going to have an honest and open relationship with the people that are working for them, and that was certainly true of the two presidents I worked for. I think to his credit, Obama really liked and respected people who would challenge him, fight with him. At the end of the day, he got elected, he was the president, and he called the shots, but he wasn't paranoid about having people who were tough with him and certainly not sycophants around him.

"He never put his thumb on the scale"

DM: Chris, it's April 2008. You started planning, and you got an office in DC. What did you do?

CL: Originally it literally was just me. I think it became very apparent we needed more people. At some point, John Podesta, probably in June, came on [as transition chair]. John wasn't doing it full-time, but we would go over and meet at his offices over at the Center for American Progress. Then I hired a bunch of research assistants. We had no place to work from. Fortunately, the Obama campaign had a DC fundraising office that they were vacating, and so we took over their office. It was about a stone's throw from the U.S.

Senate above a Subway sub shop so you would smell the fresh bread from Subway every day.

DM: How many people did you hire preconvention? And then between the convention and the election, how large was the transition team?

CL: The entire time before the election we probably had no more than ten people on payroll. It was a lot of research assistants. On top of that, there were probably fifty to seventy people volunteering. It was a relatively small operation because we had no money; any money we used to pay people came from a pool that John Podesta separately raised from some donors.

DM: With seventy people, how did you make sure that it remained confidential?

CL: It is pretty remarkable that we did a good job at that. It's something that John Podesta instilled in all of us. I think we knew that we are doing important work, and these were professionals we had chosen who were either very close to the president—people like Julius Genachowski, another one of our law school classmates, who became chairman of the Federal Communications [Commission]—or somebody like Susan Rice or Carol Browner. These were professionals, and they all understood the importance of secrecy.

DM: After the conventions, Josh Bolten, who was then chief of staff for President Bush, said: "Our transition in and the Clinton transition out was not perfectly smooth. President Bush has asked me to run the smoothest, most effective, most coordinated transition out ever." He started reaching out to you and also to the McCain campaign. So you were literally in the same room with the McCain people, talking to the White House, coordinating. What was that like?

CL: It was awkward. But we understood the importance of it. This was going to be the first transition post-9/11, and Josh, while I'm sure he would have preferred that Senator McCain succeeded [Bush], never played favorites. He never put his thumb on the scale. He understood that this was an edict that had come down from President Bush, and he wanted to carry through. I give Josh and his deputy chief of staff, Blake Gottesman, great credit for the way they conducted this whole operation.

DM: Let's go back to the postconvention, preelection period. What type of people were you recruiting to the transition team? What were the major areas of work, and how did you organize it?

CL: It's a couple of things. First of all, policy. One of the important things we did with all of these research assistants was to catalogue every policy promise that candidate Obama had made—and he had made a lot of promises. They didn't all line up, and they weren't all internally consistent, but we wanted to see what we had. On top of that, we organized into probably a dozen different policy work streams, everything from education, immigration, healthcare, and then we fleshed out not only what he had promised but what we would introduce as legislation, what we might do as regulation.

There was a personnel front to identify potential people, not only to serve in the Obama White House but in each of the agencies. We had an agency review team: a couple of days after Election Day, we would essentially airdrop into virtually every major agency in the country a group of people who would quickly fan out, get the lay of the land, understand what's happening at the agency, and come back and report. Those would then be integrated not only within our policy proposals, but the materials we put together for the incoming cabinet members to help them prep for their confirmation hearings.

DM: Martha Kumar wrote a great book on the Bush-Obama transition, and she said that you had 517 agency review people go into the agencies the day after the election, which is just incredible.

CL: Probably not the day after, but I would say that the instruction was, "Election Day is on a Tuesday; we open [the formal transition] on Wednesday." I would say, in almost every instance, by that following Monday there were people on board in most of the agencies.

DM: One of the other things you did was focus on the White House staff, getting that in place before getting the cabinet and the subagencies right in place. Why did you do that?

CL: That was something we learned from the Clinton transition. Clinton, back in '92, '93, focused on his cabinet and then belatedly did his White House staff. I think most people view that as one of the reasons why they stumbled out of the gate. We wanted a cabinet member in place along with some key political appointees around him or her, but not necessarily the people that needed to be confirmed. You certainly wanted that person to have a chief of staff, a communications person, a legislative affairs person. Some of those jobs are confirmed, some of them are not confirmed, but you could certainly put them in place on day one so that even if there was a lone cabinet member with no other assistant secretary, they would have a core group of people who could help them.

"I would step that up further"

DM: The Obama transition into office is widely seen as the best transition in the history of the United States. But, what, looking back, are the things that you could have done better in 2008?

JP: Well, I should say that the transition was co-led; we really haven't talked about this. Valerie Jarrett and Pete Rouse were cochairs of the transition. Particularly in the period before the election, they were working on the election while I was working on the transition, but subsequent to that, they were full partners in this.

We were credited with doing a pretty good job of getting senior-level personnel into the administration. I would step that up further. If you look particularly at PAS, the presidentially appointed, Senate-confirmed nominees, I think we had something like a hundred done in the first three months.

I think you could make quick decisions, make good decisions, accelerate that process, and pressure the Senate to act and really be fully engaged in getting your people inside the government. That's something I think that was particularly slow under President Clinton. We got the cabinet done right away, and then the rest took forever. We improved upon that with Obama, but I think you can really jack that up. The other thing that we laid the groundwork for, but it didn't happen, was that we accelerated the process on judicial nominations.

DM: You were involved in the Clinton, Obama, and Hillary Clinton transition efforts. How were those different based on the personality of the principals?

JP: The one thing that I would say was quite different was that Bill Clinton prioritized spending all those early days on selecting his cabinet, spending an enormous amount of time on it. I think he made very good choices, but he did that to the exclusion of picking his White House staff, which he did really right at the end. With the exception of a few people like Mack McLarty [his first chief of staff], he didn't get around to putting people in White House staff positions. I think to some extent it was because when you're a governor of a state, your cabinet essentially is your staff; they're the people you're interacting with on a daily basis. When you're president, the team that you're working most significantly with, the team that plans your communication strategy or your legislative strategy, your national strategy, is your White House staff.

It turned out it was a very long-serving cabinet, it was a great cabinet, but I think that he tripped up in not spending more of his time on his White House staff early. I raised that with Senator Obama the first time I saw him. We discussed this and really built the White House staff first, which helped him then fill out his cabinet. Obviously, he had some ideas about who he wanted in the cabinet, but I think that was a better way to run the transition.

DM: You were chief of staff in the Clinton White House during the *Bush v. Gore* recount in 2000. How was that transition? How difficult was that when you were supporting Gore and nevertheless you had to hand over power to the Bush team? What did you do as chief of staff to make that a smooth transition?

JP: First of all, we tried to be professional regardless of who was coming into office and prepare the groundwork for that with respect to the work that agencies do, giving people a real sense of what the challenges are, what the opportunities are, what the budget looks like, what the problems that need correction are. We took that responsibility quite seriously and professionally. My deputy at the time, Maria Echaveste, ran that process throughout the government. We were well prepared in November to do that. As it turned out, the winner wasn't decided until December, when the Supreme Court in the famous five-to-four *Bush v. Gore* decision essentially ended the counting in Florida and Vice President Gore conceded.

That was the first thing we did; it was professional and well prepared. It was a brief, and because of that, Andy Card and Josh Bolten, both of whom later became Bush chiefs of staff, were working on the transition during that period of time. Because this was closer to Christmas and the holidays, Governor Bush didn't come to see President Clinton until the first week of January or February. While the president hosted Governor Bush for a one-on-one session in the residence, my deputies and senior team hosted Andy and Josh in my office for a very long lunch talking through what President Clinton viewed as the big challenges President Bush would encounter on January 20.

We tried to as rapidly as possible hand things off. One of the things that we didn't do in 2000 that the Bush team prepared and did in 2008 was a tabletop exercise with the National Security Council. I raise that because I think both in my meetings with Andy and Josh, I know in the president's meeting with President Bush, and in the national security briefings that Sandy Berger had with Condoleezza Rice, we had been seized by the threat of what was going on with al-Qaeda and bin Laden. I think we imparted that information, but I think one of the effects of that truncated period of time was that we were unable to really put the focus of their security team on the threat of bin Laden, that was well-documented in *The 9/11 Commission Report*.

Some changes, including changes to transition laws, were made as a result to try to better prepare, particularly in the national security arena, for the handoff. President Bush took that very seriously. I saw the effect of that in both the ability to accelerate security clearances before the election to be able to work and connect our national security team to their national security team, and doing a tabletop exercise about terrorism in the early days of

2009 with the incoming team. I think that was very helpful to the Obama team coming into office.

DM: The other thing that President Clinton and you did during the recount was that you authorized then governor Bush to get the most extensive, full intelligence briefings available as if he were going to be president-elect. You and then-president Clinton felt that that was sufficiently important and that he should get the benefit of that, which I think is very admirable.

JP: I think we made that decision maybe a couple of weeks into the period of the recount. By late November we definitely said it was our responsibility as the outgoing administration. Obviously, we were still hopeful that Vice President Gore could prevail in the recount, but whatever the outcome we had to do as good a job as we could to prepare both sides. Vice President Gore was already receiving those briefings, but we enabled the CIA to fully engage with then governor Bush and his team, including Steve Hadley, Condoleezza Rice, and maybe some others to be able to fully get access to the highest-level secrets so that they could begin to prepare what they were thinking about and how they were going to approach the big security challenges that the country was facing.

DM: What about the Hillary Clinton transition preparation?

JP: We ran an even more full-blown preelection transition. Over the years, it's become more acceptable to be serious about working on the transition before the election. I think that in Hillary's case, we probably had a bigger team than I even had in 2008 because it was just more politically acceptable. It wasn't viewed as presumptuous or measuring the drapes or whatever metaphor you want to use.

One of the things that we were able to do was take her promises on the campaign trail and think about how we would really be able to execute against those in a context in which we weren't certain what the composition of the Congress was going to be. We were able to map that out in a way that the documentation was useful to the Biden team. Unfortunately, we didn't get to utilize it, but at the end of the day it was helpful to the Biden people as they were thinking about their transition.

"Preparation matters"

DM: Let's go to 2012. Chris, you and the deputy chief of staff were asked to prepare as if Obama was going to lose. Was that a very unpopular thing to do in the White House, and what did you actually do?

CL: No. President Obama was very publicly grateful to President Bush for the cooperation that was provided to us in 2008 and pledged that same level of cooperation to his successor. It's always awkward when you're preparing for the eventuality that you lose, but we understood that was an important part of government. We went through the process of bringing agencies together, meeting with the White House staff, making sure that everyone had done the transition planning that they needed to do to ensure a proper handoff. That's the right thing to do, whether you're transitioning out after four years or after eight years.

DM: One of the things the Obama administration did, which was, I think, best practice, was they set up a process for the Justice Department to clear lots of the people in the Romney campaign, so they'd have security clearances. In case they won, they would be ready to go.

CL: This follows on what happened in 2008. Before Election Day 2008, we cleared more than a hundred people who had security clearances that could work on the transition staff, because obviously there's a lot of national security materials at that point that you have access to. But if you're going to serve on an agency review team in a national security agency, like the Department of Defense, they're not going to let you look at anything unless you have the clearance. So it's the clearance not only to be a part of the transition, [but also] the precursor to eventually working in the administration.

DM: One of the things that you did after the transition was you worked with the Partnership for Public Service, and you gave the Partnership a bunch of documents from the Obama transition. Why did you do that?

CL: Because this is literally one of the most important things that can happen in government, and I didn't think I should be the keeper of all of the transition documents in my attic, which is kind of the case right now. It shouldn't be the case where I go meet Jim Johnson, and he reaches into his closet and pulls out a big box.

Preparation matters. I am proud of the fact that we ran what is, as you say, considered one of the best transitions in history. It's in part because we prepared, but we were also flexible. I'll give you an example. I said we had probably a dozen different policy work streams, and if you were called in the fall of 2008, the most important thing happening was we were having a financial crisis; we were having a housing crisis. So you take these twelve work streams, and eleven of them get pushed to the back burner. The most important thing you have to focus on is the economy.

Again, let's use the D-Day analogy. You can plan all you want, and if the weather is bad at one of the beaches and you have to come up with an alternate landing site, that's what you have to be prepared to do. We prepared, we were flexible, but we also had people who were smart and experienced and who had served in government before. When you have the benefit of John Podesta being your transition chair, you have Carol Browner who had been the EPA administrator, these people had run agencies. These people knew how government worked, and they were able to sort of see around corners, anticipate problems, and then, when problems came up, quickly solve them.

"As soon as he takes his hand off the Bible, they have to be operational"

DM: In 2008, the United States faced a financial crisis and two wars. There was enormous collaboration on TARP, on the auto bailout, on the financial crisis. Today [in 2020], we're facing multiple crises. We have a financial crisis. We have a health crisis. What lessons learned are there from 2008 to 2009?

JP: To pick up on Joe Biden's message, we also have a racial justice crisis and a climate crisis, and we need to address all of them. They're interconnected, they intersect with each other, and we have to connect with all of them. Just to praise the Bush team for one more minute, I think the president recognized fairly early on that the two wars, that's what dominated his presidency in the last few years, and that's what he was thinking about. He wanted a smooth transition, no matter who was elected. He gave that clear message to Josh Bolten and Joel Kaplan, Josh's deputy. They couldn't have given us better support, because they were thinking, "We've got this national security crisis that we're dealing with." Then the financial crisis occurs. We only have one president at a time, so we tried to work smoothly with his team. I think they tried to preserve optionality for us, so that the range of decisions that might be made by the Obama team were preserved. We had done the same, by the way, in 2000 for the incoming Bush team.

They could have cut that off and changed that dynamic had they so chosen, but they didn't. We're coming into a transition [in 2020–21] where you have a very erratic decision-making structure in the White House. It's a very challenging circumstance, but I think the Biden team understood that right from the get-go. It does take the commitment of the president, the president's chief of staff, and the rest of the White House structure to make it work smoothly. They'll just have to deal with whatever comes their way, but they have to integrate an approach that from the get-go has a White House that's up and running in crisis mode to deal with a pandemic, but they've also got to be working on these other issues and problems simultaneously.

So whether that's the economic recovery, dealing with the kinds of investments that the [former] vice president has promised the American people, dealing on day one with racial justice issues and with the climate issues that he's talked about in the campaign, he's got to integrate that and have a plan to go right out of the gates. He's got to have a team that can manage a crisis. Virtually as soon as he takes his hand off the Bible, they're going to have to be operational.

Notes

1. For more detail on this transition and the thinking behind it from the Bush perspective, see the interview in this volume with Josh Bolten and Denis McDonough.

2. For a scholarly view, see Martha Joynt Kumar, "The 2008–2009 Presidential Transition through the Voices of Its Participants," *Presidential Studies Quarterly* 39, no. 4 (December 2009). Most of the practitioners we spoke to pointed to the Obama transition as the gold standard they strove to meet. For a more critical account from a participant, however, see Reed E. Hundt, *A Crisis Wasted: Barack Obama's Defining Decisions* (New York: Rosetta, 2019).

Romney's Ship That Didn't Sail

GOVERNOR MIKE LEAVITT

> We don't know when the next transition to an open White House will oc-
> cur. But when that occurs, it will be vitally important that the incumbent
> president show the same kind of statesmanlike approach to this. It's seri-
> ous business, transitioning the leadership of the free world while at the
> same time doing battle with adversaries around the world.
>
> —Mike Leavitt

SO FAR, this book has looked at transitions that actually took place. In
this interview, we consider one that did not—but whose planning phase
shaped the future.

Mitt Romney's 2012 transition is well worth studying in detail. A former businessman, consultant, and governor (and now senator), the meticulous Romney was serious about preparing to be president, and his
transition team was deeply ambitious. They did not just plan for the first
one hundred days; they planned for the first two hundred days. They built
a federal government in miniature. They planned to appoint nominees
two and a half times faster than had the Obama team, then the record
holders for most confirmations during the first one hundred days.

This ambition was facilitated in part by statutory changes, in the form
of the Pre-Election Presidential Transition Act of 2010, sponsored by Senator Ted Kaufman and championed by the Partnership for Public Service,
which empowered the transition to receive federal resources prior to the
election and, importantly, helped dispel the stigma around early transition planning.

Guided by an understanding of past mistakes, the Romney team worked
to develop processes to minimize conflicts between campaign and transition. They ensured that campaign staffers would be integrated into the
transition after the election. Major personnel decisions for the transition
were only made after receiving input from senior Romney campaign aides.

Crucially, they decided that only the campaign would ever generate policy. The transition would simply prepare to implement it. While we will never know how successful these measures may have been in 2012, these best practices were adopted by future transitions.

Just as Bush helped Obama in 2008, Obama resolved to help his potential successor in 2012. In a welcome departure from previous practice, he directed his staff to offer full support to the Romney transition team. This cooperation strengthened Romney's preparations further.

To lead his transition, Romney chose a seasoned planner: Mike Leavitt, a former Utah governor who had served in George W. Bush's cabinet. Leavitt has a well-earned reputation in Washington for being a technocratic workhorse who prizes bipartisanship. Better yet, he enjoyed the deep personal trust of his candidate, having met him while working to save the 2002 Salt Lake City Olympics. Following allegations of corruption and bribery, the Games were in a precarious financial position. Leavitt brought in Romney, then one of the leaders at the investment firm Bain Capital, and over the following months, the two men worked closely together to salvage the event. That trial by fire helped forge a lasting bond between them.

After being tapped to lead the transition, Leavitt began building out his team, reaching out to talented individuals like Chris Liddell, who had been chief financial officer at Microsoft. (Liddell would later play a critical role in the Trump administration's outgoing transition as described in Liddell's interview later in this volume.) In the spring of 2012, Leavitt's team began its work.

For the second cycle running, the Partnership for Public Service hosted a small conference at which transition veterans advised representatives from all the major-party candidates. At that event, veterans of Obama's transition, including Agency Review Co-Chair Lisa Brown, a senior White House official at the time, offered advice to Leavitt and his team. These conferences not only allow the Partnership to share best practices; they also build the sense of the transition as an occasion for bipartisan cooperation.

One question that lingered in my mind was whether the Romney transition effort was too big. They built a mammoth operation with hundreds of former officials, and I always wondered how they would have managed all those egos and ambitions if called upon to integrate them with the campaign. Leavitt and I debated this point on more than one occasion, but as he said, his theory was never tested—their ship never sailed.

Although Mitt Romney lost the 2012 contest, Leavitt and Liddell were determined not to let their work go to waste. They had begun the process without access to institutional knowledge or previous transition documents; according to Leavitt, they had little more than "a couple of boxes of very old records that really couldn't help us." They wanted to make sure that future transitions would not suffer that disadvantage. Their book would become a Bible for subsequent transition planning efforts.[1] By documenting his work, Mike Leavitt became as important a contributor to the art of transitions as any other figure in the last forty years, a fact that Congress recognized when naming the Edward "Ted" Kaufman and Michael Leavitt Presidential Transitions Improvements Act of 2015.

"You put a goat in the stable"

DAVID MARCHICK (DM): How did you get to know Governor Romney, and what formed that bond of trust between you?

MIKE LEAVITT (ML): We actually became acquainted first through the 2002 Winter Olympic Games. I was governor [of Utah] at the time, and there were complications in the management of the games. We needed someone to come in and to essentially turn a problem around. I conducted a search and found Governor Romney. We had met once. I didn't have a preexisting relationship or friendship with him, but we had many common friends. He agreed and did a great job. In the course of that, you bond a bit. You go on a fifty-mile hike together, metaphorically.

After I served as governor, I spent some time in the federal government. Romney was governor of Massachusetts during that period. We worked together on a number of quite notable things. When we had both concluded our service, he ran for president, and we became very good friends in the course of that process.

DM: He's running for president, and then he calls you one day and says, "In case I win, I want you to run my transition"?

ML: I was actually working with the campaign, where I had spent a substantial amount of time for three or four months. People asked me what I did. I'd tell them that there's an old horse racing trick that when you've got a thoroughbred, if you want to settle them down, you get a goat and put the goat in the stable. That tends to calm the thoroughbred down. I tell people I was the goat because that was my job.

DM: You had been governor three times and had been HHS [Health and Human Services] secretary and EPA [Environmental Protection Agency] administrator, but you didn't really know much about transitioning to the presidency. So how did you get up to speed? How did you learn? What did you do?

ML: The truth is, I couldn't find anyone who did. There was nothing, aside from a couple of books that tended to focus on the drama in the actual transition and not so much on preparation. I interviewed anyone I could find to begin to understand what needed to be done. I called a couple of very capable people like Chris Liddell, who had been chief financial officer at Microsoft and at General Motors as the vice chairman. He had recently left there and had time and agreed to become what turned out to be the executive director.

DM: Did he know Romney?

ML: Yes, he had known him, and he had been working a bit with the campaign. We formed a very close relationship. We ended up with a little group of four or five people, and we spent from about the middle of April until September working in a very quiet way with a small group, literally whiteboarding out what a transition would look like. We had to devise objectives, we had to think through and game it out and develop plans. In some ways, part of the problem had been that there was no template for this, so we concluded very early we would keep good track of what we did. People could learn from our mistakes. I think on balance that turned out to be a good strategy.

"We're all going to leave our swords at the door"

DM: One of the things you did early in the process, I think with Chris, is that you attended a conference hosted by the Partnership for Public Service in Tarrytown, New York, talking about presidential transitions with people that had done it before. Do you recall what you learned, how that affected your thinking?

ML: It was a tremendous service that the Center did because we were able to speak in a quite thoughtful and collaborative way with people who had done transitions before. It was a situation where we had Obama administration people, we had people who had been with the Bush administration. I recall a phrase that was used, we're all going to "leave our swords at the door" and have a discussion about something very important to the American people. I thought at the time that this would inspire Americans if they could see the seriousness with which this was being taken, and to see opposing campaigns and administrations actually working together.

I had been in the cabinet when Bush 43 transitioned to the Obama administration, and I was instructed by George W. Bush that we were going to make this the best transition of power ever. The Bush 43 transition led by example: by the time we got to the point of the 2012 election, Barack Obama issued a very similar kind of standard. I worked with the White House extensively; they were very open. There was a big difference in 2008 when Bush was leaving, because there was no vice president running; there were two candidates running. In 2012, Romney was running against Obama.

DM: So you met with the Obama people. They had a process to engage with you. Was that odd? Was there total distrust between the Romney people and the Obama people since you were running against each other?

ML: Well, you'd think there would be. Very early on, I made contact with Denis McDonough, who was [then a senior White House official and later] chief of staff for President Obama. We had a straightforward conversation that was essentially, "Let's acknowledge that we have different points of view and that we have different objectives, but that we also have a mutual responsibility."

DM: Do you think we can have the same dynamic [in 2020] as we did in 2012 where you had President Obama working collaboratively with you, even though Governor Romney and Obama were opponents? Is that something that's possible in this polarized environment?

ML: Time will tell. Is it possible? Yes. Is it preferred and important? Yes. Personally, I think no person should run for president of the United States without understanding and shouldering this as part of the obligation. And again, I think George W. Bush deserves huge credit for having started a pattern that was emulated by President Obama. We don't know when the next transition to an open White House will occur. But when that occurs, it will be vitally important that the incumbent president show the same kind of statesmanlike approach to this. It's serious business, transitioning the leadership of the free world while at the same time doing battle with adversaries around the world. It's a time when there's great opportunity for mischief, when those who will challenge our country would see an opportunity to test our mettle.

"We needed a sophisticated team"

DM: How did you establish the goals that you wanted for the transition? And what were those goals?

ML: We first established a series of things that a transition needed to accomplish. One was we had to put a team on the field. The second was we needed to carry out what the candidate had laid out as campaign commitments. It was our responsibility to be prepared to do that. We also came to appreciate the fact that after the election and until the inauguration, there is no White House staff to serve the president-elect, and so we had to form a means of being able to do the care and keeping of the president-elect. We knew that the attention would shift and that the eyes of the world would shift, and we needed a sophisticated team, so we made that a very real part of it.

   We also recognized that if we were going to accomplish the things that the president-elect or the candidate had proposed, we would need to work with Congress. So we began to develop relationships with the Hill.

DM: Let's dig into some of these. Start with the Hill. Most candidates would have said, it's presumptuous for us to talk to Congress until we win. Actually, it's one of the great innovations that you led, which is to talk to people on the Hill about getting people confirmed quickly in the priority positions. Why did you do that? Weren't you worried about being seen as too presumptuous?

ML: One of the benefits of the 2012 transition was that we were under an obligation put forward by the Presidential Transition Act of 2010 to do this. Prior to that, candidates had been essentially required to do this under the cover of darkness because their opponent would routinely charge them with measuring the drapes at the Oval Office, and it became a campaign issue. We were very careful to make it low-key, but we did have the mandate. We would play very directly with the Congress. We had candid conversations that we were in the process of planning a transition. We acknowledged what this is and what it isn't, but said, "We are going to need your help." And we knew that one of our primary objectives in putting a team on the field was that we needed to work our way through a whole series of processes that would start with clearances and then would move into confirmation hearings that were required. We had established ambitious goals that we could have a couple hundred people in place within the first one hundred days.

DM: And that would have by far set a record, right? Because Obama had sixty-nine [Senate-confirmed appointees] at a hundred days.[2] So, you had ambitious goals to exceed that by more than two and a half times.

ML: We did. And we knew we'd have to streamline the process for that to occur, so we worked with the Senate, for example, and said: "What can we do to consolidate? Can we only have one set of forms for nominees for example? Can we prioritize?" They were cooperative, and we made some progress. I think progress is still to be made, but they were very willing to work with us.

DM: One of the things that was interesting about learning about your process and your effort is that you were from Utah, and Governor Romney was living in Boston, but you said, "We have to do this in Washington." Why is that?

ML: I was of the view that the talent pool that's typically required of experienced people resided here. Our vision of a transition began around the idea that we needed to create a miniature version of a federal government and that we needed experienced people who could essentially run through processes on issues that would approximate what they would go through if the government was in full standing. You could walk down the hall and have the Department of Interior, the Department of Treasury, the Department of State, the Department of Health and Human Services. You would have former officeholders, or former staff people, who were highly conversant with the issues and the processes that you would deal with after everything was in place. That turned out to be very helpful, particularly as we planned for the execution of the first two hundred days—because we planned a two-hundred-day horizon as opposed to a one-hundred-day horizon.

"There's always tension in the campaign"

DM: One of the problems in the past has been the tension between transition teams and the campaigns, and the clash that inevitably happens between those two entities. Because the campaign people say, "We're working our hearts out, we're getting a candidate elected, and we're doing the work." And the transition teams are busy in Washington planning. Then if the candidate wins, you have a clash over jobs, over egos, over structure. What was your plan to avoid that? Do you think that, had Governor Romney won, you would have avoided that?

ML: As I interviewed people and read about the transitions prior, it was evident to me that the primary obstacle was to make sure that what happened in the transition would be seen as having continuity with the campaign and that the trust levels would be sustained. I went to great effort to assure that that was the case. The first was that we adopted the philosophy that the campaign dealt with policy, and we dealt with planning implementation. The campaign didn't have to worry that we were originating policy that was going to be contrary to the candidate, or that there were people who were going to insert their own agendas into that process.

The second thing is that I spent one day a week in Boston at the campaign. We developed processes where no significant decisions were made that did not include the senior people from the campaign. We vetted major assignments with the campaign. We asked them for assistance in being able to identify the right people. We called upon those deeply involved in the campaign, which made a huge difference.

DM: Was there a lot of tension?

ML: Well, there's always tension in the campaign. It's chaotic, but we dealt with it. We dealt with it directly in an upfront way. Another thing we did that I think was important was that we acknowledged that there were people in the campaign who were there because they wanted to have a role in the administration. We made very clear to everyone that there would be no assignments made until campaign leadership was integrated into the process. We had a plan to integrate the campaign leadership into the transition. We did everything we could to give people comfort that we weren't a rogue organization operating on our own.

DM: How often did you talk to the candidate?

ML: I would typically spend less than an hour a week, but I would go where Mitt Romney was. Generally, it would be an hour on the plane in between campaign stops. I had a briefing process that I would go through, and if there were policy issues that I needed his advice on, I would discuss them with him there. With the exception of one other conversation that was a couple of hours long, right at the beginning, that's the way the pattern was established. He didn't want to think about it. He wanted to know it was happening but didn't want to burn any calories focusing on something like that until he had won.

DM: And that's why his trust in you was so important. He basically said: "I don't want to deal with this, but Mike Leavitt is taking care of it. I trust him. It's going to get done."

ML: I believe that's true. We had interagency processes, if you will, going on inside the transition. I would sit in where he would sit. Therefore, I needed to be able to express his philosophy and to have a sense of how he would respond to things. I'm sure I got a few things wrong, but for the most part I knew what was in his head and to a large degree what was in his heart. If I didn't, I would ask and I would proceed. We don't have the benefit of knowing how all of this would have come out, but candidly, I'm quite confident that we had anticipated this enough that the distrust issue would have been minimized.

"Everything was green—we were ready"

DM: Obviously, the election outcome wasn't what you wanted. What did you do then? How did you feel and what was your retrospective on this project?

ML: I'll start with the retrospective on the project. I've been involved in public policy for many years in different roles, and I would say that this was among the most challenging things, and maybe the most exhilarating experience I have had in a concentrated period of four or five months.

DM: I've heard you say this before, and you were a three-time governor, secretary of health, and head of the EPA, very prominent positions. But you said this was the most exciting, interesting, challenging thing you've ever done.

ML: I was given an opportunity to essentially stand up a government. Now, there's obviously a constitution and laws and history and tradition, but bringing this together was a circumstance where I was required to call on my knowledge of lots of different issues. My knowledge about how state, local, and national government works, the experience I had working with members of Congress, having been a cabinet member myself, having worked at the White House. It also involved a heavy dose of foreign policy. It was a very interesting experience.

You can't go through it without the belief that first of all, you're doing something important, and second of all, that your candidate has a very good chance to win. This is a live-fire exercise: you're playing with something that has real consequences. I felt that every day. Now, there were days when it felt like there was more certainty that this would actually be implemented than others. But I remember going to Boston for election night. I had with me the boxes of paper that would be put in front of the president-elect the next day starting at three o'clock. A whole series of decisions that needed to be made.

We had a planning construct that I thought was extraordinarily useful. It was a system we called a one-page project manager. We had the whole federal government down onto one page of things that had to happen. Of course, there were 104 pages underneath that, but we had designed a tick-tock, in essence, of what decisions needed to be made when. We were ready, everything was green—we had a red, yellow, green readiness dashboard. On election night, everything was green—we were ready.

DM: You'd really never lost an election, as I recall. But all of a sudden, you're part of this losing effort. You are a pretty even-keeled guy, but what were your emotions that night?

ML: It was profoundly disappointing, for all of the reasons that anyone who's ever been involved in a losing campaign knows so well. One of the things I learned from it is that someone has that experience every four years. It's a great service, actually, to run as a candidate, to support a candidate. Even though it was unsuccessful, a lot of good came from it.

DM: You deserve enormous credit for innovating and creating the gold standard for transition planning. Then after the election, even though it was a disastrous outcome for you and for the governor, you did another thing that was really innovative, which is that you decided to write a book and publish materials on your transition planning effort. Why did you do that?

ML: We knew going into it that we had a unique responsibility. We were the first campaign to ever formally operate under the Presidential Transition Act of 2010, so we were pioneering in many ways. Yes, we had a statute, and yes, there were a few letters of guidance that had been issued, but to a large extent we had to work our way through a lot of unique problems and questions.

We made a decision early on that we were going to document everything as well as we could. We were offered nothing from anyone other than a couple of boxes of very old records that really couldn't help us. We concluded that there was an opportunity here to lay out at least a construct that would be improved on as time went on. Then, at the end, we had three months we hadn't planned on because we had not been successful. We had this great ship that wasn't going to sail, and we concluded that we should spend that three months and a little bit of the money we had left over and write a book that would at least form the basis for others to start. A lot of good work went into it. We included all of the various patterns we used in the general plan. I think it's proven to be useful. The Center [for Presidential Transition] has made good use of it. They have supplemented it with the work of others, but I think when it comes right down to it, it did lay a foundation for future campaigns.

Notes

1. *Romney Readiness Project 2012: Retrospective & Lessons Learned* (Los Angeles, CA: R2P, Inc., 2013).
2. Sixty-seven individuals moved through the Senate confirmation process in the first one hundred days of 2009. Two individuals were formally confirmed for two separate roles.

Trump Dumps His Transition

GOVERNOR CHRIS CHRISTIE

> They still haven't recovered. . . . Once you give away that 150 days or so you can never get it back.
>
> —Chris Christie

ON THE morning of April 20, 2016, presidential transitions became front-page news. The *New York Times* featured a cover story describing a Center for Presidential Transition event at which representatives from the five active major-party presidential campaigns (Hillary Clinton, Ted Cruz, John Kasich, Bernie Sanders, and Donald Trump) met to discuss the serious business of transition planning.[1] That afternoon, Donald Trump called his longtime friend Governor Chris Christie of New Jersey, who had ended his own presidential bid two months previously, to ask if Christie would chair the Trump transition effort.[2] Following his usual modus operandi, Christie went all in.

Governor Christie started his effort with methodical research. He consulted the Center for Presidential Transition, as well as a who's who of Republican transition veterans, including Chris Liddell, Andy Card, Dick Cheney, and James Baker. He recruited a strong staff, headed by his talented gubernatorial former chief of staff, Rich Bagger. Bagger and Christie followed the Romney model, focusing on the four pillars of transition planning: appointments, policy, agency review, and president-elect support. They also laid out a sequenced postelection agenda for Trump and a methodical approach to engaging foreign leaders postelection.

Mike Leavitt, in his illuminating foreword to the book *Romney Readiness Project 2012: Retrospective & Lessons Learned,* sets out eight qualities a transition team leader should possess. Among them: "A personal history with the candidate that has created mutual respect, confidence, and trust between them . . . A trusted relationship with the campaign's leadership . . . Not a job seeker."[3]

Christie matched many of these characteristics, as well as a number of further criteria outlined in the Center's transition guide (which builds on Leavitt's list).[4] He was a peer of the candidate, experienced in government, with proven planning skills. However, as Christie described in his memoir, he was not above ambition. In Leavitt's terms, he could be described as "a job seeker." And he encountered two other major problems.

First, according to Christie, candidate Trump never supported serious transition planning, repeatedly telling Christie it was "bad karma" and a waste of time. Trump and Christie were "so smart," the candidate told the governor, that they could work out the entire transition in a couple of hours after his victory party.[5] It was an uphill battle to prepare the type of methodical process the Center recommends, but Christie and his team kept their heads down and did the work.

Second, contrary to another admonition of both Leavitt and the Center—and in the end fatally—Christie lacked support among Trump's key advisors, particularly son-in-law Jared Kushner, who reportedly had a personal score to settle with the governor. Two days after Trump's surprising election win, campaign manager Steve Bannon fired Christie, apparently at the behest of Kushner. Not only was Christie himself ejected; all of the binders prepared by their team were physically thrown in dumpsters—about the clearest imaginable violation of the rule that early planning is invaluable for a transition. (Bagger quickly resigned after Christie was fired.)

The results were predictably negative for the Trump presidency. His executive orders, drafted in haste to replace the more considered documents drawn up by the Christie team, were swiftly nullified by the courts. Appointments fared even worse. At the one-hundred-day mark, Trump had secured only twenty-eight Senate confirmations of his most senior appointees. Two years into his term, Trump had withdrawn forty nominations upon public scrutiny, 74 percent more than either Presidents Obama or George W. Bush.

My interview with Christie was as colorful and entertaining as any conversation with Governor Christie is bound to be. In some ways, Christie represented a prototype Donald Trump: a pugnacious political showman with an uncanny ability to make news. Almost as soon as he took office as governor of New Jersey in 2010, Christie's combative press conferences and town halls became must-watch TV—much as Trump's would six years later. Even the title of Christie's 2019 memoirs, *Let Me Finish*, demonstrated his desire to have the last word.[6]

But the surface similarities between Trump and Christie belie big differences. Whereas Trump had never before held political office, Christie had worked his way up to governor through stints as a local politician and federal prosecutor. While Trump built a largely homogeneous electoral coalition, Christie attracted large numbers of African American and Latino votes (the Republicans, he told me in our interview, "cannot just be a party of Whites"). And he demonstrated his ability to put state over self at key moments—notably when he appeared jointly with President Obama a week before the 2012 election to reassure victims of Superstorm Sandy.

At the start of his term as U.S. attorney in 2001, Christie made courtesy calls on New Jersey federal judges, including one named Maryanne Trump Barry. At the end of the discussion, Judge Barry asked Christie if he would be kind enough to have dinner with her little brother, Donald. In classic style, Trump and Christie ate at the center table—*the* table— at an opulent restaurant in the Trump International Hotel at Columbus Circle. On Christie's behalf, Trump ordered lamb and scallops. Christie hated the first and was allergic to the second. Nevertheless, that encounter started a friendship and alliance that would last for two decades.

Despite being a Republican in a blue state, Christie became a successful two-term governor and a fixture on Sunday talk shows, fêted as a future presidential candidate. In 2015, Governor Christie declared his candidacy and was instantly proclaimed a front-runner by newspapers and pundits. What he did not know was that he would soon be vanquished by the man he had first met over lamb and scallops. After his loss, Christie endorsed Trump and became a major campaign surrogate. Why? "Because I knew he would win," Christie told me. "It was that simple."

During our interview, the Center for Presidential Transition benefited from Christie's advice. Later, I faced his ire. Early in the tense postelection period of 2020, when the Center advocated for quick ascertainment of the outcome of the election, Christie called—clearly agitated—saying I had it all wrong and that we were playing into Trump's hands. If we pushed, Christie explained, Trump would only fight harder to stay. He was right.

In the history of presidential transitions, Chris Christie should be remembered favorably for overseeing an organized transition process amid the chaos of the Trump campaign; for doing what was right for the country; and for doing so even when the ultimate consumer of his work simply had no interest in preparing seriously for the most important job in the world.

"We only have one president at a time"

DAVID MARCHICK (DM): You grew up in New Jersey, you went to the University of Delaware, and there you got the political bug. What was it that attracted you to politics and policy?

CHRIS CHRISTIE (CC): I really got the political bug back in 1977, when I was fifteen years old and a local state legislator who was running for governor came to my junior high school to speak. I just fell in love with the guy; I thought he was amazing. He lived in my hometown, and that night, I was saying to my mother over homework: "I just really want to work for this guy. I want to try to help him be governor. I think he'd be a great governor."

She said: "Well, we know where he lives. Why don't you go up and volunteer for his campaign?" And literally my mother drove up this guy's driveway, I went to the front door, knocked on the door, and the person who answered the door was Governor Tom Kean. He was Assemblyman Tom Kean at the time. He came out and spoke to my mother and volunteered to have me travel with him that night to the VFW hall in Oradell, Bergen County, New Jersey, where he did an event and I handed out leaflets for him. And that's when I really got the political bug, Dave. That was February 1977. The fascinating thing is that thirty-two years later to the month, in February 2009, he endorsed me for governor.

DM: Let's fast-forward to George W. Bush's election: How did you end up getting involved with George W. Bush?

CC: My law partner at the time, a guy named Bill Palatucci, had run George H. W. Bush's campaign in New Jersey in 1988 and 1992, and I'd gotten to know George W. Bush during that period of time. When George W. decided to run for president and he was putting together an organization, he reached out to Bill because he needed somebody to help him organize New Jersey. So he asked if we would do it, and we organized a trip to Austin, Texas, with a group of legislative leaders to meet with George W. Bush. And from there, after about six of those visits to Austin, George W. asked me if I would be the lawyer for the campaign in New Jersey. I agreed to do it, and we went from there.

DM: Then he appointed you U.S. attorney, and you became famous nationally for putting politicians in jail for corruption. New Jersey has a history of that, some might say. Didn't that make you very unpopular with the political establishment?

CC: Yes and no. It made them fearful of me. Many who were honest respected me for doing it, and for those who didn't like me doing it, we learned to have a very gentle kind of détente in terms of our personal interactions. We did 130 political corruption cases during my seven years as U.S. attorney. We were 130 and 0, we didn't lose one, and we had some very, very big targets during those years. I think it just helped set a whole new tone inside the state.

DM: You went on to win two terms as governor, and as I look back at your record, one of the things that's amazing is that you won 25 percent of the African American vote, and more than 50 percent of the Latino vote, which is not typical of Republican candidates today. I know George Bush did really well with the Latino vote, but is there a Chris Christie–like figure in the modern Republican Party that appeals across the aisle and appeals to people of color?

CC: There better be. Because if there isn't, then there won't be a Republican Party twenty-five years from now. We cannot be just a party of Whites; we have to be a party that appeals to minorities in much greater numbers, whether it's Latinos, African Americans, or Asian Americans. We have to do a much better job at that. I worked very hard to gain that credibility with those communities in my state. What it shows you is that if you're willing to work very hard at it and you're willing to listen, then you can gain the support of folks who some people say are not reachable for Republicans.

DM: You became nationally famous, on the cover of *Time* magazine a couple of times, and in 2012 Mitt Romney asked you to keynote his convention. Fast-forward to a few days before the election: it's a tight race, and this terrible storm hits New Jersey; the president of the United States calls and says, "I want to come to New Jersey." That visit became controversial right before the election. So tell us what happened then, and why did that become controversial?

CC: The destruction in New Jersey was extraordinary. We lost 365,000 homes in twenty-four hours. This was a brutal storm, and on the day of the storm, the president called to offer his assistance. He signed the advance emergency declaration and did everything that I asked him to do. The next day, Tuesday, one week before the election, he called and said, "Governor, I want to come and see the damage for myself."

I had a decision to make. I knew it was a week before the election. I'd been the keynote speaker for Mitt Romney, and I'd raised more money for Mitt Romney than any political figure in America that year. I said, "Of course, Mr. President, you want to come and see it, I want you to come." The reason I made that decision was because my job is to be governor of New Jersey; my job was to make sure that the people in New Jersey were taken care of.

If all you do is see the picture of the two of us shaking hands on the tarmac outside Air Force One, some people drew certain conclusions. I made mistakes in my eight years as governor, but that wasn't one of them. I'd do the same thing over again, exactly the same way. We only have one president at a time, David. You treat them with respect, and that's all I did.

"We'd better get to making him better quick"

DM: Fast-forward to 2016: You're one of the leading candidates. You declare for president. You have lots of support. Did you at any time think that Donald Trump, who was your longtime friend, would run and then beat not only you but everybody in the Republican Party, including some very prominent people like Jeb Bush and Marco Rubio and others?

CC: Absolutely not. Donald had not given me any type of indication that he was going to run at all. Even when he started to run, when he famously came down the escalator, I did not take it seriously. I thought it was a publicity stunt. He had played around with the idea of running for president a number of times before, so I didn't take it seriously. But it was a very unusual year.

There is a story about my wife going door-to-door in New Hampshire for me. She went to a Republican home and knocked on the front door; a woman in her early seventies answered the door. My wife said, "Hi, I'm Mary Pat Christie. I'm married to Governor Chris Christie."

"Oh my goodness, we love your husband. He is so smart and articulate and tough. I mean, we're voting for Trump, but I hope he makes your husband vice president or attorney general."

"If you love my husband so much and think he's so smart and articulate and tough, why are you voting for Trump?"

The woman grabbed my wife's hand and said, "Oh dear, we don't need another politician."

That was about two weeks out from the primary, and we were in second place in the polls. In New Hampshire we had gotten the [*Manchester*] *Union Leader* endorsement and would have gotten the *Boston Herald* endorsement, so we were feeling pretty good. But I heard the story from my wife, and I came back to the hotel and my campaign manager, and I said, "We're dead."

DM: Trump surprised everybody. You dropped out, and then you decided to endorse him. In your book, I noticed that at the time you endorsed him, you were the first major political leader to do so. I think the major people that had endorsed him at that time were Jesse Ventura, Ted Nugent, and Kid Rock. Why did Chris Christie join that list?

CC: Because I knew he was going to win. It was that simple. I watched this guy lose by a whisker to Ted Cruz in Iowa, beat the best Republican field I had seen in my lifetime in New Hampshire by double digits, and then go and win in South Carolina by double digits. And I said, "It's over." And by the way, if it was anybody but Donald Trump, so would everyone else. They just couldn't come to grips with it. I understand; I've studied politics. I've watched it my whole life, especially presidential politics.

Republicans called me and asked, "How could you endorse Trump?"

I said: "He's going to be the nominee. We'd better get to making him better quick, because we want to beat Hillary Clinton." My goal was to go in there, endorse him early, and do everything I could to make him a better politician, a better candidate. That's why I did it.

"You don't have a day to waste"

DM: Fast-forward to May: Trump is the presumptive nominee, and he taps you to run the transition process. How did you get involved; how did that come about?

CC: He gave me a call in early May. He felt like it was bad luck to run anything about transition before you had actually won, but he knew that legally he had to do it. So he called and asked me if I'd come in and see him and talk to him about it. In the interim, Corey Lewandowski, who was the campaign manager at that time, called me and kind of previewed the meeting for me and said: "He's serious about this. He wants you to be the key transition chairman and set up the government for him. Are you willing to do it? Because if you're not, then I'll just cancel the meeting and we'll move on to something else so that you don't have to have that kind of awkward discussion with him."

I said: "No, no, I'm happy to do it. I think it'd be a really interesting project for me." I came in to see Donald Trump, and he offered me the job.

DM: What did you do next? Who did you seek advice from, and what advice did they give you?

CC: I first reached out to Chris Liddell, who had, along with others, run the Romney transition preparation in 2012. They were very generous in sharing all kinds of information with me, so that was great. I met with Andy Card, who along with Vice President Cheney ran the transition for the George W. Bush team. I met with Vice President Cheney as well. He was generous with his time. I met with Jim Baker, who was instrumental in the Bush 41 transition and in the Ronald Reagan transition. I also met with a number of other folks who were involved around the periphery in those transition efforts going back to Ronald Reagan.

What they said to me was that you don't have a day to waste. The government is bigger and more complex than it's ever been. If your candidate wins, he is going to be less well-versed in the intricacies of how government operates than any president of our lifetime. You're going to have to have an even more detailed plan to have him prepared in the seventy-three days between election and inauguration. All of them gave me that same general type of advice. The next thing I did was to get a really smart, capable, talented guy to be the executive director of the transition. I went back and recruited my old first chief of staff, Rich Bagger. Rich agreed to take a leave of absence to run a transition with me from May until November. That's how we began.

DM: You talked to this all-star group of people—Jim Baker, Andy Card—they'd run the government before, but there was tension because candidate Trump didn't want to spend a lot of time or money on transition. How did you convince him that it was worth you building a really good team?

CC: I don't know that I ever did, Dave. I think that what happened basically was he became convinced that he had to do this legally, and he just tried to stay as far away from it as he could. The only time I ever really spoke to him about it after that was on rare occasions where he read something in the news about the transition, and he would call and give me some reaction to it. Each time he called, he'd say to me: "Chris, you're wasting a lot of time on this. You and I are both so smart that if we win this thing, we can do the entire transition if we just leave the victory party two hours early."

It was clear that the president had no real appreciation at that time for just how difficult putting together a government was going to be. I just said: "Well, I don't really care about that. I can deal with that after the election is over. My job is to make sure that he's going to be prepared and that he's going to have every resource in front of him to be able to make good choices and to have those good choices reflect ultimately in effective governance."

DM: During this whole process, you were working with an executive committee on the Trump campaign. Who was on that committee, how did you report to them, and what were those conversations like?

CC: First of all, that was not the way it was supposed to be. The original agreement between me and the president was that I would report to him and to him only. When he did not want to be involved in the transition, he delegated it to this executive committee. The chair of the executive committee was really Jared Kushner. On the executive committee were Ivanka Trump, Eric Trump, Donald Trump Jr. Initially, it was Paul Manafort along with Jeff Sessions and Steve Mnuchin. Ultimately, Manafort was out, and Steve Bannon replaced Manafort. This group met every Monday at Trump Tower, where we reported everything that was going on in the transition to them. We gave them a briefing on Friday in writing about what we were going to cover on Monday and an agenda and a full briefing behind it. That was what ran the meetings on those Mondays, and we did this just about every week from about late June through to November.

"From promise to accomplishment"

DM: The Trump transition postelection has been criticized for being chaotic. What's not well-known is that you, Rich, and the team did a really good job planning and you worked closely with the Partnership for Public Service. What were the main things that you focused on in that planning process? What were the biggest tasks?

CC: There are so many, but I would say first was to listen to what the candidate was saying on the campaign trail, and then give him a roadmap to achieve every one of the things he was talking about on the campaign trail in either a one-hundred-day or two-hundred-day plan. First was laying out those individual promises that Donald Trump was making on the campaign trail, and then putting groups together who were expert in that area to be able to prepare white papers that would say, "Here's how you get from promise to accomplishment."

The second big piece was putting together the landing teams and blueprints for each department in the federal government. That way you would have a group of people who were qualified to go in there beginning the day after the election and get a feel for what the Obama administration was doing in that department at that time and what you would need to do to change those things to meet what President Trump's priorities would be.

The third piece was personnel. Bill Hagerty, who had run personnel for the Romney transition, agreed to come in and run personnel for our transition.

We were looking at cabinet-level, subcabinet, and White House staff. I recruited fifteen of my former colleagues as U.S. attorneys to come in as volunteers to do the high-level public-source vetting of all these potential candidates. We did a lot of outreach to people in the campaign and people in the corporate world and the nonprofit world to get recommendations for people for different positions. We then vetted people and put together an entire list of folks for each cabinet and major subcabinet position that the president would be asked to fill. All of that was done between May and the Monday before the election. On that Monday, we turned over twenty volumes of materials that met those three major tasks to the Trump campaign for them to be ready to begin to execute on Wednesday if Donald Trump was successful on Tuesday.

DM: You also laid out kind of a sequencing of his priorities. I think your recommendation was for him to focus first on tax cuts, then infrastructure, and then Obamacare. Why did you suggest that sequencing, and what happened?

CC: The reason I suggested that sequencing was because I felt it gave him the maximum opportunity to run the board and get all three. Republicans had been in the wilderness for eight years under Barack Obama, so, first off the bat, you wanted to unite Republicans. The best way to unite Republicans of all different stripes is with reduction of taxes. I think you do the tax cut first to make Republicans get a big win on the board and unite Republicans behind you. Then, I said, "Let's do an infrastructure bill," because an infrastructure bill had the possibility of uniting Republicans and Democrats. This way, you bring Democrats along, you give them a real opportunity to have input into what the infrastructure bill looks like and how the money is going to be spent. You bring them together with Republicans and show that you're not the boogeyman. Only then do you move on to what would be the most difficult task of all, which was grappling with the healthcare situation and Obamacare in particular.

DM: What do you know now that you wish you knew then?

CC: Make sure that you do all the vetting you need to do on your landing teams way in advance. Decide early on whether you're going to let any lobbyists be on those teams. I'm agnostic on it. I don't think there's any problem with having lobbyists on those teams, but everybody has a different point of view. Make sure you set your policy because having those landing teams, you're going to have to have really good people, smart, experienced people, who are literally ready to go in the day after the election.

Have all that stuff squared away and the rules laid out right in the beginning so that nobody can raise any issues that can trip you up in the beginning of an administration. I don't think you can ever spend enough time on personnel, because in government, personnel does turn out to be policy to a large extent. And so, make sure that you have a number of fully publicly vetted appropriate recommendations for the president-elect so that this process can be much easier for him than it would be otherwise. Those are two things for sure.

"They still haven't recovered"

DM: Let's go to the day after the election. You've done all this work, you're coordinating with this executive team, which included a bunch of Trump family members. I guess Steve Bannon talked to you, and what happened there?

CC: It was actually a couple of days after the election. The day after the election, I ran my first transition meeting. The meeting went fine. We started to lay things out. One of the more unusual moments was when I handed over to Jared the list of foreign leaders and what order they should be called. He said, "Well, we're not going to pay much attention to this."

I said, "Well, the order that you call them back in is very important, it's traditional."

He goes: "Well, Donald was an unconventional candidate. He's going to be an unconventional president." That was a key moment when I knew that the transition was not going to run the way I had planned for it to run.

The next day, we had a transition meeting, and when the meeting concluded, Steve Bannon asked if I'd come see him in his office. We sat down, and I said, "What's up?"

He goes, "We need to make some changes."

"Okay, what changes are we making?"

"You."

"Are you kidding me?"

"Nope. Vice President Pence is now going to be the chair of the transition, and you're out."

"Well, I'd like to know who made this decision and why."

"It really doesn't matter. We just expect you to comply."

"Well, that's fine, Steve. I know it wasn't the president-elect. But there's a big crowd of press downstairs in the lobby so I'm going to go down there right now. I'm going to tell them that I've been fired. I'm going to tell them that you did it because you're the only person who I know has anything to do with it. Have a good time dealing with the incoming phone calls."

I started to get up to walk out. He said, "No, no, no, don't leave" and that we could talk about this. He ultimately said to me that the reason I was being fired was because of Jared and that ever since he had gotten on board, sometime in August, as he put it, "The kid has been taking the axe to your head. And I think the boss just got tired of defending you."

DM: One thing I've never really understood is that you worked closely with the executive committee, which included Trump family members. They were part of the whole process, so they were presumably part of your work product. But then, they kind of tossed all that work—which was good work—in the trash. Why did that happen?

CC: I think they were feeling very arrogant at the time. They'd won a race that most people didn't think they could win, and now they thought, "We're going to run a transition in an unconventional way and watch everybody react to that." I also think that there was no doubt that there was a piece of personal animus and revenge involved on Jared's part, because for those of your listeners who don't know, back in 2004, I prosecuted Jared Kushner's father, Charles Kushner, and sent him to jail for two years. I do think that there was an element of that as well.

DM: You had done all this work; everybody that at the Partnership and other places that worked with you said you did a great job. Rich Bagger, anybody that knows him knows he's a very competent kind of nonpolitical, serious lawyerly type. What was the impact of losing all this work at the start of the Trump administration?

CC: They still haven't recovered. As you can see, in the beginning of the Trump White House there were either lots of empty seats or ones that were filled out with lots of Obama holdovers. If that was in the White House at the National Security Council, you can imagine what it was like in all the departments. So you have people there who are hostile to the president personally, but he had just been elected and then he would wonder why he couldn't get things done. It just has impacted this administration in every substantive way. They've never caught up because you can't catch up. Even if they win a second term, they won't catch up because once you give away that 150 days or so you can never get it back. Those are 150 very important days.

"What to do in year four"

DM: You were a two-term governor, and obviously you were a successful two-term governor. What did you do in year four to prepare for a year five of your governorship? What would be your advice to do in year four, year five?

CC: You have to run a campaign, and you have to continue to run the government, but in terms of preparation for a fifth year or a second term, what we did was we went back and looked at the campaign promises of 2009, when I initially ran. We looked at other issues that came up spontaneously during the four years and listed all of them and then said: "Okay, which one of these did we accomplish? Which ones did we not accomplish? Which ones did we try to accomplish, but weren't able to get it done?"

When you get those three categories of items, you can then meld those categories together to make it a second-term agenda. You can't be constantly backward-looking. You have to look to what you did in those four years and issues that came up like Superstorm Sandy that you would have never expected. Then, you have to look at the things you promised but didn't get done for some reason and see if you can get them done in the second four years. I think that would be a very useful way to look at it for anybody who's a current sitting government executive seeking reelection.

Notes

1. Julie Hirschfeld Davis, "In an Age of Terror, an Early Start on the Presidential Transition," *New York Times,* April 20, 2016, https://www.nytimes.com/2016/04/21/us/politics/in-an-age-of-terror-smoothing-the-transition-to-the-next-presidency.html.
2. This is how Chris Christie recalls the sequence of events. Michael Lewis reports that Christie approached Donald Trump with the idea rather than vice versa in his book *The Fifth Risk* (see Michael Lewis, *The Fifth Risk: Undoing Democracy* [New York: Norton, 2018], 17).
3. *Romney Readiness Project 2012: Retrospective & Lessons Learned* (R2P, Inc., 2013), 3–8.
4. Center for Presidential Transition, *Presidential Transition Guide,* 4th ed., April 2020, 58, https://presidentialtransition.org/transition-timeline-and-guide/
5. Chris Christie, *Let Me Finish: Trump, the Kushners, Bannon, New Jersey, and the Power of In-Your-Face Politics* (New York: Hachette, 2019).
6. Christie, *Let Me Finish.*

Trump's Transition Out: The Good, the Bad, and the Ugly

CHRIS LIDDELL

> We really don't want to ever have this situation again.
>
> —Chris Liddell

ON JANUARY 6, 2021, the day of the Capitol insurrection, Chris Liddell, then Trump's deputy chief of staff, came within a hair's breadth of resigning. But together with a mutual friend, former Bush 43 chief of staff Josh Bolten, we encouraged him to stay. Resigning with fourteen days left, we suggested, would not make a meaningful enough statement compared to the cost. His work at the White House, however, might smooth the transition.

In 2020, a year chock-full of challenges, Chris Liddell had perhaps the worst job in Washington: planning the transition out of office for a president who neither wanted to leave nor recognized the outcome of the election. To be fair, Liddell had other important responsibilities: he served as deputy chief of staff for policy and led the planning for a potential Trump second term. But this one component of his job—planning Trump's exit and facilitating Biden's entrance—would test Chris's considerable skill, grit, and ethical core.

My work with Chris Liddell began exactly a year before, in January 2020, when Josh Bolten and I had eggs and sausage with him in the White House mess. The primary focus of that discussion was planning Trump's second term. Josh, himself a second-term chief of staff, noted that very few presidents took seriously the task of planning in year four for a potential year five. Instead, Josh advised, Chris should approach year four like a transition.

That was the easy part of the conversation. Bolten, a seasoned and measured Washington pro, was used to raising difficult questions. Near the end, Josh turned to Chris and asked him what he was planning in case Trump lost. Chris paused, looked down at his empty plate, and said, "I guess I need to figure that out."

That breakfast began a series of meetings, walks, phone calls, and late-night texts with Chris, often in collaboration with Josh. One night in September, Josh and Chris joined me for dinner at my house, outside and socially distanced to protect each other from COVID-19. When a monsoon-like summer rainstorm overtook the dinner, we moved to my garage, where, for three hours, we discussed five possible Election Day scenarios. Chris's "nightmare" was a non-landslide Biden win that Trump refused to recognize. The nightmare came true.

Nevertheless, Chris did an exceptional job coordinating the administration's efforts to implement the Presidential Transition Act. Along with trusted aide Nick Butterfield, Chris organized the White House Coordinating Council; authorized the creation of the Agency Transition Directors Council; reviewed and approved regular reports to Congress; and provided detailed guidance to agencies on preparing briefing materials and succession plans.

To anyone who has read the preceding interviews in this book, the above sounds ordinary—almost antiseptic. But if Trump had known the details of this work, Chris would surely have been in the president's doghouse, if not worse, regardless of the White House's legislative or constitutional requirements. Chris, Josh, and I developed a strategy: first, keep preelection transition planning low-profile, out of the press; second, embrace the career staff—which Chris did, speaking to federal transition coordinator Mary Gibert directly instead of through myriad layers of political officials; and above all, keep the issue of transitions out of the Oval Office. In this way, we hoped to create space for Chris Liddell to quietly do his important work.

This strategy almost blew up with a mistake I made. I had briefed the press many times—all off the record—that preelection transition planning was going well and by the book. On September 23, Nancy Cook of *Politico* called to say she was doing a story on the effective planning on transition in the White House. Would I comment on Chris Liddell's role? I demurred in order to consult Chris and the Biden team. Both said it would be helpful to the strategy. So, speaking on the record this time, I told Nancy that Chris and his team were "very, very focused on implementing the law and doing it by the book, and they are doing a good job."

Seems innocuous? It wasn't. The next day, *Politico* posted a story titled, "Trump Team Plots His Departure—Even If He Won't."[1] The story quoted me and generally praised the job Chris was doing. My stomach churned. In came an email from a longtime friend and Biden transition advisor, Jeff Peck, inadvertently copying me along with a large group of top Biden officials. "Marchick knows better than this," Jeff wrote. He was right. All night I texted Chris to see if he still had a job. In classic Liddell humor, he told me, "I think I will just avoid the Oval Office for a few days."

The story, however, was accurate: preelection transition planning was the most organized and efficient part of the White House, and Chris had done an excellent job.

That was the good. The bad came soon after the election, when Emily Murphy, the administrator of the General Services Administration, refused to "ascertain" the "apparent outcome" of the election. When Murphy finally relented on November 23, Chris faced another monumental challenge: corralling agencies to cooperate with the Biden team. Most cooperated, but some, despite Chris's best efforts, simply refused. The holdouts included the Office of the United States Trade Representative and, scarily from a national security standpoint, the Department of Defense.

The ugly, of course, was what Mitch McConnell deemed an "attempted insurrection" at the Capitol on January 6—surely the bleakest day in modern transition history.[2] That day, protesters supporting Donald Trump violently stormed the Capital building in an attempt to reverse the election results, leaving several dead.

I hosted Chris on the podcast on January 19, 2021, Trump's last full day in office and one of Chris's last official acts as a government official. The next morning, Trump left the White House as the only president to have been impeached twice, with a lower favorability rating than any of his modern predecessors—even post-Watergate Richard Nixon was more popular. Trump never recognized the outcome of the election, never paid the courtesy of congratulating the president-elect, and—for the first time since the departure of another disgraced president, Andrew Johnson—refused to attend his successor's inauguration.

History will judge the roles of those close to Trump, and when it does, Chris Liddell should be viewed favorably. He tried to create order amid chaos. He pushed for the faithful implementation of the Presidential Transition Act. Ultimately, he facilitated the exit of a president who lost the election but refused to leave. In so doing, Liddell helped preserve democracy.

"Transitions should build on each other"

DAVID MARCHICK (DM): Let's start with how you became interested and involved in transition. You were a business leader. You had a distinguished business career, and then all of a sudden you find yourself running a presidential transition in 2012. How did that happen?

CHRIS LIDDELL (CL): In 2012, I had just finished the General Motors IPO and had left the company. So I had a pause in my career, and I'd always wanted to do public service. The 2012 election was kicking off, and I volunteered to the Romney organization and said, "Look, I'm happy to help in any way." That was relatively early on. I got to know Governor Mike Levitt, and he was asked by Mitt to set up the transition operation, and Governor Leavitt invited me to join him. We started literally as a two-person team. I thought the transition concept was fascinating, and it suited my sort of planning and thinking, so I agreed to join him. That was back in March or so of 2012. With his help, we built up to a staff of something like five hundred people just before the election. It was sort of a startup on steroids. I learned an enormous amount and very much enjoyed it.

DM: After Romney lost, you decided to do something unique. Most transitions are done in secret. They're done in the background, as they should be, and then people just kind of go off and do their thing. You said, actually we should take the learnings and publish them. Why did you do that? And why did Mike and Romney think that was a good idea?

CL: One of the benefits of losing is you end up with a bit of time on your hands, and Mike and I wondered how we should use that time. We felt that some of the work that we had done was extremely good, even though it clearly didn't have the chance to be implemented. We felt that transitions are a really special part of the American presidential election tradition, so we wanted to document it. We had learned from previous transitions and benefited from this, and we wanted to build on that. We believe then, and still do now, that transitions should build on each other and that the expertise and knowledge that's built up from one should be passed on to the other. We've benefited from previous ones. We wanted to contribute back and hopefully be useful for the future.

"I didn't want the election and the transition to be a significant disruption"

DM: Let's move to this year. You had two jobs. As in any reelection, the second part of your job was very difficult. But let's start with the first part of your job. Traditionally in year four there's some planning for a potential year five. How did you approach that job in case President Trump had won reelection?

CL: I've benefited from the knowledge of the previous chiefs of staff, and they were incredibly helpful in some of their comments, thinking about how to prepare for a potential term two. The first area that I wanted to focus on was policy. I really wanted policy to be a continuum rather than a significant change. Back in January 2020, we had an off-site with all of the major deputies here at the White House and sat down to discuss not only the policy objectives for the year of 2020, but how they would flow into 2021, in particular some of the most significant legislative ideas. As you know, after an election is a period where you can potentially get some really significant legislative work done.

So we started to build the platform for the policy initiatives that we would have put in place in 2021 had we won back in [November] of last year, and I started to work on how what we did in 2020 would flow through to 2021. I didn't want the election and the transition to be a significant disruption. I wanted it to be a continuum from one to the other.

Focus area number two was actually exactly the opposite, which was people. With a White House, the structures and processes to some extent start to mold around the people here, and it's quite hard to change them. Those people are in place. So what I wanted to do on the people side was think about not only a changing of people, which you inevitably have between one administration and the second term, but think about how we could structurally change the White House in some interesting ways to make it significantly more efficient.

I've benefited from having worked here for four years, so I really have understood how the place could work in a much more detailed fashion. I hit some plans around how I wanted to quite significantly change structure, working operations, and cadence for the White House, which really required a change in some of the people. We were expecting those people to go just in the natural course, so that really was a chance for a disruptive and very positive change that I would have implemented in the transition to the second term.

DM: Governor Christie was on this podcast. He obviously led the preelection transition work in 2016 for President Trump. But, you know, he said—and there've been lots of documents about this—that both as president and a candidate in 2016, Trump is not really a planner. He doesn't like transitions and didn't want to spend a lot of time. Did he get involved in this work you did on a potential second term? Did he focus on it? Or did he just say kind of what he did in 2016, which was: "I can figure this out. I don't need a lot of planning"?

CL: It was mostly staff-run. I don't think that is peculiar to President Trump. From what I've heard from previous chiefs of staff, generally speaking the president spends most of his time focused on policy and day-to-day, as they do when they're campaigning as well. So it was really staff-driven.

"This can happen again"

DM: Let's turn to preparations for a potential handover to President-elect Biden. For anybody in the White House, it's difficult to plan for your boss's departure. It seems like an impossible job. I mentioned that we're going to talk about the good and the bad and the ugly. I think what most of our listeners don't know is that in your work preelection, which was really under the radar, the president was not involved at all. There was very little press, and it was very smooth. There's something called the Presidential Transition Act, which lays out a bunch of requirements for the White House and the agencies to execute prior to the election. And you did that. Tell us what you did and how you did that. How did you keep that from going off the rails?

CL: As you said, the Presidential Transition Act is very useful in that it sets down a series of markers. Those markers are useful to force activity and to make sure that we stay on track toward Election Day. Way back in April of last year, we sent out an initial memo to agency and department heads providing guidance on what their obligations were, and that kicked the process off and signaled to people most importantly that we were expecting them to do what was set out. In May, we set up the White House Transition Coordinating Council. Again, this is required. Again, just signaling as much as possible that this was business as normal.

Then there were a series of meetings, just to report that we were on track. But mostly we worked with the GSA [General Services Administration] in particular, who were then working with agencies to put together the briefing books and all of the requirements that we would need once the election happened. We had these main markers. Below the surface of those markers, we were working away steadily to make sure that we were as ready as possible and trying to emphasize that, despite the politics out in the open, the transition side of things should continue as normally as possible.

DM: You did two things in an effort to make sure that the preelection transition planning part was not politicized. One is, you said, "I want to work directly with the career officials at GSA led by Mary Gibert, who's the outstanding transition coordinator of career federal civil servants" [Gibert is interviewed later in this volume]. Second is, "I'm going to take essentially what Obama did in 2016 and just do that." Why did you pursue those two things?

CL: Firstly, I call out Mary Gibert, who is an unbelievable professional. It's been a delight to work with her. As soon as I met her, I knew we were in good hands. Part of that is personality: she was just such a pleasure. She's so professional in everything that she did. It was important for me from a continuity perspective to have career people there, ones who had some experience from the past and who are professional and not too deeply politicized. As you said, transitions should be as apolitical as they possibly can be. The career people really do a great job, and if you were lucky enough to find someone like Mary, you were in really great hands.

The other aspect was precedent. I think precedent is good. We only have a transition every four years, and there haven't been that many in the modern age with the scale and complexity of what we have. So building up a body of precedent is very useful. You need to occasionally change the approach, but just going back to what the previous person did, who went back to the previous person before, I think helps to depoliticize it, because you can basically say, "Look, this is what they did, this is where they drew the line."

There's some judgment done, and every time one of those judgments comes up you want it to be as smooth as possible. Precedent is helpful for that. Circumstances change, so sometimes you have to change the precedent, but if we can build up a body of all of it, I think that's incredibly useful. That way it will become mechanical, and people don't have to think about the politics of the decision they're making.

DM: One of the things that Ted Kaufman and Yohannes Abraham [respectively chair and executive director of the 2020 Biden transition] talked about on the podcast was scenario planning. They essentially said, "All right, let's take every possible scenario and try to anticipate it." I think you did the same thing. You and I had many, many discussions over the months about what might happen, what might happen smoothly, what might happen not smoothly. As you approached preelection [planning], what were the scenarios that you planned for in your mind, that could possibly happen on the day after the election?

CL: As we discussed, the scenarios were a clean victory for the Trump administration; a clean victory for the Biden administration; and a disputed situation. In the disputed case, we considered a dispute for a relatively short period of time and a dispute for a long period of time. Clean loss and clean victory clearly would have been relatively easy to deal with, and there's plenty of good precedent on that. I've been involved in some of that, so I had a very clear idea of what needed to be done either way. Obviously, all of the systems and processes are set up for either of those scenarios.

On the disputed situation, I started to build some scenarios around that. As I said, there was the short version, where a week or two passed and then we moved on, and then there was an extended one. In the short one, I wasn't too concerned about that. Having lack of access to the agencies would have been a nuisance to the incoming administration but not that significant initially, mainly because there's so much for the incoming people to do straightaway, they have to choose. For a period of time, it's incredibly inconvenient and annoying but not that significant to the final outcome. If you have that situation, some of the things that a clean victory or clean loss would allow don't happen.

The real issue is the one that we started to face, which is that it dragged on and on and on. As the transition goes on, it becomes more and more critical that the president-elect gets intelligence briefings, that the teams start to get into the agencies and the components of the White House. Unfortunately, the scenario I was most worried about was the one that came into play.

DM: I remember one conversation where we basically said, "This is a nightmare scenario, and it's much worse than we ever could have even imagined." We'll come back to that. But we talked about the good; let's go to the bad. The election occurs on November 3. That following Saturday, all the networks called the election for [Biden], but then the GSA administrator, Emily Murphy, refused to ascertain the outcome. The president of the United States did not recognize the outcome of the election, even though it was clear. You had no role in the GSA determination. What happened then, and what were you doing during this three-week period when this whole ascertainment debate was going on?

CL: That was probably one of the most frustrating periods that I've ever seen. Essentially, we were just on hold. We couldn't do anything. Clearly, I wanted to get on with it. We were ready to go. But until the GSA administrator ascertains, it's impossible really to do any of the things that are set down. Emily Murphy was in a terrible position, and for that period of time we were literally sitting on our hands ready to go, having done all the work but not able to do anything.

DM: What were the conversations in the White House at this point? The outcome of the election was clear. History shows that this was not one of the closest elections. It wasn't even one of the closest elections in the last forty or fifty years. What is the conversation in the White House where you have a president basically saying, "I don't recognize the outcome"? How did that work?

CL: I don't want to get into the ins and outs of the election itself. I was sitting there trying to decide how we were going to make a transition work on a compressed timeline. I was hoping that we would resolve it as quickly as possible so we could get on with it. I had no connection with the GSA administrator, and so I was really in her hands as to when she did that.

I think that raises a wider issue, which is that we really don't want to ever have this situation again. We need to look at a solution where the incoming administration can get access to a lot of the things that they would do and should do as a result of the Transition Act, regardless of the politics and the dispute associated with the election.

We have to think about the fact that this can happen again. With a dispute going on, we need to be able to split and let the legal processes play out as they should or could but at the same time not slow the transition planning down. It's something certainly I'd be happy to work on with the Partnership [for Public Service] or anyone who feels the same way. We should have legislation that allows a provisional assignment, for example, for the president-elect to start getting security briefings, for a lot of the time-sensitive issues to start regardless of whether the actual formal election has been settled or not. I think those two could be running in parallel, to my mind. That's the big lesson from those initial weeks.

"This should just happen as a matter of course"

DM: Let's fast-forward: Pressure builds; the election [result] further clarifies. On Monday, November 23, about three weeks late, Emily Murphy issues the ascertainment letter, and the agencies work with the Biden team. Then what did you do?

CL: We were literally ready to go on a day-by-day basis. Mary [Gibert] and I were talking pretty regularly and saying: "Are you ready? Are you ready? Yes, yes." So as soon as we got the ascertainment, she went into action, contacted the Biden transition team, and we [set up] access to a number of the agencies the next morning.

It wasn't quite as smooth or quite as comprehensive as it would have been had it been the day after the election; the incoming team had to get themselves back up again. But we pretty much straightaway went into action. And again, I pay compliments to the GSA team and all the various agencies that had put together the briefings. They were ready to go. A lot of that preparatory work meant that we could kick-start the engine straightaway.

DM: Overall, the Biden team has said that most agencies cooperated, but there were a few that just refused to cooperate, [for example] the Office of the U.S. Trade Representative, the Department of Defense, the Office of Management and Budget. In the memorandum of understanding between the Biden team and the White House, there's an escalation clause. When they escalated these problems to you, you would call the agency heads and say, "Hey, you're not cooperating." And they would say, "We don't want to cooperate." How did that go? What were those conversations like?

CL: Just before we get into the problems, I want to recognize that 90 percent–plus of the agencies and components went about the job really well. I don't want it to be lost on people that there were a lot of good actors out there who really tried hard and did the right thing. There were some situations where there were some reluctant people, but I rang them up, and we managed to smooth it over and get on. I don't want people to come away with the impression that there was a significant resistance across the whole of the government. That was not true. There were some agencies that were uncooperative. I tried my best, but I didn't really have the teeth to do it

Again, I think that's an area where you do have an unusual situation where you have the outgoing administration in charge of the transition to the incoming one, and that relies to some extent on goodwill. When that goodwill is absent, it's hard to make it happen. I'm not a great fan, generally, of regulatory fixes or deterministic processes, but this is an area I want to think about again and try and come up with some solutions based on how we can take away some of the discretion and need for goodwill and make it a little bit more prescriptive.

DM: Tell me if you agree with this: Most agencies were eager to cooperate and did, but there were some agencies that were reluctant, and you essentially pushed them and prodded them, and they moved to be cooperative. And then there were a handful of agencies that basically just refused; even with your pushing, it didn't have an impact. Is that an accurate statement?

CL: Yes. Maybe "refused" is too strong. But certainly [some] did the absolute minimum, and that was really not good enough under the circumstances.

DM: And the difference here was that for example, with Obama and Bush, you had a president of the United States that basically instructed all of their cabinet agencies to cooperate, and here you didn't. So you were basically doing as much as you could, but without the president's direct intervention or instructions, which made it impossible for you to push some agencies.

CL: I don't think we should have a situation where that's needed. This should just happen as a matter of course and as a matter of expectation. It shouldn't be a situation where you're requiring goodwill and arbitrary decisions to that extent.

"My duty was to be here"

DM: We've talked about the good, we've talked about the bad. Let's go to the ugly. I think that we anticipated a lot of the problems that would happen, but what happened on January 6? It was one of the most disturbing days in American history. It was an insurrection. There will be criminal actions. There's been an impeachment. History will judge what happened. Where were you when this broke, and what were your reactions? What did you do?

CL: Ironically, I was in the West Wing and working on transition matters when it all broke, and I saw it on the television screen at the same time as everyone else. I guess I was horrified initially and heartbroken afterward. From the transition point of view, it made everything exponentially more difficult as well.

DM: There were some press reports that said that you considered resigning on that day. How did you think about that? How did you weigh the pros and cons, and why did you decide to stay?

CL: There were some people we saw that wanted to resign and just have nothing to do with the event or anything associated with it. And I respected those people who decided that it was their opportunity to leave and that was their protest. I thought long and hard about that and came to a different conclusion. I felt that in the following couple of weeks leading up to the inauguration, it was probably more important that I was here, because when you look at a transition, the closer you get to an inauguration, the more critical it gets. So to walk away when the very most important time was coming up, and at a time when tensions had gone through the roof, I just didn't feel like that was my duty. My duty was to be here. The easy thing would have been to leave that day and never come back. But the slightly harder, and I think more appropriate, thing to do was to stay.

DM: There have been other events throughout the administration, like Charlottesville. Were there discussions or consideration of resignations at previous events? Or was this so bad that it rose to the level where people said, "I just can't be here"? How did this event compare to previous problematic events during the Trump term?

CL: This was unprecedented. Clearly there had been other times where there'd been issues, but this was unprecedented across the board. I want to pay respect to some of my other colleagues who stayed on, people like Robert O'Brien, the national security advisor, and Pat Cipollone, the general counsel. There was a core of us who felt collectively it was our duty to stay. So I think this was much more significant and broad-based than previous issues.

DM: Going back to the scenarios, this was so much worse than any worst-case scenario that you or I imagined. We thought the whole denial of the outcome might have happened for two weeks, but Trump still hasn't even called Biden. What's the mood at the White House today, a day before you leave?

CL: We're down to a core staff now here, a skeleton staff. I think everyone's focused on tomorrow [i.e., the inauguration of President Biden]. On a slightly more positive note, the relationship with the Biden transition team has been as good as it could possibly be throughout this period. It's been challenging at times and particularly in the last couple of weeks, but most of my interactions over the last few days and up to today have been very much about how we land the plane as well as we possibly can tomorrow at twelve o'clock.

Those of us that are left here are really focused on that, and that's as constructive as we can possibly be. I want to call out Yohannes [Abraham, executive director of the Biden transition], who has been tremendous to work with, and Jeff Zients before him, who was running the transition at an operational level. People should feel good that the operational people here, people like Robert O'Brien, have been dealing with their counterparts. That relationship has been, if anything, strengthened over the last couple of weeks because of the adversity that people have been feeling. I think the mood here is, everyone wants to get through tomorrow. We're all praying for a peaceful and successful day.

"I would have pushed pretty hard for some legislative changes"

DM: You've just been through this incredible four years and even more incredible seventy-seven days of the transition. We have one more day left.

You anticipated a lot of problems, but the outcome and the events were much worse than I imagined. What do you know now that you wish you knew before? How would you approach what you've done differently with 20/20 hindsight?

CL: That's a really tough one, and I think I need time to reflect. Again, my focus has been, in the last couple of weeks in particular, just getting this done as well as we possibly can for the country. I guess my initial reaction would be that I would have pushed pretty hard for some legislative changes in the months coming up to the election. Because I think even from the middle of last year, it was quite clear that the chance of a disputed election was going up. We hoped that wouldn't happen, but there were signals relatively early on. I think with some goodwill on the Hill, we could have said, "Look, this might happen, and if it's going to happen, this is what we need to do." Perhaps we could have avoided some of the initial few weeks where nothing happened and that set us back. Maybe predicting some of the things that did happen, not clearly the riot on January 6 but all the other aspects of the dispute beforehand, knowing how badly it played out, then maybe I would have pushed a lot harder for that.

DM: Do you think a legislative fix would have helped? The attitude, the approach of the president has been so unusual and so outside of norms that I'm not sure better legislation would have fixed this problem.

CL: I'd like some time to reflect on that and come up with some suggestions. But the concept of having a provisional ascertainment or conditional ascertainment would have at least got the transition off to a slightly better start now. That wouldn't have solved the disputed election aspect of it—that's a different discussion—but the transition side of things could have at least gotten off on a relatively good footing straightaway. We could have gotten the president-elect intelligence briefings sooner than we did. At least it would have perhaps taken the temperature down a little bit, though it wouldn't have solved the bigger issues that we faced.

DM: It's been a very, very difficult time for our country and a tragic time in many, many respects. You and I got together with Josh Bolten about a year ago to start this process. Since then, we've had a global pandemic, a racial reckoning, a deep recession. We had multiple COVID outbreaks at the White House, which you've been spared of, thankfully; a tough election; and an attempt to overturn the results of our democracy, which is unprecedented. I realize you want some time to reflect, but what are your thoughts on this last year as you prepare to leave office and as President Trump prepares to have his last day in office?

CL: This has personally been the toughest assignment of my life by a distance. None of us want to go through what we went through in the last few weeks again. Maybe I can finish on a slightly more positive note, if that's possible. Despite just about every possible bad scenario that you can think of for the country, I believe we will have a successful and peaceful transition tomorrow. The institutions of this government have held. It's hard to imagine a more difficult set of circumstances, but at twelve o'clock tomorrow President-elect Biden will become President Biden. The incoming transition team will be here, set up, ready to go. I think we've covered every possible scenario. So in the most difficult circumstances that are humanly possible, the institution of the United States government and the transition associated with it I think will be successful.

Notes

1. Nancy Cook, "Trump's Team Plots His Departure—Even If He Won't," *Politico*, September 24, 2020, https://www.politico.com/news/2020/09/24/trump-presidential-transition-421465.

2. "Pence says 'violence never wins,' McConnell decries 'attempted insurrection' as Congress resumes electoral count," *Associated Press*, January 6, 2021, https://apnews.com/article/6ecdf2a62072a2acf3baa8147d7b60cf.

Biden's Organized—and Perilous—Transition to Power

SENATOR TED KAUFMAN

> No other transition has ever taken place with this set of challenges: a pandemic, a recession, a racial justice crisis, an unpredictable president, and political polarization.
>
> —Ted Kaufman

COMPARED TO other transitions, the Biden team enjoyed what one might almost call an unfair advantage. Their candidate arguably came to the race with more relevant experience than any other candidate for president in the history of the United States. Indeed, Biden had been a key player in two momentous presidential transitions before: Bush-Obama, which set the gold standard for transitions, and Obama-Trump, where one side was ready for the party and the other was uninterested in attending. While those transitions presented their own challenges, the 2020 transition was unique. Only in 2020 did the incoming president simultaneously face an economic crisis, a global pandemic, a racial justice crisis, and a constitutional crisis.[1]

On Election Day 2020, around eleven million Americans were out of work.[2] The COVID-19 crisis approached a new milestone: more than 172,000 Americans would die during the interregnum.[3] Amazingly, despite multiple crises facing the nation, Trump focused almost exclusively on litigating the election results. The hollowed-out federal government lay in disarray. And Trump, by refusing to accept the election result, delayed Biden's transition and precipitated an unnecessary political crisis—the worst in decades.

Luckily, Biden had a secret weapon in the shape of his transition chair, former senator Ted Kaufman.

When the Center started talking to the Democratic candidates for president in January 2020, it gave them a checklist of early actions, the first of which was to pick a transition chair. Center staff emphasized the need to select a senior figure close to the candidate—a peer, if possible. An individual with significant government experience, including transition experience. Someone who is organized and has strong relationships. And someone "above ambition," who was not looking to position themselves for the future.[4]

Ted Kaufman had all of the above and more.

Kaufman started working with Biden in 1972, when Biden was a Delaware County Council member running for Senate; since then, he has been Biden's most trusted advisor and closest friend. Kaufman represented Biden on the 2008 Obama-Biden transition. After being appointed to succeed Biden in the Senate, Kaufman worked with the Partnership for Public Service on two amendments to the Presidential Transition Act, one of which was named after Kaufman and Romney Readiness Chair Mike Leavitt. He also served on the Center for Presidential Transition's Advisory Board and participated in each of its quadrennial transition conferences—first giving advice to other transition teams, then receiving it when he launched Biden's.

Quite apart from any personal loyalty or partisan alignment, Kaufman cares deeply about the art of transition planning. In October 2019, Max Stier and I awkwardly asked Kaufman if he might step off the Advisory Committee for the 2020 cycle, out of concern that other Democratic candidates might not want to see Biden's closest advisor in that role. He understood, and he graciously stepped aside—on condition that he could rejoin in the event that Biden did not make it through the primaries.

In February 2020, Kaufman asked us for a detailed briefing on getting the transition started. For two weeks, I worked with Dan Hyman and Livi Logan-Wood, two staff members at the Partnership for Public Service, to put together a timeline, a checklist of early decisions, and recommendations for how to structure the transition. This was just as the COVID-19 crisis was beginning, and I was nervous about traveling on Amtrak. Instead, we took a car to Wilmington, spent more than three hours transition planning with Kaufman and Mark Gitenstein, and bumped elbows—no hand shaking—on the way out. The next day, virtually the entire country shut down.

Anticipating the many problems Biden would face, Kaufman broke up his team's workflow into two streams: one for the conventional problems—appointments, policy, agency review, and president-elect support—and another for "unconventional challenges," foreseeing President Trump's future posture as well as pandemic-related logistics issues. What if Trump delayed ascertainment? What if the Biden team could not access agencies? What if the FBI, the Office of Government Ethics, or the Office of Personnel Management were instructed not to process Biden personnel files? The transition team anticipated each of these problems and developed strategies to mitigate them.

In addition, Ted Kaufman made three other consequential decisions which would separate the Biden transition from previous efforts.

First, he formed a strong leadership team. He hired Jeff Zients, formerly CEO of the Advisory Board Company and head of Obama's Office of Management and Budget and National Economic Council, as a de facto CEO for the transition. Jeff is one of the most organized and impressive professionals I have met in my thirty years in the private, public, and legal sectors. Jeff, in turn, hired Yohannes Abraham, a rising star and Obama alumnus, as executive director—in effect, chief operating officer to Zients's CEO. Over the next nine months, Kaufman, Zients, and Abraham pulled together the best-organized and most effective transition team yet.

Second, Kaufman studied and followed best practices from previous transitions—and went out of his way to avoid their mistakes. He started earlier than any other modern transition besides that of George W. Bush. He raised funds; developed strong ethics requirements; shaped the transition around the candidate's preferences and personality; established a culture that put the campaign first; and avoided leaks. Kaufman, Zients, and Abraham studied every modern transition, asking themselves key questions: What were the pain points? What were the mistakes? How do we avoid them? They methodically attacked all of these risks: campaign-transition tension; vetting challenges; postelection integration with the campaign; and an artificial divide between the policy and agency review teams. Through regular communication and collaboration, they fully integrated the policy teams from the campaign and the transition.

Third, Kaufman built a transition team and strategy commensurate with the challenges Biden would face. They attracted scores of experienced former officials like Cecilia Muñoz, Avril Haines, Carlos Monje, and Suzy George. They built the largest agency transition team ever—more than six hundred officials covering one-hundred-plus agencies (Obama held the previous record with sixty-two agencies). Moreover, given the government's disarray, and anticipating a slower-than-normal Senate due to a combination of Republican control and COVID, they developed a new personnel strategy—one that emphasized non-Senate-confirmed officials on an equal footing with those that receive Senate confirmation. In this way, the Biden transition team sought to send as many officials into their departments as soon after Inauguration Day as possible, thereby allowing a faster start on implementing Biden's agenda.

History will judge the successes and shortcomings of the Biden presidency. But based on my studies of transitions past and present, it was clear to me that the Biden transition was likely to be among the most effective. Future Republican and Democratic campaigns will study the Biden transition for cycles to come. And Joe Biden should forever be grateful that one of the nation's experts on transition—Ted Kaufman—was ready to launch his transition to power.

"I would never again believe that anything was impossible."

DAVID MARCHICK (DM): I always like to start these by talking to people about their backgrounds. You were in engineering for DuPont, and I understand you worked on a product called Corian, which was used for bathroom sinks. So how exactly did you go from bathroom sinks to working for Joe Biden in 1972?

TED KAUFMAN (TK): It's a really fascinating discussion. In 1972 I was involved in the Delaware Democratic Party but only as a volunteer. I was working full-time at DuPont in finance. At that point, I had met Joe Biden in the early months of 1972.

In the spring of 1972, his sister, Valerie, called and asked me to talk to the candidate, Joe Biden, about getting involved in a Senate campaign. When I met with him, he asked me if I would help him. I told him I would absolutely help him. The main reason was that he was concerned about criminal justice reform as well as taking care of folks that had less in our society. He was really talking about what I saw were really great issues. Lots of times there are people—especially in Delaware—who run to have a platform to talk about issues. So, I said I was happy to help him. But I also told him that I thought he had no chance of winning.

It was simple. Back then, the incumbent Republican, Senator Caleb Boggs, was beloved throughout Delaware. He was a two-term governor, a two-term member of Congress, who was running for his third term in the Senate. If that wasn't bad enough, every major elected office in Delaware was held by a Republican. I'll never forget that. Biden listened, he smiled, and he welcomed me on board. He then went on to win Delaware's Senate seat by 3,600 votes. That night at the victory party I swore that I would never again believe that anything was impossible.

"An undercover kind of operation"

DM: You have become kind of a transition guru. How did you actually get involved in transitions?

TK: The way I got started is, before he was actually elected, the Obama team started a transition. Biden told then candidate Obama, "I'd like to have Ted Kaufman and Mark Gitenstein as cochairs of the vice-presidential transition and be involved in the president's." Mark Gitenstein had worked for then-senator Biden for years, had been his chief counsel on the Judiciary Committee, and was an old friend. The Obama people could not have been more welcoming. They really had an incredible operation. A few days after the Obama campaign won the election, Mark and I went with Vice President-elect Biden to Chicago to meet with President-elect Obama and his staff to begin selecting the cabinet. Which was incredible. I mean, to sit with an incoming president and actually talk about who should be in what positions in the cabinet was just an incredible, remarkable experience.

DM: I understand in that race—John Podesta told me this—that Obama was pretty focused on the transition. He spent time on it. But Biden, when he was running for vice president, I guess he was superstitious and didn't want to spend a lot of time on transition. Why was that?

TK: I don't know if it's superstition. It may be Irish—we both had Irish mothers. The other thing was that he just never took his eye off the ball during the campaign. He concentrated like a laser to make sure all his time and effort went into winning the race. But he did understand that transition was something we should get started on, and President Obama asked him to put some people on. So, he did ask Mark and me to work with John Podesta, Chris Lu, and the others. They were the all-star team on transitions—many of them had been involved in Bill Clinton's transition. We started meeting with a very extensive transition team that was working for Obama. It was very much an undercover kind of operation. You had to keep it secret, but it was quite gigantic.

"We could not do that with a corporation"

DM: What were the main things that you learned from that transition that you applied to this cycle?

TK: When you look back on it, they really sound kind of obvious. The first thing is start early on transition. This is the most complex transition you can ever have. I mean, if you went to the head of a major corporation and said, "You're going to take over an operation that has six to eight million people and hire four thousand people to do it all in two or three months," they would say they could not believe it. We could not do that with a corporation.[5] So we had to start early.

You had to have someone lead the transition with the total trust of the candidate. The recent Trump transition was the worst case. They signed people to work on the transition, but meanwhile, the candidate and other important people in the campaign were not looking at what was going on in the transition. Governor Chris Christie spent months preparing and went into detail. But right after the election, the team that had been most responsible for the winning campaign came and sat down and tried to learn about transition in two or three days. And what happened, and it's happened many times, is a sense of frustration set in, and the campaign people just took over the transition. And of course, in President Trump's case, he fired Chris Christie.

The next thing we learned was that the transition should not create problems for the campaign. You can have a transition that is busy: for instance, you are raising money for the transition at the same time the candidate is working to raise money for the campaign. But, if you are not careful, you can be calling up people to ask for contributions more than once. That is the most obvious and simplest, but there are a bunch of reasons why you have to have really good interaction with the leaders of the campaign.

I also learned the important role that the outgoing president plays. How important it is if the president plays or does not play. In 2008, we were in a crisis with two wars going on. The president; his chief of staff, Josh Bolten; and the entire Bush team were 100 percent cooperative. They helped us every step of the way.

"There were some obvious things you could do to make it better"

DM: Let's fast-forward: You are appointed senator and you take your experience from the Obama-Biden transition to make transitions better. You sponsored a bill to amend the Presidential Transition Act of 1963. What led you to do that?

TK: It was really kind of simple. The transition is so important, and I just saw that there were some obvious things you could do to make it better. I had a lot of help every step of the way, thanks to the Partnership for Public Service. You are the folks that really keep track of all the data and know who the good people are and prepare all the presentations. So I turned to the Partnership when I was going to write the bill. I think it is fair to say that both President-elect Joe Biden and the Partnership believe that effective transition is essential if you're going to have an effective presidency. And they are absolutely right.

It just made a lot of sense to put together a bill. The other thing that is kind of interesting about this is that freshmen senators do not usually get an opportunity to actually write a bill and get it passed. So it was great for me to be able to do that. Now, I had worked in the Senate for over twenty years. But it was incredible how the other senators—both Republicans and Democrats—helped me.

DM: You actually were involved in two bills. Talk about what those two bills did.

TK: In 2010, as I said before, the Senate passed my bill. What it did was move up the date for transition teams to get access to office space, computers, and phones and funding from the government. Prior to this legislation, the GSA [General Services Administration] support only kicked in after the election. The transition is the biggest and most complex organization in the history of the world, but you are supposed to do it in seventy days. What my bill did was increase it from seventy to more like 140 days. Instead of getting the financing to help after the election, you got it after the convention [the Democratic and Republican nominating conventions, held in the late summer of a presidential election year].

The other thing that is really hard to believe now is that if you were caught at the convention working on the transition, people would say, "they're over-confident." The term they used to use, that became a term they used in all the news stories, is that they were "measuring the drapes" in the White House. Once my bill passed, since everything started by law right after the convention, people did not have to worry about those kinds of stories.

DM: And then your second bill was 2015, when actually you were out of the Senate, but I think Senator Carper sponsored that legislation and got it through. And then he named it after you and Mike Leavitt.

TK: That is exactly right. Tom Carper is an old friend. He is the senator from Delaware. He was a key person in the 2015 bill and asked me to get involved, and then he suggested Mike Leavitt, who was governor of Utah and held two cabinet posts in the Bush administration and is really a very impressive person. It was a surprise at the final hearing in the Senate committee to pass the bill when Senator Carper asked to add an amendment making this bill the Edward "Ted" Kaufman and Michael Leavitt Presidential Transitions Improvements Act of 2015. It was great.

"This transition would be like no other"

DM: The Partnership has hosted meetings on transition every four years starting in 2008. Tell us about your experience in those meetings.

TK: In 2008, I was involved as a representative of one of the candidates [Obama].

In 2012, after I had written the bill and I had been involved in 2008, I was in a conference they had for the candidates. The Romney team was led by an incredibly impressive governor—Mike Leavitt—and Chris Liddell. And a bunch of representatives from the Obama White House were also there.

In 2016, I participated in a session with five campaigns. It is hard to believe really looking at where we are today, but all five campaigns—the Clinton campaign, the Sanders campaign, the Trump campaign, the Cruz campaign, and the Kasich campaign—all sat around the table. The Partnership hosted John Bolten, Chris Liddell, a lot of folks involved in previous campaigns. And everyone actually sat and listened and talked. There was not a bit of rancor or anything else. It was really fascinating.

In 2020, I participated, but instead of being an expert, I was the one getting the advice. And I will tell you, the advice was great. It was an incredibly vital event to help us in our transition.

DM: What were the things that you took away from that conference that you have applied to this transition?

TK: Start early. Shape the transition to the candidate's preferences. No matter what, what you want is somebody that believes in what the candidate believes in and understands what the candidate's preferences are, somebody that has absolute discipline on information and leaks.

The second thing was that the conference also reinforced our view that this transition would be like no other. I thought the 2008 transition was the most difficult because of the Great Recession, but it was nothing like this. No other transition has ever taken place with this set of challenges: a pandemic, a recession, a racial justice crisis, an unpredictable president, and political polarization. I realized that we had to build off the best work these past transitions had done and do much more to ensure the Biden administration was ready to govern.

DM: One of the things I remember from that conference involved Mary Gibert—who is the career federal transition coordinator and a really incredible person. I think Mark Gitenstein [a member of the Biden-Harris Transition Advisory Board] said, "Mary, the country is shut down and operating on Zoom." This was early in the COVID crisis; we really did not know what was going on. Mark said: "Are you planning a Plan B? If we are still remote in November, what is GSA going to do?" Mary said, "We're planning that to be Plan A." I remember I kind of gulped and thought that was not good. What was your reaction when Mary said that?

TK: It was a real eye-opener. When we started the transition, we were just about a month into the period when businesses and schools had been shut down, and we had no idea how long that would last. We also were just learning to be efficient on Zoom and other platforms. We realized we needed to plan for a virtual transition, which would increase the degree of difficulty considerably. But, thanks to good planning, coordination, and communication, it has been seamless.

The other thing that Mary's comment reinforced was that the career officials working throughout the government are nonpartisan patriots, they just want to do a good job. And that is something that Mark and I knew from our years of working in government to be absolutely true. The civil service in the United States government is full of people exactly as Mary described them. And we knew that Mary was prepared for a Trump reelection or a Biden win. Her team and other career officials across the government would do a great job on the transition.

"What happens in the transition stays in the transition"

DM: When did you start working on the plan for the Biden transition?

TK: It was in the spring. Candidate Biden and I had been talking, at this point not about the transition, but about the very concerning campaign. I think I maybe mentioned the transition in passing, but not anything saying we ought to start or not.

Then he called me and said: "I have been thinking about the transition. I think we ought to get started right now." I replied, "If you learn one thing from these Partnership for Public Service get-togethers, it is that you can't start too early." It was really one of the smartest things we did.

DM: What was the first thing you did?

TK: The first thing I did was to call my cochair from the 2008 transition, Mark Gitenstein. We got together a group: Mark; Dana Remus, who was the chief counsel of the campaign and is going to be the chief counsel in the White House; Jeff Peck, who is a staff director on the Senate Judiciary Committee; Darla Pomeroy, who worked in a number of different positions and was very successful in business; and Chris Schroeder, whom I taught with at Duke Law School for twenty-six years and [who] probably knows more about the laws of what we do than anybody I've ever known.

DM: But then you decided to bring in Jeff Zients. How did that decision get made, and why Jeff?

TK: We did a search. We just talked to a lot of people about who would be the best person for the transition without really giving away that we were even starting to transition. We wanted somebody with lots of successful experience—not experience in transitions, just experience in management, who was highly organized and totally discreet. We talked about it with Anita Dunn, who was very much involved in the campaign, and she used to be [Senator] Bill Bradley's press secretary. The three of us all decided that Jeff Zients would be the ideal person to do this. Again, he was someone who was highly successful in business and who then in the Obama White House ran both the Office of Management and Budget and the National Economic Council.

I talked it over with the [former] vice president, and he agreed. He knew Jeff and felt the same way we did about Jeff's many talents. Then we asked Jeff who would be the best person to be executive director, and he right away said Yohannes Abraham. Yohannes had worked with him in the White House and was teaching at the Harvard Kennedy School. He has run the day-to-day operation of the transition and has done a fantastic job since then. I have met dozens of people that know Yo, and every one of them talks about how incredible of a talent he is, and I know from firsthand experience. The four of us established the Joseph R. Biden Presidential Transition, and we worked together closely for the following eight months.

DM: Another early moment of the transition, which was indelibly sealed in my mind, is when Dan Hyman—another fellow from the Partnership—and I drove up to your house. We did not want to take Amtrak because of COVID. And we spent three or four hours with you and Mark talking about all the key architectural decisions for the transition. It was at that meeting that you started talking about some of the rules that you want to establish for the transition. Maybe you could just mention some of those rules.

TK: They are really about values. The first rule was that the transition does nothing to hinder the campaign. Until Election Day, the campaign is by far the most important part of the Biden effort. We talked with the campaign and cleared everything we did all the time. In addition, we met every Saturday with Anita Dunn, who was involved in the campaign, and Bob Bauer, who was the legal brains of the campaign, and talked about the campaign. We told them what we were doing on the transition. They gave us especially valuable advice on whom to talk to, what could be effective.

The second rule was: what happens in the transition stays in the transition. We knew that there would be incredible interest in what was happening in all parts of the transition, and especially who was going to get positions in the administration. If you have spent any time in Washington, it is like the greatest parlor game for the period of the transition. Everyone in the transition took that responsibility seriously, and we had very few accurate reports [in the media] of what was happening on the transition. We had a lot of reports of what was happening on the transition, but little of it was accurate.

The third rule was that policies are made on the campaign, not in the transition. This is really important. I do not know how other transitions did this particular piece, but one of the things we had learned was that the transition is not about making policy; it's about getting to the bottom of what President Biden would want to do when he became president. One of the things that was valuable for this—another advantage of having been involved in so many Senate campaigns and every Biden campaign—was that there was a detailed record of what the candidate had said publicly on all the policies. What we did was collect all the policy statements he made from the campaign into what we called the campaign promises book.

Then, what the transition did on policy was they took the campaign promises book and they sliced and diced it, so that people in each agency knew what the Biden policies were for that specific agency. What Senator Biden had learned earlier was that if you wanted to accomplish anything when you were in office, it was really essential that you talk about it during the campaign, especially for a president. After the election, one of the big advantages of it is that if somebody opposes your bill, you can say: "Why? The American people voted for my bill. Like I said, 'Build Back Better'—they voted for a very comprehensive program. I'll just do what the American people elected me to do." Whereas if you talk about an issue that you have not talked about in the campaign, you are on your own.

The fourth rule was that transition staff should mirror the United States. President-elect Biden's most important commitment was having administration that reflected America. And I must tell you because of the incredible number of highly qualified people interested in serving the transition, this was no problem.

DM: Going back to your second rule, it is really incredible: I have reporters call me all the time saying: "I do not get anything out of the Biden team. They do not leak. They are totally disciplined." I will give our listeners one story. I talked to you almost every day during the transition, sometimes several times a day. I remember the day that Biden tapped Senator Harris as his vice-president designate. There was lots of speculation over who was going to be picked and when it was going to be, so I called you and said, "Ted, I am not going to ask you who he is going to pick because I know you would not tell me and it would be inappropriate, but is he going to do it today?" And you said, "I do not know, no comment. I cannot tell you that." He announced it an hour later. I called you that afternoon. I said: "Ted, you can at least show me a little leg. You know, you could at least say today." But: absolute discipline.

"There were two sets of challenges"

DM: One of the things I have said publicly is that future transition teams will study the Biden transition model for many cycles to come, Republicans and Democrats. What do you think are the most critical innovations you've made on this transition?

TK: I think one of the big things we did for this transition is that we broke it down. We knew right away that we were faced with these incredible challenges of all kinds. So, we knew that that transition was going to be much harder because of complex technology, changes in germane laws, and everything else. But we also realized that we were faced with an incredible pandemic, the economy was going down fast, we had a racial justice crisis. We had all the things that Donald Trump had done—domestically to the federal government but also around the world.

We knew there were two sets of challenges. One we called the conventional challenges, the ones that every president's transition faces. The second group we called the unconventional challenges. And frankly, most of the spring we spent going over the unconventional challenges. Without hard work, we came up with seventy unconventional challenges. We spent a good part of our first six months coming up with plans to deal with each one of them.

DM: I think another innovation is the way you approached the agency review teams. Let me give you some data: Obama had 349 professionals covering sixty-two agencies. You have more than six hundred agency review team members covering more than a hundred agencies. What was the rationale for doing that? And what type of people did you try to recruit for the agency review roles?

TK: Because we were going to have these gigantic challenges, you are really going to have to hit the ground running. In the first hundred days, you have to grab this thing by the throat. What can you do in order to do that? One of the most important things I have found is that if you have a difficult problem, the single best thing you can do is find somebody that can help you deal with it. We just said in the beginning: "That is not where we want to go. We want to have a lot more people working with the agencies, and we are going to cover a lot more agencies. It really it is essential that we hit the ground running."

We wanted to make sure that we had a team that looks like the United States. We wanted many people with experience, but we also wanted new, younger people. Finally, we wanted people who can maintain security. It really came out of our analysis of the unconventional challenges. The first thing we must do is have people that could really deal with these issues, as many good, smart people as we could. We did get more people, and we will do more agencies, but I think that the biggest thing is we got really incredible people. And that goes to President-elect Biden.

"They are highly qualified, they are experienced, and they are breaking barriers"

DM: How are you feeling about the appointments that President-elect Biden has made so far? How do you feel the rollouts have gone and [how do you feel about] the pace?

TK: I think it is excellent, especially on the pace. I mean, the transition is on pace to have many more White House and agency nominations than any other transition in modern history. Again, it is all built on this basic building block of, "We have got to hit the ground running on Inauguration Day."

As you look at these nominees, they are highly qualified, they are experienced, and they are breaking barriers. Let us go back to being a mirror of America: the first person of color to run the Defense Department; the first female to be the Director of National Intelligence; the first gay cabinet secretary. It is about a half dozen or more of minorities in the country that were not previously represented.

DM: I have to say the Pete Buttigieg announcement really had an impact on me because going back to Clinton, one of my close friends from the '92 campaign was a woman named Roberta Achtenberg; she was nominated for an assistant secretary of HUD [Housing and Urban Development] and is a member of the LGBT community. I remember that Senator Helms and others basically tried to block her vote because she had the audacity of introducing her partner at the confirmation hearing—really an ugly incident. Now we have the first openly gay person in the cabinet, which is incredible.

I talked to my kids about it last night. And they just did not understand: "Well, what's the issue? Why does anybody care?" But it is important that people are able to understand how difficult it was for people of color, how difficult for gay people, and for women to have a major role in the government and go through a confirmation process, because the issues would not be whether they were qualified or not; they had to do with race and gender and issues like that.

"The intensity ramps up—and then it accelerates"

DM: You came into this transition knowing more about transitions than perhaps any other transition cochair, but certainly you have learned a lot. What do you know now, Ted, that you wish you knew in the spring when then candidate Biden asked you to be the architect of the transition?

TK: A number of things. One of the things I remember from the Partnership for Public Service's conference. I wish I could remember who said it, but someone said the intensity ramps up—and then it accelerates. I have been in difficult situations, but boy, I would say nothing could have been truer. I have worked my whole life in what I think most people would think were difficult jobs, but this is the most difficult and intense workload that I have ever experienced.

Second, I am so happy we started early. I think it was Mack McLarty, Bill Clinton's chief of staff, who said if you fall behind you can never catch up. We were determined not to fall behind, and we did not. We built a great team. We put a lot of time and effort into that, and Jeff Zients and Yohannes Abraham did a fantastic job. They also brought in incredibly qualified people. So the people in this effort have been absolutely unbelievable. And finally, it all starts at the top. Joe Biden brings more experience to this job than any other person that became president in our history. He was determined to be ready on day one, given the crisis our country faces.

Notes

1. Perhaps only the election of 1876—which similarly helped spur a constitutional crisis, pivoted on issues of racial justice and took place during the tail end of an economic depression—created a comparably wide set of challenges (see C. Vann Woodward, *Reunion and Reaction: The Compromise of 1877 and the End of Reconstruction* [New York: Oxford University Press, 1991]). For an account of the economic crises faced by other incoming presidents, see Robert F. Bruner, "Harnessing the Economy: Lessons from Eight First-Year Crises from Adams to Obama," in *Crucible: The President's First Year*, ed. Michael L. Nelson, Jeffrey Georgakis Chidester, and Stefanie Abbott (Charlottesville: University of Virginia Press, 2018).
2. U.S. Bureau of Labor Statistics, "The Employment Situation—November 2020," press release, December 4, 2020.
3. Hannah Ritchie, "Coronavirus Source Data," Our World in Data, https://ourworldindata.org/coronavirus-source-data.
4. Center for Presidential Transition, *Presidential Transition Guide*, 4th ed., April 2020, 58, https://presidentialtransition.org/transition-timeline-and-guide/.
5. While around two million people work in the federal civil service, when one includes military personnel, post office employees, and contractors that total number of employees can reach as high as nine million. For a discussion, see Fiona Hill, "Public Service and the Federal Government," Brookings, May 2020, https://www.brookings.edu/policy2020/votervital/public-service-and-the-federal-government/.

President-elect Abraham Lincoln raising a flag at Independence Hall, Philadelphia, on February 22, 1861. This is one of just three photos of Lincoln's journey from Springfield, Illinois, to Washington, DC. (National Archives and Records Administration; photo by Frederick De Bourg Richards)

President-elect Franklin D. Roosevelt (*right*) and President Hoover seated in a car en route to the inauguration in Washington, DC, on March 4, 1933. The relationship between the two men was famously icy. (National Archives and Records Administration)

President Jimmy Carter looks over Stuart Eizenstat's shoulder aboard Air Force One. Eizenstat served as chief White House domestic policy advisor. (Stuart Eizenstat)

President Ronald Reagan holds a meeting with the "troika" on January 21, 1981, his first full day in office. *Left to right:* Deputy Chief of Staff Michael Deaver, Counselor to the President Ed Meese, Chief of Staff James Baker III, Press Secretary James Brady, President Reagan. (Ronald Reagan Presidential Library)

President George H. W. Bush (*left*) and Chief of Staff Andy Card (*center*) meet with Ambassador Malcom Richard Wilkey (*right*), on March 19, 1989. Card played a leading role in both the 1988 and 2000 transitions. (George H. W. Bush Presidential Library and Museum)

President Bill Clinton and former president George H. W. Bush together at a White House ceremony promoting the North American Free Trade Agreement (NAFTA) on September 14, 1993. NAFTA was a key element of President Clinton's economic agenda. (William J. Clinton Presidential Library)

President George W. Bush meets in the White House Oval Office with President-elect Barack Obama on November 10, 2008. (Official White House photo by Eric Draper)

Members of the Hillary Clinton and Donald Trump transition teams pose for a photo. The two teams shared a building in the lead-up to the 2016 election. *Left to right:* Sara Latham, Rick Dearborn, Ed Meier, Rich Bagger, Laura Schiller, Ann O'Leary, and Monica Block. (David Eagles)

Max Stier, founding president and CEO of the Partnership for Public Service, announces the launch of the Center for Presidential Transition in 2016. Stier is holding the Partnership's *Transition Guide,* which documents best practices for candidates and federal agencies. (Partnership for Public Service; photo by Aaron Clamage/clamagephoto.com)

President Barack Obama meets in the White House Oval Office with President-elect Donald Trump on November 10, 2016. (Official White House Photo by Pete Souza)

Officials from the President-elect Donald Trump incoming administration and President Barack Obama's cabinet and senior staff hold a "tabletop exercise" on pandemic planning in the Eisenhower Executive Office Building of the White House, January 13, 2017. Four years later, the world faced the worst pandemic since 1918. (Official White House Photo by Lawrence Jackson)

Governor Mike Leavitt speaks with David Marchick in March 2020 about Leavitt's leadership of the Romney Readiness Project. (Partnership for Public Service)

PART III
POLICY

What's at Stake: The Critical Importance of the Federal Government

MICHAEL LEWIS

> The federal government is the manager of a giant portfolio of risks—and many of them are potentially catastrophic. Most of us aren't thinking about most of those risks most of the time. And it's the ones that we're not thinking about that are going to cause us the biggest trouble.
>
> —Michael Lewis

HERE IS a challenge: name an area of American life that the federal government does *not* meaningfully support. Good luck. While some of the government's functions are extremely visible, like distributing Social Security benefits or providing airport security, much of its work, though vital, goes unseen. Classified defense programs intended to prevent terror attacks; ambitious investments that created the technologies behind the iPhone and the COVID-19 vaccine; incentives that make green energy affordable—all these and more play an essential role in the lives of Americans.[1]

None of it could be done without career civil servants. The career workforce, around two million strong (not counting contractors, postal employees, or members of the military), outnumbers political appointees five hundred to one; the relationship between these two types of federal worker determines a president's success or failure. And as with so much else, the transition sets the tone.

According to Lewis, by treating career civil servants as essentially hostile actors, certain leaders in the Trump administration reduced their own effectiveness across wide swathes of policy. At the Department of Energy, they sought to purge career officials who had worked on climate change.[2]

At the State Department, they derided foreign service officers, calling them "the deep state."[3] Similar clashes occurred at the Department of the Interior, the Environmental Protection Agency, and other major agencies.[4] The result: a hollowing out of the very capability and expertise the American people rely upon from their federal government.

Michael Lewis, the author of such nonfiction classics as *Moneyball* and *The Big Short*, took this story of hubris and made it a bestseller. Focusing on three cabinet agencies—the Departments of Energy, Commerce, and Agriculture—Lewis's book *The Fifth Risk* explores how Trump's poorly managed transition undermined these agencies' ability to carry out their duties, from predicting hurricanes to distributing food stamps.

The notion of "risk" has been a central theme in Lewis's career. In 1989's *Liar's Poker*, he chronicled how the investment bank Salomon Brothers aggressively created a market for opaque mortgage-backed securities, overextending itself until its bubble burst in the 1987 stock market crash. Lewis's 2010 follow-up, *The Big Short*, examined how those same mortgage-backed securities fueled the financial sector's boom in the early 2000s—only to bring it crashing down in 2008.

When Lewis turned his attention from the private to the public sector in *The Fifth Risk*, he enlisted Max Stier, CEO of the Partnership for Public Service, as his guide to the complexities of the federal government.[5] Shortly after I began working at the Partnership's Center for Presidential Transition, Max and I hosted Lewis for a dinner along with prominent supporters of the Partnership. At our dinner, and during the conversation we had on *Transition Lab* several months later, Michael Lewis drove home the kind of risks that a poorly run transition can create or accentuate.

In Lewis's account, perhaps the starkest example of the difference in attitudes between the Obama and Trump administrations played out at the Department of Energy. The day after the 2008 election, the Obama team had sent roughly thirty people to speak to the department. The Trump team, by contrast, would take weeks to arrive. Thomas Pyle, the leader of the Trump landing team, did not speak to outgoing Secretary Ernest Moniz until a month after the election. When Lewis interviewed John MacWilliams, the department's outgoing chief risk officer—responsible, among other things, for the safety of nuclear weapons—MacWilliams had still not been contacted by the Trump team, nearly a year after the transition started. Trump left MacWilliams's old job vacant until 2018.

As if to underline exactly what can go wrong when the machinery of government is mishandled, our conversation on *Transition Lab* took place against the backdrop of one of the greatest crises in living memory: COVID-19. Lewis recalled having asked President Obama, years before, what his biggest fear was. Without missing a beat, the president replied, "A pandemic." Lewis declined to write about that eventuality in *The Fifth Risk* because he thought it was too obvious; surely, he thought, adequate plans must already exist to deal with it. In 2021, Lewis published *The Premonition*, which recounts the flaws in our nation's public health infrastructure, and the failure of our government and the Centers of Disease Control and Prevention to prepare for and competently deal with the deadly COVID-19 pandemic.[6]

Lewis cares deeply about the effectiveness of our federal government. He told me that after he finishes a book, he is typically so tired of the subject that he never wants to return to it. Except, that is, for presidential transitions, a source of risk that continues to trouble him to this day.

As Lewis rightly points out, long-term structural problems plague the federal government—among them an aging federal workforce, a brittle employment system, and difficulties in harnessing new technology. Failure to address these issues will, in the long term, undermine the ability of the federal government to manage the portfolio of risks for which it is responsible. A botched transition can exacerbate these challenges, tearing at already weak seams or creating new problems altogether. By making transitions faster, smoother, and more effective, therefore, we can minimize the hazards faced by the American people.

"A giant portfolio of risks"

DAVID MARCHICK (DM): I want to start with a dinner we had last December [2019]. You were nice enough to come to our house and speak to a group of people interested in government effectiveness. And I remember the first question I asked you, which was, "Geez, Michael, you've gone from hanging out with MLB players and Brad Pitt to writing about the Department of Energy and the Department of Agriculture. That's pretty boring, isn't it?" Today, that doesn't seem so boring.

MICHAEL LEWIS (ML): It didn't even seem boring at the time. I mean, I wouldn't have written about it if I thought it was boring. Yes, it's become even more pertinent and on the top of people's minds. But I think anybody who walked into the transition that I walked into as a writer would have found it interesting—and would've had the problem I had, which is that you don't want to stop, because the federal government is so big and there are so many things going on inside that seem so critical.

DM: Well, everybody that's experiencing this shutdown from the pandemic should read your book *The Fifth Risk*. But for those who haven't read it, what is "the fifth risk"?

ML: I'll tell you how I came upon the title. I was interviewing the person who was in charge of risk management inside the Department of Energy, which was the first department I had walked into. His name was John MacWilliams, and he was just appalled that nobody had really even debriefed him at that point. This was nine months after Trump had taken office. The transition hadn't happened. The people who'd come into the Department of Energy had no sense of what there was to learn from the people who had gone out.

I asked him, "What are the top five risks that you needed to worry about if you're the chief risk officer?"

He said, "One, a nuclear weapon going off when it shouldn't go off. Two, the Iran nuclear deal falling apart. Three, North Korea is on its way to getting a missile that's going to hit us—I'm really worried about that. Four, the electric grid being attacked or compromised in some way. It's constantly under attack, and we don't really have good defenses for it. Five—"

And then he paused. He couldn't think of one. It took a while. Finally, he came up with one. He said program management. Which sounds dull but actually isn't. Long-term programs, if they are mismanaged, end up creating catastrophe.

But what he told me was you get to a point when you're thinking about risk, where you can't think of what the risk is. Because it's not top of mind. You're not paying attention to it. And I thought, "Aha! That's the risk." The federal government is the manager of a giant portfolio of risks—and many of them are potentially catastrophic. Most of us aren't thinking about most of those risks most of the time. And it's the ones that we're not thinking about that are going to cause us the biggest trouble.

DM: What's your observation on the linkage between your book and the pandemic that we're experiencing today?

ML: It's funny. When I was wandering around talking to people and thinking about what I wanted to write, I came so close to writing about the risk of pandemic, but I had two thoughts about it. One was, it's too obvious. This should be top of mind. I had interviewed Obama at one point, and I asked Obama—and this was two years ago, three years ago—what's the catastrophic risk that worries you the most? And he said, without missing a beat, "Probably disease, probably a pandemic." So I thought this was a little too obvious. I was looking for less obvious risks. Two, the infrastructure the government has to deal with in a pandemic is so complicated and cuts across so many agencies, it was going to be hard for me to reduce it to eighty or ninety pages in a book.

I didn't take that particular risk head on. However, having seen the Trump administration's response to this, and in particular having seen the fact that the pandemic response infrastructure was treated just like all the rest of the government by the transition and by the administration, I think it's a natural chapter in the book and probably the first chapter in the sequel. Even now, I think the American people are only partially aware of what the government might have done if it had been properly prepared.

"I thought of them as our greatest patriots"

DM: It seems like a boring subject to write about people that work in the government; there are stereotypes about them as bureaucrats and slow-moving. What were your observations when you met people that were long-time career federal officials?

ML: You're giving me an overhead lob to smash there. I don't write a book if I'm not energized by the characters I'm meeting. I had as my hook the fact that the Trump administration had not bothered to show up for the transition, had not bothered to show up for the briefings that were there to be had from the permanent civil service. So I had to go get the briefings. I had to get to know these people who were the subject experts.

In some cases, there were people who had left the government. In some cases, there were people who were Obama appointees. In some cases, they were just permanent civil servants. And to a person, they were extraordinarily mission-driven, extraordinarily focused. Maybe a little myopic, but passionate about the thing they cared about. And they were all to a person moving and important characters and easy to make swing on the page because they cared so much about something that mattered so much to them and to which much of the country was completely indifferent or oblivious.

I thought of them as our greatest patriots. It was as if you had a military that was off fighting and dying in our wars without anybody acknowledging it. That's how they felt to me: unacknowledged, very patriotic in the best way. An army of people who were there for a variety of reasons. Almost to a person, these were all people who could have made multiples the income they were making working for the government in the private sector. These are not people who were there because they couldn't get a job anywhere else. It wasn't anything like that.

What I would say is, if you think you know what a federal government worker is, maybe think again. When you actually meet the people doing the jobs, you think, "Thank God they're there."

DM: One of the amazing things about your writing is how you create drama around characters. Very few people would know who Billy Beane is today but for your writing. There's a fellow in your book named Arthur Allen who was a longtime career employee at the Coast Guard. How did you pick him and what was his story?

ML: Here's a perfect example of everything I just said. We will illustrate it with Arthur A. Allen. When the government shut down, in December and January of 2018–19, I thought—knowing what I knew about these people—how extraordinary it was that hundreds of thousands of them were being told they were not "essential workers" and sent home without pay.

I called the Partnership for Public Service, and I said: "Give me a list of everybody who's nominated for one of your Sammies awards [Samuel J. Heyman Service to America Medals]—distinguished government service awards—and just send it all to me. I'm going to pick one of these people to write about." And it was hundreds of people. I mean, you know, it was a grab bag of people. So, I just grabbed the first name on the top of the list. Because it was alphabetized, it was Arthur A. Allen, and it said he worked in the Coast Guard.

DM: Literally the way you picked him was he was the first name.

ML: The first one; he was the first on the list. I thought, well, it's as good as random. He was indeed at home, deemed inessential, not being paid, told that he wasn't important by this society. He had been a young oceanographer, gone to work in the Coast Guard in the mid-1970s, and as the only oceanographer in the search-and-rescue division of the Coast Guard, started to find himself being asked questions that, if he didn't know the answer to them, nobody did. A lot of these questions had to do with the movement of the water and the drift of the ocean, and how specific objects moved in the ocean, because when the Coast Guard went to look for people who were on a capsized fourteen-foot sailboat, they knew that the boat moved differently than, say, a Cuban life raft would. You needed to know how an object drifted to predict where it might be.

So Arthur A. Allen is aware that this is a problem. Then he's invited to watch a day in the field with the actual search-and-rescue people, which is supposed to be a mild day, that he was just going to observe their technology. He was down in, I think, Norfolk, Virginia. All of a sudden, a squall comes up out of nowhere, and the Chesapeake Bay is in havoc. Boats are being lost. People are calling for help from the Coast Guard. He watches, over the course of twelve hours, [and] a sailboat that has three adults and a little girl on it go missing. They find the little girl and her mom dead of hypothermia. The other two are found in a place where they never guessed they would be.

They'd spent hours and hours looking where the boat wasn't, because they didn't know how the boat drifted. When I go to see Arthur Allen in his house, and he's explained to me how he drifted into becoming the world's expert on how objects drift in the ocean, when he's telling me this story, he pulls from his bookshelf a yellowed clipping from the local newspaper in Norfolk. It's the story of this little girl and her mom dying. He starts to cry. He says, "That could have been my wife and daughter." He said, "Right then I said, 'I'm going to figure this out so this never happens again.'" He starts to freelance, to just devote himself. He lives in Connecticut, so he starts throwing objects into the Long Island Sound and measuring very precisely how they drift.

In a couple of years, he's got a catalogue of hundreds of objects. He writes the code. If you're a Coast Guard search-and-rescue guy, actually on the job, you hear that some object is lost at sea, a fishing boat, you pull up Arthur's page and you pick the nearest object that he's measured. It tells you how it might've moved.

In the weeks after he rolls out this new software to all of the Coast Guard search-and-rescue divisions, the Miami office gets a call. A man has run off the side of a Carnival cruise ship, eighty miles east of Miami. He's floating in the ocean. We know when he went off; we didn't find out for a couple of hours, but we have cameras on the ship, so we know exactly where we were when he went off. We also know that he's you know, five foot ten and three-hundred-and-something pounds. He's obese. Arthur Allen had studied a big person in the water. That person in all of human history [up to that point] would never have been found. Never. It's a needle in a haystack. They plucked him out of the water, alive, seven or eight hours later.

All the stories are written about this miraculous rescue—but no one writes, "Arthur A. Allen saved this man's life." Arthur Allen's work has saved thousands of lives of Americans lost at sea. It's not a trivial subject. The Coast Guard will tell you that every day on average, thirteen Americans are lost at sea and ten get rescued. This man is responsible for a lot of those saved lives.

You asked me, famous author, what do you think he was going to get out of talking to me? I spent three days with him. Three very full days. I was in his house. I met his wife and children, interviewed them, went to meals with him. He took me back to his old office. On my way to the airport, on my way out of town, I get a text from him, and it says: "Hey, you're an author. Why didn't you tell me?" I said, "What do you mean?" He says, "My son says you wrote a book that was a movie." I said, "Well, what did you think I was doing there?" He said, "I thought you just wanted to learn all about search and rescue." I'm like, "That's hilarious."

Now that is a very government worker story. They aren't thinking: "What's the spin? What's my media presence? What's my brand?" They're not thinking anything like that. They're thinking: "I do this job. I want to teach people how to do this job." The great sadness in Arthur Allen's life was, the government had never given him someone to train to replace him. So he walked out of his office and left all that expertise behind.

"You're going to be handed a crippled organization"

DM: Having written a whole book about transition, spent a large chunk of time on it, what advice would you have for the Biden team on what they should be doing?

ML: It should be the number-one priority, especially given the pandemic we're living with now—and who knows what crisis might emerge between now and then. I mean, you may be dealing not just with the threat of a virus and a pandemic, but things on top of that. The tool our society has to deal with these problems is the federal government. You're going to be handed a crippled organization, an organization that has, not just through the Trump administration, but through many administrations, been allowed to age, has not been managed all that well, has been hamstrung in various ways. A lot of people have retired; people who are not subject-matter experts have been put in places that require subject-matter experts.

What I would say is: "You're being handed this giant toolbox. A lot of the tools are broken, some of the tools are missing, but it's all you got. And you can fill that toolbox up pretty quickly if you're ready to go on day one."

The advice I would give them is: One, make it a huge priority. *The* priority. Two, no partisan litmus tests for most jobs. The filter is not, "Are you Democrat or Republican?" The filter is: "Do you know what you're talking about or don't you? Do you understand the subject? Do you have management ability?" Finding the right people and getting them ready to get them confirmed or have agreements with the Senate beforehand, tell them, "This is my list; start thinking about this." Speed up that process.

I think what I'd also do is have a plan in place to present to Congress to overhaul the management of the federal government. Make it easier to hire and fire people, for example. Make it easier to pay people. One of the problems we're seeing in the Centers for Disease Control is, I think, the top salary is like $180,000. The people who are qualified for those jobs can make ten times that in the private sector. So, you've a problem of not being able to pay the people who can do the jobs.

I would identify up front what those problems are and not wait a year to address them. I'd have a plan to try to address them on the first day. You might, in this environment, have a sympathetic Congress. If a Congress has watched the administration bungle a pandemic and watched millions of Americans get sick, and thousands of Americans die who otherwise might not have, they might be more sympathetic to the argument that this whole enterprise needs to be reconsidered.

DM: We're a nonpartisan organization, and we're focused on government effectiveness, whoever wins. So, what advice would you have for Donald Trump and his team, were they to win a second term?

ML: It's the same advice. They just won't take it. If you rolled me into Donald Trump's office and told me, "Look, you're not going to get anywhere if you offend him. So you should suck up to him if you want to get him to pay any attention," what could I say that he might hear? I think what I could say is the second part of that: "Look, it's so sad that you got handed this artifact from the 1940s and 1950s—our federal government—where you can't get the top talent in, where you can't fire people and hire people like you should be able to. There are basic structural problems that are not your fault at all. It was all there before you got there. One of the problems we've had in managing this horrible crisis is just the structure of the government. Let's address that."

I think that part of it they might hear. They might be able to hear and do something about it because it isn't threatening to him. But beyond that, I don't know.

"If the Partnership didn't exist, you'd have to invent it right now"

DM: Let me ask you this: You've worked closely with the Partnership for Public Service's Max Stier. You wrote about him in your book. What are your observations about the role the Partnership plays and why its role is important?

ML: You know, if the Partnership didn't exist, you'd have to invent it right now. An organization that is genuinely bipartisan or nonpartisan, whose sole interest is in making the federal government work better—there's nothing else like it. What was intriguing to me is that Max started with a very narrow ambition years ago: how do we get bright young people to want to work in government? But that naturally leads to the broadest ambition, because to get bright people, young bright people, to want to work in government, you have to make the government a place where young, bright people want to work. So, it ends up being a broad government reform effort. There's no other place that is doing this with the same level of energy.

In addition, there's no other place that has such a positive appreciation of the government and is doing whatever it can do to raise the stature of people who work in government. The Partnership is a place where, first, the conversation can happen. Second, it's a safe place where government workers can come and learn and share frustrations. Third, it's like a little lab for how you fix the problems. When I stumbled into it when I first started writing *The Fifth Risk,* I was elated, because I thought it was kind of one-stop shopping for anyone who wants to get to know their federal government. The enterprise is so complicated and so vast, you really need someplace like that to organize it for you.

Notes

1. For a discussion of the role played by the federal government in driving innovation, see Stephen S. Cohen and De Long J. Bradford, *Concrete Economics: The Hamilton Approach to Economic Growth and Policy* (Boston: Harvard Business Review Press, 2016); and Mariana Mazzucato, *The Entrepreneurial State: Debunking Public vs. Private Sector Myths* (New York: PublicAffairs, 2015).

2. Jason Slotkin, "Department of Energy Defies Trump, Won't Name Climate Change Workers," NPR, December 13, 2016, https://www.npr.org/sections/thetwo-way/2016/12/13/505440178/department-of-energy-defies-trump-wont-name-climate-change-workers.

3. Nahal Toosi, "The Revenge of the State Department," *Politico*, October 23, 2019, https://www.politico.com/news/2019/10/20/state-department-trump-051564.

4. See, for example, Mike Spies and J. David McSwane, "Inside the Trump Administration's Chaotic Dismantling of the Federal Land Agency," ProPublica, September 20, 2019, https://www.propublica.org/article/inside-the-trump-administrations-chaotic-dismantling-of-the-federal-land-agency; and Dennis Brady, Juliet Eilperin, and Andrew Ba Tran, "Staff Exodus Hits EPA under Trump: 'I Could Do Better Work to Protect the Environment Outside,'" *Chicago Tribune*, September 8, 2018, https://www.chicagotribune.com/nation-world/ct-epa-workforce-trump-analysis-20180908-story.html.

5. Michael Lewis, *The Fifth Risk: Undoing Democracy* (New York: Norton, 2018).

6. Michael Lewis, *The Premonition: A Pandemic Story* (New York: Norton, 2021).

Help Wanted: Getting the Right Team in Place

JONATHAN MCBRIDE AND LIZA WRIGHT

> On January 20, somebody blows a whistle and everybody—from the CEO to three levels down—leaves an agency. And then a new CEO comes in, and you replace them.
>
> —Jonathan McBride

> When you're in the administration at the White House, it is one massive succession planning exercise on steroids.
>
> —Liza Wright

DURING THEIR service in the White House under Presidents George W. Bush and Obama respectively, Liza Wright and Jonathan McBride became inured to flattery, pestering, and toadying of all kinds. Why? Because as directors of the Office of Presidential Personnel, they were responsible for handing out thousands of presidential appointments, from the topmost positions at the Pentagon to plum ambassadorships and seats on the Kennedy Center board. And when you are recruiting for some of the most powerful positions in the world, things can get a little colorful.

The absence of a strong team to support the leader would hamper any organization—let alone one of the size and complexity of the federal government. Roughly 4,000 government jobs are reserved for presidential appointees, around 1,250 of which must go through the arduous Senate-confirmation process. Keeping these key roles staffed with talented, hardworking individuals is a mammoth task. Every new staffer must be vetted, hired, and onboarded.[1] And because the "churn" rate among political appointees is higher than in the private sector, the hiring process never ends.[2] Not that there is any shortage of applicants; after Barack Obama's election, the transition website was deluged with more than a quarter million résumés.

All of this work is run by the Office of Presidential Personnel, known as PPO. Historically, most PPO staffers have been policy experts or campaign veterans. Liza Wright and Jonathan McBride were different, in that each of them came from a professional recruitment background. Their experience fit what the Partnership for Public Service has long considered best practice: professional search experts who can lead not just recruitment but also talent management, team development, and succession planning.

The work Wright and McBride had done in the private sector was hardly easy, but the federal government is on a whole different level. No private company turns over staff so quickly, so comprehensively, or with such a small HR department. The operational challenges are compounded by the delicate political tightrope that a PPO director has to walk. It can seem as if everyone in Washington—including the most powerful—either wants a job in the administration or wants to influence who is ultimately chosen.

Nor do the headaches cease with the end of the transition phase. Resignations tend to surge in the weeks and months after a president is reelected, creating a challenge that all second-term administrations face. A study we conducted at the Center for Presidential Transition found that an average of 44 percent of officials in key Senate-confirmable positions left their jobs within six months of a president's reelection.[3] While fresh legs can help reinvigorate an administration, if not handled carefully these resignations can threaten to derail a president's second term.

Given these immense challenges, the Partnership for Public Service made a number of recommendations to the Biden team about presidential personnel, of which two in particular stand out:

First, almost all presidents have kept PPO relatively small and only interacted with it one step removed, through their chief of staff or deputy chief of staff (the exception was George W. Bush, who personally met with his PPO director every week). The Partnership has advocated for a larger PPO with more support from the president, including a seat at the table—not on the sidelines—for key decisions.

Second, in order to manage turnover in the administration, the Partnership has argued that PPO should focus on talent management as well as talent acquisition. By cultivating appointees internally, PPO can limit turnover and retain experienced officials. The Obama PPO put a greater emphasis on talent management, working with experienced appointees to find new positions they would be willing to fill, and found that appointees across all levels stayed an average of 28 percent longer than their equivalents during the Bush administration.[4]

For decades, many political appointees have found themselves frustrated with PPO at one time or another. The complaints are common: they never return calls; it is a black box; their bedside manner is terrible. Talking to McBride and Wright, I finally heard the other side of the story. Most strikingly, Liza Wright reported getting several hundred calls a day. Acquaintances she had not heard from in years were suddenly calling and feigning close friendship. And most of the time, PPO had only bad news for them. As Jonathan McBride put it, "you are delivering way more disappointment than happiness in a job like this."

In addition to offering their own wise recommendations on the personnel process (with the perennial admonition to start early being chief among them), Wright and McBride were also kind enough to share some of their war stories, including what to do—and, more amusingly, what not to do—to get a presidential appointment. Perhaps for this reason, this was one of the most-listened-to episodes in the whole podcast cycle. PPO directors, it seems, will never want for work.

"One massive succession planning exercise on steroids"

DAVID MARCHICK (DM): Let's start off with an easy one. Liza, for our listeners who don't know, what is PPO, or the Office of Presidential Personnel?

LIZA WRIGHT (LW): The Office of Presidential Personnel is essentially the office that helps to identify and select all of the appointees that are politically appointed by the president. What a lot of people don't realize is that when a president comes into office, they have over four thousand positions that they can place—ranging from cabinet secretaries to more junior-level positions like staff assistants—to staff all the agencies and departments to carry out their agenda. In essence, the office that Jonathan and I led was the office that carried out the management of all those appointments across the administration.

DM: That's a huge operation. It's the largest takeover of any entity in the world. Jonathan, when there's a new president, how big an office is PPO, and how many people worked there when you led it?

JONATHAN MCBRIDE (JM): It varies. We had just over fifty people working full-time in our personnel office, but we also had people distributed throughout the agencies called White House liaisons that we hired. They just didn't work in the personnel office. By comparison, we hired about as many people per year as my former employer BlackRock did—and their HR department is over four hundred people. We were about fifty-three.

DM: Is fifty the right number? If you had to design this on your own, would you say you should have 100 or 150? What's the right number of people actually needed to do a good job in Presidential Personnel?

LW: Our numbers varied. Maybe fifty in the beginning, but it ebbed and flowed—it was usually between twenty-five and thirty-five within the actual Office of Presidential Personnel. I think if you had asked any one of the special assistants that reported to me, they would tell you that they felt pretty overloaded most of the time. I do think that it was a budget issue, and I do think that fifty more consistently during the nontransition times is probably a good number.

JM: The one thing I'd say is that number of fifty or so is also without a budget to hire people like Liza. In a corporate setting, you also are bringing in specialists who are helping you in executive search, filling some of your trickiest positions. You do not have a budget for that in federal government. So you're fifty people really doing all of the work, including the vetting and everything else. It's a pretty significant workload.

I don't know what the right number is. I think bigger than fifty would be good, in particular if you want to be able to search the whole country, find nontraditional candidates, and convince them to come in and serve their government. You need to have a bunch of new faces, as well as people who've done this before. You need a broader reach, and you have to come up with ways to do it. And it's hard to do that with fifty people.

DM: Both of you have professional business and HR search experience. What surprised you when you went from the private sector to recruiting for the government?

JM: The first for me was the idea that on January 20, somebody blows a whistle and everybody—from the CEO to three levels down—leaves an agency. And then a new CEO comes in, and you replace them. I think that was significant.

Second, I think if you haven't come out of the political or campaign world, the politics of all the constituencies and all the interests are at first pretty significant. While there are small-*p* politics in business, it is nothing like the various vectors—and the media scrutiny—that you get at a job like this.

Those two things were pretty surprising, but the main thing is how few people [we vetted] pay their taxes. It was really surprising to me how many people didn't pay their taxes—I didn't know!

DM: How about you, Liza?

LW: I would say the exact same thing on the nanny-tax issue [failure to pay taxes on the wages of domestic workers]—it plagued us a lot. But I will also echo what Jonathan was saying: in the private sector, companies are constantly doing succession planning. When you're in the administration at the White House, it is one massive succession planning exercise on steroids. Not only are you bringing in essentially four thousand people within those first few months of the administration; you're also having to plan because the people are not going to stay. The average tenure [among political appointees] is around eighteen months. By the time you are placing the first round of people, it's not too much later that you've got to start thinking about the succession planning exercise all over again. That was definitely a surprise.

"You are delivering way more disappointment than happiness"

DM: So you're doing well in the private sector, you're very successful. You get a call from the White House that says, "We want you to serve." And you go into the White House to get this job. Did friends all of a sudden come out of the woodwork, people you went to kindergarten with, people you hadn't heard from in years, and say: "Hey, remember me? Can I have a job in the White House?" How did that work?

LW: A lot of people would say to me, "Wow, you're the head of Presidential Personnel, you must be pretty popular." And I would say, "The exact opposite." Because at the end of the day, for every position, there could be twenty, thirty candidates that all want the job. You're getting lobbied by members of Congress, by governors, by folks in the private sector, by folks within the White House, and folks within the agencies who are not always in agreement. You've got to be the person that says: "Okay, my mission is to find the very best people to serve the president. The people who are the most qualified and who are here to serve something greater than themselves." And that is the most critical thing that I tried to home in on with my team. We tried to kind of take some of the noise out of the equation, but it's not always easy to do in such a highly political environment.

DM: How about you, Jonathan? Did you all of a sudden become more popular and funnier, taller, in better shape? Did people start telling you that you were really cool once you started working in the White House?

JM: Dave, for the record, people always think I'm cool. But I would say Liza is exactly right. You are delivering way more disappointment than happiness in a job like this. And there's an added element because we put people through a rather rigorous vetting process. There are plenty of times when you have to call somebody up and explain that they're not going forward in the process, but you can't tell them why, because the FBI, IRS, all these people are involved, and that obviously makes them very nervous. It leads to a lot of very uncomfortable situations. I still run into people periodically at parties and things like that, and they move away from me because they think that I know something about them.

DM: Let's say you want to get a job postelection. What's the best way to approach Presidential Personnel?

JM: To put it in a frame of reference, in the couple of days after the election in 2008, 253,000 people submitted résumés into the résumé database. That's not including people that already had been submitting during the campaign. If you went through those 253,000, you found CEOs of publicly traded companies who didn't know what to do, so they just put their résumé in. It's pretty overwhelming.

That's not to say don't submit your résumé—we searched that database for eight years, so being in the database is particularly important—but people who have worked on the campaign and built relationships and have had some visibility and are known to be expert on something, that's a great way to be connected. Making sure you're raising your hand through whatever connection you have to the White House is also a good thing, but there are lots of different groups, trade groups, community organizations, philanthropies who started putting together lists of people who care about their topics and their issue areas. We leveraged tons of outside groups to help us get people from all over the country. It was a very effective mechanism.

LW: What I always tell people is: do your homework. When you're in Presidential Personnel and someone submits a résumé, it's so helpful if someone has taken the steps to really research what positions in the government they're interested in and they believe they're qualified for. So in your cover letter or your email, or however you're submitting that information, make sure you're saying, "Hey, I have a strong background in international trade, and I've identified these five positions as ones that I would be interested in." The more they can help the process the better, because the floodgates open in the beginning of any administration, and the PPO is overwhelmed, as Jonathan said.

DM: What was the most annoying or difficult approach that someone made to you when you were head of Presidential Personnel? And how did that backfire on that person?

LW: Oh my goodness! There was one person that launched a campaign, and I had literally fifty or sixty phone calls that were coming and letters being faxed in. I think that was the most egregious situation; you used the word "annoyed," and that struck a specific memory.

One of my responsibilities was to handle the ambassadors. One time I had a husband and wife that came into the office and tried to pitch me on the idea of being neighboring-country ambassadors. So basically, they each wanted an ambassadorship in neighboring countries, and they thought that was a great idea. It just shows a lack of judgment.

I always appreciated when job candidates would say to me: "Listen, I have a lot of support. Here's a list of the folks that I know would be very supportive." Especially if they were on Capitol Hill, because that's certainly relevant. But we would openly talk about it. I would let them know if and when I needed to speak to those people. Or maybe if I wanted letters of recommendation. But to just have all these people start kind of [bombarding] the office with phone calls . . . things like that are not a good approach.

DM: Did someone ever say, "I'm very close with this senator," and then you called that senator, and that senator said, "Whatever you do, don't hire that person?"

LW: Yes, that happened. But also, I can't tell you how many times I would get a letter from a senator saying, "I recommend this person," and then it was quickly followed up by a phone call from them to me saying: "Oh, by the way, I sent you this letter, but I kind of had to do that. I really wouldn't recommend them." I was getting the backdoor reference saying, "The senator doesn't really feel strongly about it," or something like that. It was a lot of craziness.

JM: There were a couple of different categories. There were the people that wanted to prove that they put it in the process, but they weren't feeling strongly about it. There were people who they wanted us to call and engage, but it wasn't superstrong support. It was more that they wanted the person to be considered. And then there were people that felt strongly about it.

The only thing I would add to what Liza was saying is that giving a list of names is a great idea. That is exactly what you should do. But the other thing you need to think about is: are these people helping my candidacy? If somebody can speak to the substance of what you can do or your acumen in some way, that's great. But twenty people saying that they like you does not help. It becomes a judgment question. If you approach it this way, when you're acting on behalf of the president of the United States, are you going to show similar poor judgment?

One thing that I actually didn't love about the job was that you would see—every once in a while—someone's worst version of themselves. I remember vividly a guy who felt he was very important; we were at an event, and he didn't know who I was. He kept interrupting me and talking over me and everybody else for that matter. And at some point, somebody walks up and asked me a question about how it was going [at PPO]. I'd been in the office for probably about four or five months at that point. And when he heard what I did, he turned around and then followed me around all night, just paying so much more attention to me because suddenly he found out that I had this job. But prior to that he was treating me like everybody else in the room. Unfortunately, every once in a while, you get one of those.

"Really strong diplomacy skills"

DM: Let me ask you another difficult question. Let's say you had the chief of staff, or someone very important in the White House, pushing you to hire someone. And let's say a cabinet officer was pushing a different person for that same role in their own agency. How do you handle that situation?

LW: Oh boy. First of all, I never ever had a situation where I had our chief of staff pushing me to hire someone. But I did often have situations where people in the White House who were in charge of policy had concerns about a candidate or wanted one particular candidate, and the agency or department wanted a different person. That is one of the harder challenges. We have to walk a fine line. Our job is to find the best, most qualified people that support the president's agenda. And I think at the end of the day, we would try to sit down, mediate this, and have an adult conversation about what is really best.

Thankfully, I can't remember too many instances of that. There were definitely a few [cases] where we couldn't resolve it. We had one particular cabinet member that went directly to the president when they didn't get what they wanted. Interestingly, the president ended up siding with our judgment. We tried to listen to all the inputs, but at the end of the day—and hopefully Jonathan would agree with this—we needed the best candidate. Not necessarily who the cabinet member thought was the best, because that wasn't always in alignment.

DM: But presumably it's your job also to read the tea leaves—not all cabinet officers are created equal. For example, we had Jim Baker on *Transition Lab,* and he basically said: "When I was secretary of state, I didn't even go to Presidential Personnel. I just picked who I wanted. And that was the deal I cut with the president." So you knew which cabinet officers had more leeway than others, right?

LW: That's right. I'll give you one other example. When Hank Paulson came in as treasury secretary, he had, on the one hand, that deal with the president, but he worked so beautifully and closely with our office. He used us almost as his executive search firm. I was lockstep with him on every position we hired. But on the flip side, we had a bit of an antagonistic relationship with DoD [the Department of Defense].

DM: And that was with Secretary Rumsfeld, right?

LW: Yeah, it was. So, when I came in as head of PPO, it was already a really sour relationship, and I walked in, and it was not a good situation. But when [Robert] Gates came in [as secretary of defense], we built a great relationship. A lot of things changed in terms of how we interacted with DoD. Not to beat a dead horse, but it comes back to the abilities needed for folks in Presidential Personnel. You need people with really strong diplomacy skills who can build those relationships effectively from the very beginning.

"Our office ramped up like a transition effort"

DM: Let's talk about the differences between a first term and a second term. Two of the chiefs of staff that you worked with, Josh Bolten and Denis McDonough, were on *Transition Lab* [see their interview below], and we had a bit of a debate about the right level of second-term turnover. For Bush, if you look at the secretaries, deputy secretaries, and undersecretaries—the top three levels of positions—54 percent of those people left the government within six months of [the beginning of] Bush's second term. In comparison, during the first six months of the [second] Obama administration, 34 percent left. Denis argued that they had better retention, they had more stability, and that was positive. Josh argued that you actually wanted fresh eyes, fresh legs, fresh energy. People are tired, and you need rejuvenation in the second term. How did you two approach personnel at the start of the second term, and what did you do in year four to get ready for a year five?

LW: I agree with Josh wholeheartedly. I remember before the 2004 election getting called into the Oval Office, and President Bush and Andy Card and I had a conversation about eight or nine cabinet members that we were going to be replacing. That's a lot. So our office two months before that election ramped up like a transition effort. We had our lists ready to go so that right after the election, we could make those announcements as to who those cabinet members were going to be.

We treated it as a big transition and identified, ahead of time, lists of who we would probably lose. We identified a stoplight system, a red-, yellow-, and green-light system, where we went through all of the top Senate-confirmed positions. If someone was a red, we knew they were leaving, or we knew we wanted to have them leave. If they were yellow, we were at risk of losing them. And if they were green, then we knew that we felt comfortable that we wouldn't have to replace them. That helped us prioritize what my team could focus on, because we were trying to be more proactive and to cut down the time it was going to take to bring new people into the administration.

JM: Our approach was similar. We did a lot of preparation going into the election year. We built off what the Bush team had done. We actually had started doing succession planning quarterly with each cabinet secretary a couple of years earlier. We had that same conversation: How likely is this person to stay over? In what period of time should they be promoted to another role in the agency or across the administration? We started having those conversations about every single person a couple of years earlier. The whole point was to have a sense of where people were going to be and where there were opportunities to keep people around.

So they might have changed jobs, but they stayed in the administration. So they stayed longer. That's what Denis was referring to. We worked very hard to try to smooth out the outflows and to give really good people a chance to keep working because they had learned a lot in their first eighteen-month [or] twenty-four-month cycle. That was something that we started working on in the second year and got pretty good at by that point. We were able to predict a little bit better and then preempt and try to keep people around.

"Developing them as they get their sea legs"

DM: The Partnership for Public Service has been pushing that PPO and the government should not just focus on appointments, but they should also pay attention to effective talent management. Do you have any advice for a future PPO director on how to pursue talent management and development of personnel as a priority, along with appointments?

LW: It's a critical step because when you think about talent management, talent acquisition is a part of that. You've got to find the people, but then it's onboarding them and engaging them appropriately and in a productive way. It's developing them as they get their sea legs and as they understand what their jobs are. It's performance management, it's succession planning, it's all of these things in combination and concert. But to do that, Dave, it's going to require an investment. It is such a huge job to just onboard these people and to find these people. With a limited number of people in Presidential Personnel, they can't possibly add on all of those other areas.

There's got to be some thoughtful approach—maybe working in partnership with the White House liaisons to identify the high performers. We really tried to do that, to identify people and say, "Okay, what's their highest and best use?" Sometimes we would take them from the Treasury Department and put them over to another department. But I would advise any future administration to have people focused on that because we were spread so thin, we weren't able to do that as effectively as I would have liked.

"The best team, representing the entire country"

DM: How did you approach the issue of diversity when you were head of Presidential Personnel? Did you focus on diversity mostly from a gender and race perspective, or did you also look at geography, age, a much broader set of criteria? And what would you advise that a future head of Presidential Personnel do better or learn from some of the problems or mistakes that you made or encountered?

LW: We looked at it across the board, so it was ethnic and racial diversity and everything you just said, geographic diversity. We also looked at making sure we're bringing in people that represent different types of backgrounds. People out of corporate America, varied industry backgrounds, people out of the nonprofit sector, international NGOs, higher ed, to really have gender diversity as well. To us, diversity encompassed a really broad view.

JM: A couple of things are important. The first is establishing with the president-elect what their belief system is around this and making that clear to people as they're coming through the process as candidates for senior positions. What are the aspirations around diversity, what types of things matter, how you want to approach it, etc. We learned that having those successful conversations and having agency-by-agency high-level conversations allowed us to talk about diversity across two hundred or three hundred positions over time. Not one by one. And that makes it a lot easier to sit and say, "How do we put the best team in place, representing the entire country that it's supposed to represent?" Well, you need a year, and you need lots of positions, and you need lots of opportunities, and you need to be able to be strategic about it, like anything else.

Planning at that level, having a regular quarterly discussion to see how you're doing and keep yourself on pace, is a great way to have that conversation. There are a bunch of reasons why diversity matters, but one of the things is that you have a lot of people on the outside looking at this government to represent them. And it gives them great confidence to see people there who seem to get them better. We have a pretty broad country to represent. And there are a limited number of positions that we need to fill. You have to be strategic, and you have to start from day one.

Notes

1. For a summary of the extensive vetting process for presidential personnel, see Center for Presidential Transition, *Presidential Transition Guide*, 4th ed., April 2020, 83–86, https://presidentialtransition.org/transition -timeline-and-guide/.
2. Center for Presidential Transition statistics, on file with the authors.
3. Center for Presidential Transition, "Significant Cabinet-Level Turnover after a President's Re-election Highlights the Need for 2nd-Term Transition Planning," November 2019, https://presidentialtransition.org/wp -content/uploads/sites/6/2019/11/Turnover-Report_11.7.19.pdf.
4. Center for Presidential Transition statistics, on file with the authors.

Preparing the Government for a Transition

MARY GIBERT

> It takes a lot of sensitivity, it takes a lot of political acumen, and it also
> takes a lot of just being knowledgeable about what needs to be done. . . .
> If we have a transition, our job is to make sure everyone is ready. We try
> to approach it in a nonconfrontational and nonthreatening way.
>
> —Mary Gibert

F. SCOTT Fitzgerald wrote that "the test of a first-rate intelligence is the
ability to hold two opposed ideas in the mind at the same time, and still
retain the ability to function."[1] Transition planning at the General Services Administration (GSA) requires exactly this: the ability, while working for the incumbent president, to prepare for that individual's departure
from office. From Mary Gibert's perspective, the only way to achieve this
was by ensuring strict equity between incumbent and challenger. Gibert
served as the federal transition coordinator for the 2020 election, organizing the government's transition effort under supervision of the GSA
administrator—surely one of the toughest duties a career civil servant has
ever been called upon to discharge.

Federal agencies are required by law to take certain actions to prepare
for a transition, and since 2010, these requirements have expanded.[2] But
the GSA's mandate during a transition is unique. Between the nominating conventions in the summer and the election in November, the GSA
is required to provide office space, technology, and associated resources
to the Republican and Democratic transition teams. After the election, it
is the job of the GSA administrator—a political appointee rather than a
career civil servant—to "ascertain" the result, an administrative process
that gives the winning transition access to classified briefings and further resources. But this work went off the rails in the wake of the 2020

election, when, for more than two weeks after the outcome had become clear, the Trump-appointed GSA administrator, Emily Murphy, refused to "ascertain" Joe Biden as the winner.

Despite these issues, Mary Gibert remained the consummate professional throughout the 2020 cycle. She corralled more than twenty-five agencies identified in the statute to complete their preparation while persuading another seventy-five to undertake additional transition preparation that was not statutorily required. She worked in a balanced manner with both the White House and the Biden team. She ran toward problems like a firefighter toward a burning house, dealing with headaches ranging from IT issues to political appointees who didn't understand why the administration would do anything to help Biden prepare for the possibility of power.

In a testament to her integrity and fairness, Gibert gained the confidence of both Trump White House deputy chief of staff Chris Liddell and Yohannes Abraham, the executive director of the Biden transition team. Each felt that Gibert was looking out for their interests while protecting, as appropriate under the law, the interests of their political opponent. And they were both right.

As the size and complexity of the federal government has grown and transition preparations have become increasingly robust in the wake of 9/11, the GSA's role in transitions has been constantly enhanced to foster equity, anticipate issues, and refine the overall process. One such improvement, established under President Obama, was the Agency Transition Directors Council (ATDC). The ATDC provides guidance to agencies on transition preparations and coordinates among agencies, transition teams, and the White House. As the federal transition coordinator, Gibert led the ATDC. As essential as it is, the ATDC excludes many boards, commissions, and smaller federal agencies. Some of those excluded are rather large, like the Social Security Administration, which has more than sixty thousand employees. To solve this shortcoming, in June 2020 the Partnership for Public Service worked with the Boston Consulting Group to set up a series of Agency Transition Roundtables, something the Partnership also organized in 2016. These roundtables served as a forum for career officials across all federal agencies to share strategies for preparation, receive guidance from Gibert and her team, and gain key insights from panels of transition experts.

When I approached Gibert to be on the podcast, she was nervous. Career officials are trained to operate quietly behind the scenes, letting political appointees take the credit and face the public. I pointed out that, as federal transition coordinator, she was the only statutory officer identified in the Presidential Transition Act. Speaking publicly about her role, I argued, was critical to the transparency and integrity of her effort. She agreed and made a fantastic interviewee, although some questions were off-limits—for example, we did not discuss ascertainment, anticipating it could be a hot-button issue.

Ultimately, Gibert's 2020–21 ride was a roller coaster. Briefing the White House Coordinating Council in the Roosevelt Room in the West Wing of the White House constituted an undeniable high—most career officials never get that close to power. In contrast, the ascertainment delay stalled all of her good work, handcuffing her team until Administrator Murphy gave the green light to the transition.

Watching Gibert in action reinforced my admiration not just for her but for career civil servants across the government. They do heroic work, and they do it without fanfare. Gibert, more than most other career officials, was forced to walk on the flimsiest of tightropes above treacherous waters, facilitating the transition to power of a new president while the incumbent did not recognize the outcome of the election. When we taped the podcast in August 2020, we had no idea what Mary would face in the coming months; as it turned out, she would demonstrate the capability, commitment, and integrity to handle this delicate task with skill and grace. The Partnership for Public Service subsequently named Gibert as a finalist for its prestigious Samuel J. Heyman Service to America Medal for her work on the transition.

"The most important thing is equity"

DAVID MARCHICK (DM): What is GSA, and what does it do for transitions?

MARY GIBERT (MG): GSA is the General Services Administration, and we provide all things workplace across the federal government. We provide the physical space, whether it's leased or owned. We're often called the federal government landlord. We provide acquisition services and solutions, and we also promote management, best practices, and efficient government solutions by providing government-wide policy.

When it comes to transitions, GSA has a statutory role to provide services and facilities during both the pre- and postelection. For preelection, we prepare the two candidates should there be a full transition [i.e., a transition to a new administration]. During the postelection period, we receive funds to manage for the president and president-elect for staff, travel, and supplies. We also have an interagency coordination role. A big part of the job is to provide guidance on transition activities. That includes succession planning, briefing materials, direction, and support. There is also an Agency Transition Directors Council that I cochair with the OMB deputy director of management. I'm also a member of the White House Transition Coordinating Council, which provides guidance through myself as a federal transition coordinator to the Agency Transition Directors Council.

We also provide support to our partners in preparation for having an inauguration. That includes the military, the Park Service [which controls the National Mall], DC government, and also the volunteers who actually plan the inauguration. If needed, we also plan outgoing activities. There are funds that come with that to the outgoing president and vice president to provide approximately seven months' worth of services, to include space and support to wrap up things within their office. Following the end of that seven months, the president becomes part of the Former Presidents Program, which GSA manages.

DM: Essentially, the whole suite of transition activities has been formalized for the good of continuity of government. Prior to various amendments to the Presidential Transition Act, GSA didn't do all this; but based on various amendments to that act in Congress, GSA has a much bigger role, and there's much broader support for eligible candidates so that there's a smooth transition of power should a challenger win, is that correct?

MG: That's correct. The Presidential Transition Act itself was passed in 1963; then there have been various amendments starting around 2000. Based on lessons learned, the statute has become very specific and very clear about what needs to be done. In fact, preelection services were not provided previously—they came in the legislation that was set up in 2010.

DM: Mitt Romney, when he ran for president, was the first candidate to benefit from this whole suite of support from GSA. In 2016, both Hillary Clinton's team and Donald Trump's team received this whole suite of GSA support.

MG: That is correct. The first-time services were provided was to the Romney campaign.

DM: Some of this can get a little awkward. Rich Bagger, who was the head of the Trump team, and Ed Meier, the cohead of the Clinton team, said they were both in the same building planning their transitions, and sometimes they would get in the same elevator and kind of look at each other and then look down, and it was a little awkward. Why did you put both the Trump team and the Clinton team in the same building in 2016?

MG: We gave a great deal of thought to those when we provided the preelection services the first time, even though they were only provided to the Romney campaign, because President Obama was the sitting president. We thought about how we should do this, because in the underlying legislation, the most important thing in providing preelection services is that there is equity. We made the decision fairly early on that we would house both of the candidates in the same space to assure equity not only in terms of the amount of space, but location and proximity [to the White House]. It's worked very well for us.

DM: This is complicated stuff for someone sitting in the government. One might wonder whether you would favor the sitting president, but you're saying that you have to be totally scrupulous, totally equitable, and totally nonpartisan?

MG: That is correct. That is one of the reasons that my position is designated to be a career position. The other thing to keep in mind is, the statute over time has become very clear about what must be done, who needs to do it, and who needs to do it by certain points in time. Particularly as it relates to the preelection services, equity is specifically in the statute. Of course, no one wants to start planning for their departure if they are planning to be reelected. It takes a lot of sensitivity, it takes a lot of political acumen, and it also takes a lot of just being knowledgeable about what needs to be done and that it is statute-driven. If we have a transition, our job is to make sure everyone is ready. We try to approach it in a nonconfrontational and nonthreatening way. From the human aspect, no one wants to be thinking about this, but we have to do everything we need to do to make sure that the federal side of the house is prepared.

"The team is a lean, mean fighting machine"

DM: How long have you been working on preparation for a potential transition [in 2020–21]?

MG: We start the planning about two, two and a half years out.

DM: How large is your team?

MG: The team is a lean, mean fighting machine. That's what we like to call it. The team starts out very small at the front end. At its peak when we are providing the full postelection services, should we have a transition, it is up to about fifty people who are all directly supporting the transition. That doesn't account for folks who may be doing the build-out of the [office] space, our legal support, and HR.

DM: Let's discuss the phases of transition work. Your work actually is triggered when the candidates are formally nominated. Is that correct?

MG: That's correct. Access to the services kicks in per the statute based on the conventions and becoming the nominee. The letter of the law is that we are to provide the preelection services to the candidates within three days after the last convention.

DM: So essentially on September 1 after the second convention, the Biden team can move into the GSA space. You hand them a bunch of computers and iPhones or whatever mobile device you use, and that's when they start to get the benefit of GSA services. Right?

MG: I think it's also important to know that not only is GSA getting ready, but there is interagency coordination going on as well with our partner agencies preparing the postelection space. GSA is not the only one working at this time; all of our partner agencies are also busy preparing, and we are the conductor to make sure that everything is happening to meet our statutory guidelines.

DM: Part of your job is to work with the transition teams to provide support postconvention. Another part of your job is to chair this interagency committee to promote preparation at the agency level. What do you work with the agencies on?

MG: There is lots of coordination across government. The Office of Government Ethics has statutory requirements to prepare; there are preelection and post-election items for them. Of course, we work with the Secret Service. We work with the intelligence community to be prepared to provide the briefings. A lot of this is being prepared if we are needed to execute postelection activities. Of course, we cannot wait until we have the outcome of the election to start working on the postelection activity.

DM: One of the things you focus on is briefing books. Are briefing books generally these dense, impenetrable documents, or are they more targeted now?

MG: It's an evolution. I think that's probably the best way to talk about it. I believe last time, most everything was available online and electronically to the teams as they came in, but we also provided the option to print it out if needed. One of the things the statute did was set a specific date that those briefing materials have to be ready, which is November 1. The guidance that we will be issuing to the Agency Transition Directors Council, as well as the rest of the federal government, provides a framework for those briefing materials, to make sure that there's consistency. We are working to provide direction and guidance on that, which will come from the ATDC to our agencies so that we have some level of consistency.

"Our platform is different, but our ability to carry out the mission is not"

DM: One of the things that is even more complicated this year is COVID. Transitions are complicated enough in normal times, but now basically most of the government, particularly the civilian agencies, are operating remotely. How will COVID affect transition planning?

MG: I would say that COVID has not impacted our transition planning. We haven't missed a beat. We've kept up with all our statutory requirements. We've held meetings. Before, everything was large gatherings in person; now we go to Zoom and Google Hangouts. Our platform is different, but our ability to carry out the mission is not.

One of the other things that I would emphasize is the services that GSA provides in partnership with our other federal agencies. The physical space is only one of them. One of the other key features that we provide to the candidate and in the postelection environment is a secure internet and IT environment. The same environment that GSA uses is also available to our customer, either through preelection or postelection, so they will be able to operate wherever they may be, using the same suite of tools that we have within the government. They will have their own secure network for that.

DM: You're planning for either a traditional transition where they operate in their space preelection or postelection, but you're also preparing for a remote transition in that the Biden team can use Zoom or Google or whatever technology you use, and there could be a remote transition?

MG: Another item of note would be: in past transitions, just talking about the last one, for example, the number of devices that GSA provided to the preelection and postelection process exceeded the number of seats that were available in the space. So before COVID, there was a great deal of work going on in previous transitions without folks all being physically there.

DM: So you're saying that in every transition, there are some people in the office, but there are a lot of people that have iPhones, iPads, computers, whatever device they have, and they're operating within the agencies that are operating remotely. And that will be the same this year?

MG: Correct. Perhaps it will be on a larger scale. It will be up to the customer either pre- or postelection to determine what that looks like, but there's a platform available, and it's not a new practice.

DM: What about the issue of bringing people in? One of the biggest challenges associated with a new president is they appoint four thousand people. It's the largest takeover of any organization anywhere in the world, and GSA coordinates that activity with all the different agencies. Do you anticipate that being more difficult because of COVID?

MG: No. Right now, not just GSA, but the other federal entities are bringing new people on board remotely and virtually. Certainly not to that scale, but we won't be doing it for the first time, and we have the ability to plan.

There is a memorandum of understanding that lays out the rules of engagement. It talks about who can come, when they would come, what the process looks like, who they deal with, how that process all works. That is all coordinated with our other federal partners including the Department of Justice and the [Office of the] Director of National Intelligence.

DM: One other aspect of a new transition effort is something called the agency review process. The transition team brings together somewhere between five hundred to one thousand people who are experts in government. They go into all the agencies to meet with career officials and political officials to find out what the big issues are, what the big problems are, what is coming down the pike in thirty, sixty, ninety days. Usually these people fan out all around the government to have meetings with officials in those agencies. In this environment, will that all just be done remotely?

MG: That is exactly what will be addressed in the MOU [memorandum of understanding]. The MOU is informing, in a postelection environment, those agency review teams, the process to get on the list to get access. We will also be addressing with the agencies whether they want to come into the office, because we don't have a crystal ball to know what phase [of COVID] we may or may not be in. Certainly, there will be an option for in-person as long as it's safe. All of that will be outlined in the MOU so the incoming president-elect understands the rules of engagement. We will also make sure that our agencies understand what they need to do to be prepared, as well as the limitations on what can be shared.

DM: So it sounds like a big part of your job is just preparing for every contingency. You don't know who's going to win, so you have to prepare for both sides winning. You don't know what stage the pandemic will be in, so you need to prepare for both a traditional in-person transition or a remote transition. So your job has become much more complicated just because you prepare for every eventuality.

Let me close with this question, Mary. Transition is just a huge task. The peaceful transfer of power is one of the bedrocks of the United States. Ken Burns was on our show, and he remarked that we've had 223 years of transitions since George Washington handed the reins to John Adams. There's never been a president who has refused to leave office. What do you think the biggest misconceptions are about transition, and what do you think every American should know about how the government is preparing for this transition?

MG: The first thing is planning starts not too long after the [incumbent] president actually takes the oath of office. We start two, two and a half years out with our planning and our preparation. The statute lays out when we must do things, what must happen.

At GSA, we take that role very, very seriously. I would say to the American public that the federal entities, the federal government is in good shape. The planning is on track. Our budget is on track. Our activities are on track. We're on schedule. We're meeting all of our statutory requirements.

Notes

1. F. Scott Fitzgerald, "The Crack-Up," *Esquire*, February 1936. John Lewis Gaddis uses the same quote to make a similar point in his *On Grand Strategy* (New York: Penguin, 2018), 14.

2. For a summary of these requirements and detailed recommendations for best practice, see Center for Presidential Transition, *Agency Transition Guide: A Comprehensive Guide to the Activities Required during Agency Transitions*, 2nd ed., June 2020, https://presidentialtransition.org/publica tions/agency-transition-guide/.

The Art of Agency Review

LISA BROWN

> Setting up these teams, figuring out what the work product is that you want, training everybody, getting them into the agencies, figuring out the collaboration and intersection between the policy group and the agency teams, between personnel and agency teams—all of that is just a massive organizational effort. You can't do that in the seventy-seven days between the election and inauguration.
>
> —Lisa Brown

THE UNITED States government was established in 1789 with just three departments: State, Treasury, and War. Today, there are fifteen cabinet departments, sixty-six independent agencies, and hundreds of smaller subagencies. Accurate counts are hard to do—the government is that big—but at the time of writing, the *Federal Register* lists 455 agencies and subagencies.[1] An incoming administration must not only understand this vast apparatus; it must know how to use it to realize policy promises made on the campaign trail. That is the unenviable job of agency review.[2]

For Barack Obama's 2008 transition, the task fell to someone I have long admired, Lisa Brown. Her team's performance stats—seventy-seven days; 349 agency review team members; sixty-two agencies—put them firmly in the big leagues. Like any good coach, Lisa Brown trained her players with offensive and defensive strategy, teaching them to keep their eyes on the ball by identifying immediate opportunities to address campaign priorities, all while safeguarding the president-elect's first one hundred days by anticipating issues that might threaten forward momentum. With her colleagues Melody Barnes and Don Gips, each of whom went on to take top White House posts, Brown's team prepared and executed a gold-standard agency review.

The process pioneered by Brown, Barnes, and Gips remains notable for several reasons.

First, their preelection preparation was comprehensive. Access to non-public information is restricted before the GSA ascertains a winner, but Brown's team conducted thorough research in the public domain to develop context and understand major issue areas before landing in the agencies. This helped to ensure their readiness to engage with career agency officials immediately after President Obama was declared victorious.

Second, their briefing materials were readable. Josh Bolten once joked to me that a major benefit of the shortened Bush transition was that the agency review teams wrote fewer documents that no one would read. Recognizing this, Brown focused on producing usable, digestible materials. A series of two-page executive summaries provided the president-elect with an overview of opportunities and pitfalls. Behind each of these, a more comprehensive twenty-page roadmap outlined the agency review team's deeper assessment of key issues and priorities facing the agency. Here, the audience was incoming agency heads and their teams. Finally, a still-more-comprehensive "user's manual" provided updated information on organization, technology, and budget, among other areas.

Third, they structured their organization well, streamlining chain of command, categorization of agencies, and general guiding principles. A senior team of eight "captains" presided over sets of agencies grouped by theme. They recruited experienced individuals—often former civil servants—to lead and staff teams for each agency. Brown engineered this arrangement to ensure that workflow would not be interrupted by transition officials leaving to take up posts in the administration.

Fourth, they catalogued agencies into tiers based on priority and size, dividing work streams within each according to critical subareas. On the ship of state, nailing down a creaky plank can be just as important as tending to the sails: overlooked minutiae often become major issues. Brown's in-depth approach, characterized by a thorough division of labor, allowed the transition team to anticipate opportunities and surprises at every level.

Finally, in all their efforts, the team hewed to a single maxim: "No-Drama Obama." Recognizing that the administration's relationship with career officials might undermine or elevate President Obama's four years in office, Brown counseled her staff to adopt an attitude of patriotic duty rather than partisan gloating.

As Brown points out, however, all this excellent work would amount to naught without personnel to implement it—both in the administration and on the transition team itself. In both places, she identified the lack of staff as a pain point.

Brown once confessed to me that she was a "transition geek." Echoing Mike Leavitt, she said that of all the roles she had occupied during a meteoric career in the public and private sector, she found her work on the transition the most challenging and rewarding.

"You don't want gaps"

DAVID MARCHICK (DM): What is an agency review team, and what do people on that team do?

LISA BROWN (LB): The president, as you obviously know, oversees over a hundred government departments, agencies, commissions, and boards. When he or she takes office, they are then in charge of all of those agencies. The goal of agency review is that when they actually start governing on Inauguration Day, they are ready to hit the ground running. What that means is that the agency teams collect information about each agency—critical information that the president and his or her senior key advisors need to make strategic policy, budgetary, and personnel decisions.

Transitions are a time of vulnerability. You don't want gaps when one president leaves and another one comes in, particularly if it's a time of crisis. You want to make sure that when the new team comes in, they have the information they need to handle the crisis of the day, and then also to start implementing the priorities of the new president. If you think about COVID, in many ways, that's a good example. We want to make sure during the transition that the president-elect knows exactly what the government has been doing, what plans are in place, so that when they come into office, they and their secretary of Health and Human Services [HHS], the Centers for Disease Control and Prevention, etc., can move straight in and continue fighting what is the biggest crisis we're fighting today.

DM: Agency review teams are only activated should the challenger win. Secretary Clinton had four to five hundred people lined up to do this work on the day after the election. Obviously, she didn't win the election, so the agency review people put their pens down, but they were ready to go.

LB: Right. That's actually a good point, because there is work that is done preelection, and the Partnership for Public Service has been superhelpful. The Partnership has briefed both candidates at that point and [both candidates'] teams. Then, postelection, you can actually go into the agencies. But there's a lot of preparatory work that is done before you even know that you're going to be the person who wins.

DM: Let's walk through your timeline. You were tapped to do this in 2008 in the summer?

LB: Yes, it was, if I recall correctly, early July.

DM: So you're tapped to do this. And then the first thing you did was recruit people that could be leaders and recruit other people. It's kind of like a large pyramid that you want to recruit and recruit and recruit. What did you do?

LB: That's exactly right. The way that the Obama-to-Biden transition was structured, Don Gips and Melody Barnes [interviewed elsewhere in this volume] were cochairs with me of agency review. The three of us, the first thing we did was to set up a structure. We had an agency review working group that had [ourselves and] eight other individuals, each of whom was responsible for a group of agencies. Each of those individuals chose a person to lead each individual agency review and to put together the team for each individual agency.

DM: How many people did you recruit to be ready the day after the election?

LB: I recall we had over five hundred people total and that there were about 350 who actually went into agencies after the election.

DM: You have a great memory, because I looked it up. Here's the data: the Obama-Biden team had 349 people that were cleared to go into the agencies. There were a lot of people that didn't go to the agencies that were supporting that team. You covered sixty-two agencies. In 2016, the Trump team had 328 people that were cleared to go to the agencies, and they covered forty-two agencies. The 150 people that didn't actually go into the agencies: what did they do?

LB: A lot of research is done preelection. We had a team of people that were doing research on each of the agencies, the nitty gritty of their budget and their authorities, how many people do they have, what are all their divisions. Some of it would have been those, and some of it may have also been that there were people that worked preelection that then didn't actually go into agencies postelection.

"What is going to hit you in the face"

DM: What type of people did you recruit? Do they all have to have had federal experience before, or were they just smart people that can figure it out?

LB: We had seventy-seven days between the election and inauguration in which to get our head around what was going on in each of these agencies. So there's a real premium on having people who are knowledgeable about the agencies, and that tends to be people who have worked there previously.

DM: Were these all volunteers? Were some of them paid?

LB: Ours were all volunteers. And I should say one other thing, which is, we were really careful preelection. The transition effort was distinct from the campaign effort. We wanted people who were on the campaign to do what they were supposed to be doing, which was to go win the election. In the meantime, you had a separate team of people who were working on agency review. After the election you could incorporate some of the people from the campaign.

DM: Mike Leavitt, the former governor who ran the Romney transition team, was on *Transition Lab,* and he made it clear that the campaign makes policy, and the transition prepares to implement that should their candidate win.

LB: That's exactly right. The other big thing that the transition teams do is iden-tify for each agency what is going to hit you in the face when you walk in the door. What are the things that are going on that you're going to have to handle immediately? [It is also critical to] identify those things that you may want to change really quickly. The work of the agency review teams is aimed at the early part of the administration. It's aimed at the day you take office and the first hundred days. It's [about] prioritizing issues for that period of time. Then the cabinet member has the chance to go into the agency, and things evolve over time. But part of how we were trying to prioritize issues was to be able to focus on the key issues at the beginning of the administration.

DM: Because presumably, once there's a cabinet officer that's been there for three, six months, they have their sea legs. They're ready. They're moving forward and not just looking at information that was developed during the transition or prior to the election. You were recruited in July, and then there were eight leaders of essentially clusters of agencies. You had an economic cluster, a foreign policy cluster, etc. And those eight people recruited indi-viduals that would lead sixty-eight agencies. Is that the way it works?

LB: Yes. We allocated all one-hundred-plus departments, agencies, commis-sions, and boards, but we tiered them. So Department of Justice and Treasury and HHS: those are tier-one agencies. A lot of the boards and commissions were in tier three. The Treasury review team could handle a smaller commis-sion or board that's related to Treasury; you wouldn't need a full, large team the way that you do for the big agencies.

DM: For a big agency, say Treasury, Justice, Department of Defense, and State, how big would that agency review team be?

LB: When you think about how large an agency is, this number is not going to sound all that large, but it was probably about twenty.

DM: You have a lead, and then you have people assigned to policy, you have people assigned to personnel. How did you organize each team?

LB: They were more organized by area, particularly with a large agency, because there are subagencies within these large agencies. At the Department of Justice, for example, you would have somebody that was focusing on the Office of Civil Rights. You'd have somebody focusing on the criminal division. It was more about the substance of the agency. Within that substance, obviously policy was a big piece of it. But the transition had separate personnel and policy teams. The way that we integrated policy into the agency review was that we mapped each of candidate Obama's promises to the agencies. If I'm going into Treasury, I know exactly what candidate Obama has said about Treasury, and what I need to think about how we are going to go about implementing that quickly.

DM: Let me ask you what may be a sensitive question. There are thousands of people working on the campaign. Presumably, many of them want jobs. Presumably, many of them would say, "Geez, if I'm not on an agency review team, I'm not going to get a job." What is the correlation between people serving on agency review teams and going into the administration?

LB: There is a pretty high correlation with people who've been on the teams who go into the agencies, but there are also a number of people who serve on the teams because they worked at the agency before, care deeply about it, and then go back to their academic perch or whatever else that they're doing at the time. I think what's important for campaign folks to remember is that there are a lot of government positions—positions that are filled after the president takes office. So you don't have to be on an agency review team in order to get a job.

DM: We pulled the data on the Obama agency review teams. Of around 120, 130 leads at different agencies or coleaders, about 50 percent had worked in the agencies they were reviewing for you. About 20 percent went on to serve in Senate-confirmed roles in the first two years of the administration. Another 10 percent went on to serve at some point in the future. What's also interesting is what you said is that a lot of the people, they want to help, they want to do this, but then they want to go back to their normal lives. About 45 percent of the agency review leads never went into the Obama administration. So it really is a mix of people that may want to go in and people that just want to help and then want to go back to their other lives.

LB: It's great that the data backs up what my impression was.

"No-Drama Obama"

DM: One of the things that we're very focused on at the Partnership is the career workforce, really the guts of most agencies. What we advise is humility. Agency review teams, when they come in, they're heady, their chest is out, they may be a little peacock-y. They just won the election, and they think they're pretty smart. Did you tell all the agency review people on your teams: "No egos, be respectful"? What was the culture that you could try to create?

LB: "No-Drama Obama" and "No Ego" were very important. Part of what we emphasized to the teams is that they were essentially raising the flag as they went into the agencies. They were representing President-elect Obama. So it was really important how they comported themselves. If you've ever worked in the government, you realize how critically important career employees are. They are the ones who know how to get things done. You need them to be your friends. You need to be collaborating with them. The worst thing that you could do during agency review is to go in and alienate the career staff, because you will find that it is much harder to get things done when you take office.

DM: How do the career officials at the agencies receive the agency review teams? Are they happy to see them? Are they unhappy to see them? Are they rolling their eyes because they've been through many political bosses, and this is just another one?

LB: I have found that career employees are professionals, and they are accustomed to a change in political administration. Those who are in the more senior positions have been through a number of different transitions, and they tend to be very professional about it. They care about the mission of their agency. They care about the work that they're doing. They do want to partner with you to get that work done.

DM: What type of back-and-forth is there typically between those agency review people and both the political-level people and the career level people in the agencies?

LB: The way that we structured this was, in the preelection work that was done, part of your job was to identify questions. You knew that there was an issue at an agency, but you didn't know exactly what the status of it was. All you would know is what's public. So you would go into the agencies with essentially a series of areas that you were expected to dig into to learn more about, because what you do get access to postelection is nonpublic information. There's a lot of government work that isn't in the press every single day. To really understand the status of usually the more sensitive work of an agency requires talking to people who are working on it day to day.

DM: Would they be cooperative, or do they kind of have an attitude like, "Why are you asking me this? You're not really the people that are going to be in this agency. I'll wait for the cabinet secretary to be here."

LB: As a general matter, they were cooperative. There were a couple of bumps, and usually it was over access to particularly sensitive information. We had a whole protocol for clearance to get access to classified information. If you've got nonpublic information, you also had to sign an agreement that you couldn't disclose that. Sometimes there were debates over what couldn't be shared.

DM: The Partnership has worked on improving this area of the law. Since you did this in 2008, there have been a couple of amendments to the Presidential Transition Act. The main one was called the Ted Kaufman and Mike Leavitt Presidential Improvements Act. When you [led agency review for] Obama, you and the Bush administration signed a memorandum of understanding that governed the way this worked, that was signed postelection. Now, that MOU is required preelection. Second is that the agencies now are required to have a career official in charge of this process and chart the transition for each agency. The one thing you did have in 2008, which was a 2004 innovation that was post-9/11, was access to get people security clearances. On your team—I pulled the data—you had about 170 people that had security clearances that went into the agencies because DoD [the Department of Defense], the CIA, [the Department of] Homeland Security, and other agencies are sharing classified information with the agency review teams.

LB: You're exactly right. We had our lists of people to go into the agencies, and they had clearance before the election so that they're ready to go the day after the election. And let me add one other thing on the question earlier about career staff. President Bush and his team in the White House really set the tone for collaboration, even though we didn't have the statutory provisions that you've described. They wanted to ensure that it was as seamless a transition as possible. Now, this was after 9/11, so they had a real sense of responsibility to the country. Having them set that tone with the agencies I'm sure facilitated the response by the agencies as well. I think much of what worked [from the Bush-Obama transition] ended up being codified in the statute, with some earlier dates, which is terrific.

"You can't do that in seventy-seven days"

DM: You start in July recruiting eight team leads, and then you and those team leads each recruit people to essentially perform this agency review function for sixty-two agencies. What were their instructions? What are the deliverables that they had to give to you, to the transition team, and then eventually to the cabinet secretary-designate?

LB: We were very clear about exactly what we wanted from the teams. I think this is important, because you need to get the information in an organized and digestible way. If you think about the president-elect digesting memos on each of these agencies, it's really helpful for the information to be in exactly the same format for each agency and prioritized in the sense of the question, "What does the president-elect and cabinet-[designate] really need to know?" So we had what we affectionately referred to as a two-pager, a twenty-pager, and then a much larger user data file.

I think of it as having an offense piece and a defense piece, because part of it was to identify the strategic priorities and opportunities at the agency. What are the major commitments that the president-elect has made that relate to that agency? What's the strategic vision for the agency? What are the opportunities for very quickly starting to implement the promises and priorities of the new administration? On defense, what are the major looming issues? Is there legislation pending you have to worry about, are there important regulatory issues, litigation that's going on where you may want to be changing position?

One other piece that goes through this is budget priorities, because the audiences for this were the president-elect in terms of informing his decision about cabinet, the group that's going to be putting together the budget, and then the cabinet nominees. So our work product was also used in helping to prepare cabinet nominees for their hearings.

DM: So the president-elect would actually review some of these memos, or you all would summarize and take kind of the salient parts and put that in a memo for the president-elect?

LB: Some of this information is needed quite early. I think the biggest lesson that I learned through this process was to expect that the work product is going to be needed sooner than you think it is. This was one example of that: I remember giving the candidate—this is preelection, so he wasn't even president-elect yet—all of these memos as he was thinking about his cabinet appointments. We gave him the two-pagers.

DM: Who's the ultimate audience for this vast amount of material that the agency review teams produce? The president will read some summary of the top agency priorities and issues. Is the next audience the cabinet secretaries-designate?

LB: Yes, that's exactly right. As they prepare for their confirmation hearings, the cabinet secretaries-designate absorb this information. And again, I can't say frequently enough how important it is that you prioritize the information that you are giving to these individuals, which is why we did these outlines— so that what is received is usable. The large data file we compiled, I always thought of as more of a resource for the senior team in an agency when they go in. It is so comprehensive. It's helpful as a resource, but not necessarily helpful as you are trying to get your head around the question, "What are the most salient issues that I'm going to have to manage at this agency?"

DM: In every transition there are lessons learned and things get better, and people like you say, "I wish I did this better," and that's codified in law. It's also shared with future transition teams, whether Republican or Democrat, which is one of the great things about this area, that it's truly nonpartisan, good-government-oriented. What were the major headaches or pain points you had in the agency review process in 2008?

LB: I think we were in the in-between era where it was still a little bit considered to be "measuring the drapes" if you focused on transition. We worked in complete secrecy for a period of time. One of the wonderful things the Partnership has done is to say: "No, it's not measuring the drapes. It's being responsible." Because setting up these teams, figuring out what the work product is that you want, training everybody, getting them into the agencies, figuring out the collaboration and intersection between the policy group and the agency teams, between personnel and agency teams—all of that is just a massive organizational effort. You can't do that in the seventy-seven days between the election and inauguration.

DM: Looking back, what do you know now that you wish you knew when you started the agency review process?

LB: You need to anticipate demand for your work product quite early. The preelection work that you do is vital, and it is supplemented with the postelection work. Postelection, you really do want to get people into the agencies very quickly so that you get that information fast to inform policy and to inform personnel, particularly confirmation hearings. The sooner you have all of that information, the better.

The other area that I think needs to be backed up is personnel. The personnel process is a real challenge. When you think about the number of critical appointments that are being made and getting those people into agencies, and it has, to date, always ended up being a logjam. So, I think [that] thinking earlier, not just about your cabinet nominees but also about the other political appointments that you're going to be making in agencies, would facilitate getting people into agencies sooner.

DM: I'll just give you some data. There are 4,000 political appointments, 1,250 of which need to be confirmed by the Senate. The Obama team had the fastest launch of any transition team. At day one hundred, of the 1,250 nominees that need to be confirmed by the Senate, they had 69.[3] The Trump team at day one hundred had 28. These are cabinet secretaries at some departments, deputy secretaries at others.

LB: I'm going to add a couple other things on the "lessons learned" side. One would be to do your best to integrate policy teams with the agency review teams. Melody Barnes, who was one of the cochairs and ran policy for the campaign, mapped all the promises that candidate Obama had made against the agencies. Integrating policy and agency review is important.

The other challenge that we encountered, and I don't know how you fix this, is that roles evolve over the transitions. Melody and Don and I are running agency review. Early on after the election, Melody is announced as the incoming domestic policy advisor, I'm announced as staff secretary, and Don is working on personnel matters. You risk losing continuity if you aren't careful. You have to think about how you create a structure with enough redundancy that the critical work continues and the system can absorb somebody starting a new role.

Notes

1. Federal Register, "Agencies," https://www.federalregister.gov/agencies.
2. For a detailed summary of the process, see Center for Presidential Transition, *Presidential Transition Guide,* 4th ed., April 2020, chap. 5, https://presidentialtransition.org/transition-timeline-and-guide/.
3. Sixty-seven individuals moved through the Senate confirmation process in the first hundred days of 2009. Two individuals were formally confirmed for two separate roles.

National Security and Transitions

MICHÈLE FLOURNOY

> There's a sense of vulnerability and that we really have to do this as professionally and carefully as possible.
>
> —Michèle Flournoy

"ETERNAL VIGILANCE is the price of liberty" is a worthy aphorism, even if it was not, in fact, Thomas Jefferson who said it.[1] The need for vigilance does not lessen during elections or transitions; indeed, it is likely that our adversaries see the transfer of power as a prime chance to strike us at our most vulnerable.[2] In recent years, the threat has only grown with the advent of cyberattacks and cyberespionage; in 2020, the hacking of major campaigns began more than a year before the election.[3]

More than any other sphere in which the government operates, therefore, national security requires cooperation between incoming and outgoing administrations—a fact of which both sides were more than usually aware in 2008, the first transfer of power since the 9/11 attacks. The day after the election, with Republican John McCain having conceded defeat, President George W. Bush gave a speech at the White House Rose Garden in which he told the nation: "We are in a struggle against violent extremists determined to attack us, and they would like nothing more than to exploit this period of change to harm the American people. So, over the next seventy-five days, all of us must ensure that the next president and his team can hit the ground running."[4]

Under orders from the president, Bush administration officials offered unprecedented cooperation to the incoming Obama transition team, culminating in a series of "tabletop exercises" designed to walk prospective Obama appointees through simulations of various potential crises, including major terrorist attacks. For the first time in history, members of the incoming and outgoing administrations formally collaborated to discuss the critical decisions that would have to be made in such circumstances.

In addition to the heightened need for cooperation, a presidential transition poses at least two unique challenges when it comes to national security.

First, classified briefings are not made available to an incoming transition team until after the election result has been ascertained, typically a little over two months before Inauguration Day. Gaining access to this information almost inevitably reshapes the transition team's understanding of potential threats; it is telling that even as seasoned a professional as Michèle Flournoy was surprised at the array of dangers presented in those initial briefings.

Second, the tremendous scale of the turnover can in itself expose significant vulnerabilities in the country's national security. In just the Office of the Secretary of Defense, there were, as of 2020, 112 positions reserved for political appointees, 44 of which require Senate confirmation. Unfilled seats at national security–related agencies contribute to real or perceived national weakness, making personnel issues into matters not just of government policy but of national security.

From the point of view of appointments, the early days of the Obama Defense Department represented a template for best practice. On January 8, 2009, Obama named four officials—in a batch—for senior Senate-confirmed roles at the Pentagon.[5] Those officials had a joint confirmation hearing on February 5, and they were in their seats, confirmed as a team, on February 9. In parallel with that process, and knowing that a full slate of Senate-confirmed officials at Defense would take time (ultimately, given the scale of the transition, it took more than two years), the administration instead moved to appoint deputy assistant secretaries and other nonconfirmed officials, ready to assist the most senior appointees.

One of the four top Defense officials Obama announced on January 8, 2009, was his nominee for undersecretary of defense, Michèle Flournoy. A preeminent national security expert and defense policy advisor, Flournoy is no stranger to swift action and strategic decision-making. In the fall of 2008, then-candidate Barack Obama called on Flournoy to exercise these skills in executing the peaceful transfer of power. A member of the hundred-person cohort precleared for transition work in anticipation of a potential Obama win, Flournoy was ultimately designated colead of the Defense Department agency review team.

In that role, Flournoy counseled her team to approach outgoing Bush administration officials with humility, professionalism, and respect, marking a significant departure from the posturing of previous transition teams, whose postelection swagger has often alienated career agency officials. Flournoy's approach paid extra dividends when Obama asked Robert Gates, Bush's secretary of defense, to stay in his post. Obama appointed Flournoy as undersecretary of defense for policy, which, at the time, made her the highest-ranking civilian woman to serve at the Pentagon.[6] In the run-up to the 2016 presidential election, Flournoy condensed her vast experience into nine lessons for the incoming administration in an essay for the University of Virginia's Miller Center.[7]

Flournoy has been a trailblazer for women in the defense world, dozens of whom she has directly mentored. Following Joe Biden's election win in 2020, Michèle entered the transition as the odds-on favorite for secretary of defense. Instead, President-elect Biden selected General Lloyd Austin, who thus became the first African American ever to serve as defense secretary. Austin was an exceptional and groundbreaking choice, and he broke the glass ceiling for African Americans at Defense. Michèle Flournoy would have done the same for women—and may do so in the future.

For Flournoy, diversity is not just about ensuring fair representation. In a *Foreign Affairs* article written shortly after the start of the Biden presidency, Flournoy pointed out that "developing a military force and a civilian defense cadre that look more like the American people they are sworn to protect is not just a social good; it will lead to teams that are likely to make better decisions and drive progress toward an even higher-performing military."[8] In the national security world, better decisions and higher performance can literally translate into matters of life and death—proving that diversity, too, is a national security issue.

"We tried to avoid that swagger"

DAVID MARCHICK (DM): What was your job as colead on the agency review team?

MICHÈLE FLOURNOY (MF): The first thing was to put a team together. Some people were assigned who had already worked on the campaign who had identified themselves as experts in defense. I was given a list of people to incorporate, and then, based on my assessment of what we needed to cover, I started suggesting additional names of people we could bring in who would be helpful. I remember meeting at my house to do a mini-off-site to try to come up with a strategic plan of how we were going to work, what were we going to cover, how were we going to divide up the labor, what were the deliverables going to be, and how were we going to use the very limited time we had to do a good job for the president.

DM: You had worked in the Pentagon; you knew a lot of people there. During the campaign, you knew you would have a role in the transition. Did you talk to people in the Pentagon, or was that a no-no?

MF: That was a no-no. There's really no official contact with members of the transition team until the White House and the outgoing administration and the incoming administration negotiate a memorandum of understanding governing the transition. And then you're invited into the department. But I want to say upfront that to their credit, the Bush administration, at least in the Pentagon, did an incredibly professional job on the transition. We were received with red-carpet treatment and very well supported.

DM: Did you come up with lists of people that could be good candidates for different roles, or was that separated from the agency work?

MF: There was a separate person who was in charge of putting together the slates of candidates for different jobs. We certainly made suggestions. But that was a separate effort.

DM: Secretary Bob Gates writes about this in his book. In any transition, people that come in think they're smarter, they're better. They have a little swagger, and they say, "We're in, you're out." Did you have that swagger, or did you try to avoid that swagger?

MF: We tried to avoid that swagger. We talked as a team about approaching this professionally and with some degree of humility. We were there really to listen and learn and then start formulating our own suggestions. Many of us knew Gates, and I think he commanded a lot of respect. It was very clear that he was brought in late in the Bush administration to try to turn around the Iraq War, and that had been his focus. So I don't think there was too much arrogance walking in the door.

DM: One of the unusual things about that transition was that you went in, and you're meeting with Gates, and he knew something that you didn't know at that time, which was that Obama had already asked him to continue on as secretary of defense. Was that awkward for you, or did he hint that maybe that was happening?

MF: Nope. He had a great poker face. He did not let on at all. Eventually it became known, but the truth was we were deep into doing an assessment of what was happening in the department. Where were things going well? Where were they not going well? What was the president going to inherit and on day one that we would need to highlight from the start? What would the first hundred days look like? and so forth.

We just were going about our work, and then once it was clear that Gates was the appointee, we developed a briefing for him. And the main message was: He used to go up to the Hill in the Bush administration and say, "My top three priorities are Iraq, Iraq, and Iraq." We basically made the case to him that in this new incarnation as secretary of defense, you've really got to broaden the aperture. There are lots of issues with the budget, with the program, with modernizing for the future and other areas that you've got to take on.

DM: This was the first transition in decades where there were two wars going on. How did that affect your transition?

MF: It gave us a great sense of responsibility and urgency, to really understand where we were on Iraq, but also on Afghanistan. Remember once Iraq started in 2003, Afghanistan essentially became an economy-of-force mission. And frankly, it started going downhill. President Obama inherited a deteriorating situation, Afghanistan, that required immediate attention, so we did spend a fair amount of time on that.

DM: Now Obama ran in part against the war; he voted against the Iraq War. Gates was one of the people that was brought in to fix all the problems, but wasn't it awkward to deal with a secretary who became your boss, when the president had basically run against the policies that Gates was formerly implementing? How did that work?

MF: Well, I think Gates had been brought in to try to change the trajectory of the war, and that did happen on his watch. By the time Obama came in, the Bush administration was already implementing a phase transition approach, which means that they had built up the Iraqi security forces. They were starting to hand off responsibility for certain provinces as certain conditions were met. A lot of the core thrust of the Iraq review was to continue that process.

"The chemistry on the team"

DM: One of the things that you've talked about post government experience in the Obama administration is the importance of teams. You wrote a great essay for the University of Virginia's Miller Center on transitions, and you said that the president not only needs to pick great people, but he needs to pick teams of people that work together. Why is that so important?

MF: Because the chemistry on the team, the complementarity of skill sets and experience, can make things go very smoothly or very badly depending on the composition. Pay attention to that, trying to ensure that you have people who can work well together. Not that you have groupthink—you want a diversity of backgrounds and experience and perspectives—but you want people who are able to check their egos at the door and focus on the mission and work together as a team.

DM: One of the things that Gates and you did was send up a slate of candidates to the Hill, which we think is best practice. I think that the president sent up five or six nominees for the Gates Defense Department under Obama in early January. They were confirmed very quickly. Was that something that you did by design? Or is that something that just happened?

MF: Because of the sense of urgency that we had two wars ongoing, even before the election, or just after, there was a deep discussion with the Senate Armed Services Committee, and they basically said, on a bipartisan basis, "Look, we're going to put priority on confirming your top team quickly because we understand that a gap is dangerous for us."

I would have loved to have seen that from an interagency perspective as well. I ended up going to Afghanistan on day five because I had spent a lot of time in Iraq but never in Afghanistan, and I had the benefit of having access to an aircraft that could get me in there. Had I known then what I know now, I would have invited all of the other deputies from other agencies who were going to be involved in the Afghanistan review to come with me, because I think that it would have been very useful to do a fact-finding tour together. But a lot of them weren't in place. And again, it just wasn't exactly known who was going to be on that team.

DM: One of the best practices in transition planning has been the security clearances for the agencies. And that stems from the 9/11 Commission report, which looked at what happened on 9/11. A lot of the Bush people were not in place in September after President Bush had taken office, so [the commission] recommended that transition teams postconvention get as many people cleared as possible. I guess in the Obama campaign there were about two hundred cleared. How does that process work, and does that lead people to think, "Oh, I'm going to get cleared, so I'm in a good position to get a job"?

MF: It certainly leads people to believe that the candidate wants you as part of the transition team. It's a very important practice, less important for some of us who've spent a career in the field and maintain our clearances, but for new people coming in, very, very important. And in terms of getting the transition team jobs, I think you have to do it in its own right. There are some people who can't serve in the administration, but they want to help the president by just working on the transition. But I think most of the people who work on the transition did a good job, and those who wanted to serve were able to find jobs.

"There's a sense of vulnerability"

DM: Is there something unique about that transition on the national security side that is distinct from transitions in the civilian agencies? There are more vulnerabilities. That's more pressure. What do you think is unique?

MF: At a time when you're involved in active combat operations overseas and there are active threat streams in terms of, at the time, terrorist attacks against the United States, there's a sense of vulnerability and that we really have to do this as professionally and carefully as possible and as urgently as possible. So I do think it's different.

DM: Do you think our adversaries think that there's a vulnerability in the country during a transition that they could take advantage of? Did you see evidence of that?

MF: Sure. I mean, there were active threat streams on Inauguration Day that people were worried about. We've seen in other cases attacks happen as transitions occur. So yes, it's a time where thousands of people are literally walking out the door, and their replacements have not walked in yet.

DM: How do you deal with that?

MF: One thing is you try to accelerate the confirmations of people coming in. I do think it's a good best practice to designate certain key positions and ask people to stay in their jobs and do a direct handoff to their successor. Don't just leave the job open, but ask people to be holdovers. Something that's now in law is you have the outgoing administration host the incoming administration with a tabletop exercise. They did one [in the] Bush to Obama [transition]—again, very well done—where you had, left and right seat, cabinet official and cabinet nominee doing a scenario-based exercise about an attack on the American homeland.

DM: Many of our listeners won't know what a tabletop exercise is. What is that?

MF: It's basically a scenario-based structured conversation where you walk through the stages of a scenario and the critical decisions that would have to be made at each stage of each step along the way, so that if on day one or day two something happens, people have some idea of the resources at their disposal, how decisions will come to them. They've been through it at least once before.

"You need to have an honest broker"

DM: One of the things that presidents-elect need to decide is how their structure of government will be organized. Will there be a strong White House? Will there be a government run by cabinet agencies like President Carter did, which didn't work so well? The Bush administration had a very tight, centrally controlled government, and the Obama administration, many would say, tightened that even more. One of the things you write about in your Miller Center report is that the agencies should be given much more latitude in the national security space. Was that recommendation based on your experience, and why do you think that's important?

MF: The role of the NSC [National Security Council, a coordinating body within the Executive Office of the President] is to support the president in his or her decision-making to run the interagency process, the NSC process, to tee up options for a decision, to staff the president as he makes those decisions, and so forth. But when it comes to policy implementation, that's why you have presidentially appointed, Senate-confirmed cabinet secretaries who have responsibilities and authorities in law to drive that policy and execution. The best way to actually ensure policies are faithfully executed is to hold those cabinet members and the other political appointees accountable as opposed to having a small White House staff trying to get inside an agency as large as the Pentagon and do the job for the secretary.

DM: What would you advise a new president on how they should structure their NSC versus the national security agencies?

MF: First of all, you need to have the NSC as an honest broker; that is, ensuring that you get the best available information to inform your decisions—including any dissenting views, because dissenting views can help you make better decisions, can help you mitigate risk if you're ruling against that dissent. But you also [need to] have role clarity and [need to] sit down with your top team, your cabinet secretaries, your national security advisor, and talk openly about the questions, "What is the division of labor? What do you need from each person, what's their lane, what are they accountable for, where should they not stray into the lanes of others?"

"You get that first brief and realize, Wow!"

DM: What were the biggest surprises that you dealt with when you came into the administration after carefully planning a transition in 2008?

MF: That's a great question. I think you never fully appreciate the extent of what's happening operationally, particularly in the classified domain, until you get that first brief and realize, "Wow!" I saw some of this in the newspapers and so forth. But the extent of the threat streams we were seeing against the U.S. homeland in terms of potential terrorist attacks at the time was much more concerning than I had had a sense of from the outside, for example.

DM: And did you think the new team was ready when you got there and saw these horrific threat streams?

MF: I do. I think most of the people in senior positions had some experience before, and there were a number of both career professionals and people who were asked to stay on, people like [Assistant Secretary of Defense] Mike Vickers, [who] were very deeply expert on counterterrorism.

DM: You stayed in your position three-and-a-half-ish years. Is that about the right time to serve? These are exhausting, high-pressure jobs. Your husband had a high-pressure job; you had three kids. Was that about the right time? Do you in hindsight look back and say, I wish I stayed longer or I stayed too long?

MF: I wish I could have stayed longer. We had one child who had some health issues that required attention. But actually, the average turnover for a political appointee is something like between eighteen and twenty-four months, which is way too fast. You have to be in one of these jobs three, four years or more to really have enduring impact on the institution. You can change policies quickly, you can be part of those processes. But I was trying to add a big human capital strategy when I was in policy, in OSD [Office of the Secretary of Defense], and I was working hard to try and change the culture and how we take care of people and how we develop people. That is not something you do overnight. It takes time. So I would argue for longer commitments if you can get people to make them.

"It was the gray-bearded priesthood and me"

DM: When you started your career, you were interested in defense and national security policies, you had a distinguished academic background. Did you think that you would achieve these great heights in government service?

MF: I had no idea. What I always tell young people is that you can't plan this. I felt very blessed to have the opportunity to serve and particularly to have the opportunity to serve people like Barack Obama and Bob Gates and Leon Panetta [Obama's second secretary of defense, 2011–13]. I tried to share it with my family as much as possible and tried to, even on the hard days, step back and be grateful for the opportunity.

DM: You were excellent in your job and have an impeccable reputation. You [were] the most senior female to ever serve in the Pentagon. When you started your career, did you think you were going to be a trailblazer for women in the national security space?

MF: I didn't set out to be that, but I did find myself from the beginning in rooms where I was the only woman. I started my work working on nuclear issues, and it was the gray-bearded priesthood and me in a lot of my early jobs. I think that got me prepared for it, but it also got me committed to trying to have some impact on changing it. All of the business literature says that the more diverse the teams, the better the decisions, the better the performance of the organization. So when I did have a chance to hire a team, I tried to bring in a team that looked more like America and that had a greater diversity of background and perspective and experience to help us all make better decisions.

DM: In the national security space, you've had female secretaries of state but never a female head of the Defense Department. Now we have a female CIA director. It's gotten better, but it's still one of the least progressive areas in terms of gender opportunities. Do you think that's going to continue to change?

MF: I think it's changing. When I was a young professional in the Clinton administration, I remember we had a senior women leaders' lunch, and there were, like, eight of us at the table, and everybody was staring like, "What are all the women talking about?" Fast-forward to the Obama administration, we would have filled the executive dining room with female leaders in the Pentagon. So it's getting better. It needs to get better still. And particularly, it needs to get better in terms of minority representation.

Notes

1. *Respectfully Quoted: A Dictionary of Quotations*, ed. Suzy Platt (New York: Barnes and Noble, 1993), 200, 205.
2. Kurt M. Campbell and James B. Steinberg, *Difficult Transitions: Foreign Policy Troubles at the Outset of Presidential Power* (Washington, DC: Brookings Institution Press, 2008).

3. Nicole Perlroth and David E. Sanger, "Iranian Hackers Target Trump Campaign as Threats to 2020 Mount," *New York Times,* October 4, 2019, https://www.nytimes.com/2019/10/04/technology/iranian-campaign -hackers-microsoft.html.

4. George W. Bush, Remarks to White House Staff Online by Gerhard Peters and John T. Woolley, The American Presidency Project, https://www .presidency.ucsb.edu/node/285148.

5. "Press Release: President-elect Obama Announces Key Department of Defense Posts," The American Presidency Project, January 8, 2009, https://www.presidency.ucsb.edu/documents/press-release-president -elect-obama-announces-key-department-defense-posts.

6. Kathleen Hicks's appointment to the role of deputy secretary of defense in 2021 made her the highest-ranking woman in Pentagon history.

7. Michèle Flournoy, "How to Prepare for National Security Challenges," UVA Miller Center, February 17, 2016, https://millercenter.org/issues-policy/for eign-policy/how-to-prepare-for-national-security-challenges.

8. Michèle Flournoy, "America's Military Risks Losing Its Edge: How to Transform the Pentagon for a Competitive Era." *Foreign Affairs* 100, no. 3 (May and June 2021), https://www.foreignaffairs.com/articles/united -states/2021-04-20/flournoy-americas-military-risks-losing-its-edge. This is a point Flournoy and others seeking to diversify the national security space have repeatedly made (see Michèle Flournoy, "Foreign Policy Best Practices," University of Virginia Miller Center, January 14, 2016, https:// millercenter.org/issues-policy/foreign-policy/best-practices).

What Do We Do Now? Policy Development after the Election

MELODY BARNES

> Executive orders . . . regulation . . . legislation . . . litigation. . . . It is really
> three-dimensional chess when a new administration walks in the door,
> which is why those days between the election and the inauguration are
> so important.
>
> —Melody Barnes

So you won the election. Now what? How do you take policy promises
articulated during the campaign and prepare to put them into practice?
The answer, as with everything about transitions, is complicated. First, as
Carter, Clinton, Trump, and others learned to their chagrin, integrating
campaign and transition teams can be a delicate matter.[1] Then there is a
laundry list of tasks to be performed between the election and the inauguration in order to prepare to deliver on the candidate's policies.[2]

It was that promise-to-execution process I sought to explore with Melody Barnes, an attorney, former staffer to Senator Ted Kennedy, and veteran of the liberal think tank Center for American Progress. After joining
the Obama campaign in July 2008, Barnes's duties, along with cochairing
agency review, included leading domestic policy development on both
the campaign and the transition. Later, when Obama took office, he appointed her chief domestic policy advisor to the president.

As Mike Leavitt and Ted Kaufman told me in their interviews, campaigns develop policy; transition teams prepare to implement it. Barnes
therefore served as one of the point-people to translate Obama's promises
into action. Her initial areas of focus included developing executive orders—particularly those candidate Obama had promised to issue on day
one—figuring out what government litigation the new administration

should initiate or drop, and determining which of the previous administration's regulatory changes could be easily reversed.

Meanwhile, she worked closely with White House legislative affairs
director Phil Schiliro to prioritize and sequence legislative priorities for
Congress. Together, they identified quick wins like a new national service
program and the reauthorization of the popular Children's Health Insurance Program, known as CHIP. But they also anticipated longer battles,
like the economic recovery legislation and, in particular, Obama's signa-
ture healthcare reform.

The ability of Barnes and her team to generate substantial domestic
policy immediately was facilitated by their experience during the transition. Recognizing that the country could not afford a lapse in capable
governance, transition chair John Podesta had implemented a series of
mock councils where the national security team could collaborate on policy development. As Barnes reflected, "Starting that process in the transition was not only smart, it was critical."

Barnes described the shift from the preelection phase, when transition teams eschew meetings with advocacy and interest groups, to the day
after, when suddenly they want to engage. The resulting deluge of information was, she said, "as though several trucks backed up to the transition front door and unloaded reports, documents, and lists of names."
The trick here was not just sifting through all of the information, but
making sure that everyone who supported the campaign felt heard.

In the more than 220 years since John and Abigail Adams moved into
the newly built White House, Barnes is one of only a handful of women
of color—among them Condoleezza Rice, Susan Rice, Mona Sutphen,
Valerie Jarrett, Alexis Herman, and of course Vice President Kamala Harris—to have reached the senior echelons of that institution.

Barnes grew up in Richmond, Virginia, and, while selling Girl Scout
cookies as a child, developed her love for working in the community.
From there, Barnes enjoyed a highly accomplished career, with an uncanny ability to be in the room where it happened. After law school and
a stint at a law firm, she became a senior aide to Senator Ted Kennedy,
which was fitting, because anyone who has worked in Washington for a
while knows that Kennedy attracted the best staff, many of whom have
gone on to future greatness as Supreme Court justices, national security
advisors, White House counsel, and, in Melody Barnes's case, one of the
most powerful African American women in political history.

"The first hundred days"

DAVID MARCHICK (DM): You helped design and develop candidate Obama's domestic policy platform, then you moved to the transition and helped to run domestic policy during the transition. What happened between the campaign and the transition with respect to policy development?

MELODY BARNES (MB): My role when I joined the campaign in July 2008 was twofold from the beginning. I spent part of my time on the road campaigning, which I ended up loving. I didn't think that I would, and certainly hadn't planned for that, but I did. I enjoyed engaging with people. I spent the other part of my time based in Washington, DC, working with John Podesta, Chris Lu, and others, to do pretransition planning. We started to focus on agency review teams, those teams that would go into departments and agencies to get the lay of the land after the election in those seventy-plus days between the election and the inauguration, knowing that their work and the work of others and the pretransition world would start to shape policy development. During that summer, we started to see the economy just start to swirl around the drain.

There was a recognition that that was going to be a significant issue for then-candidate Obama, should he become President-elect Obama. Even before becoming President Obama, he would have to take it on, and the elements of the campaign and the pretransition had to start to focus on those issues. As with any campaign, candidates make promises, but recognizing that there was an emergency that was going to be in our hands, people had to begin to think about that so that during the transition, we could very, very quickly pivot to addressing those issues. I give John Podesta great credit for starting to think about that and how the transition should be set up to allow for that.

DM: Preelection, the campaign puts out policy positions. The transition is working off to the side, not a lot of outside engagement with groups. Then, the day after the race is declared, what do you do? What's the transition team doing on policy? Are you starting to say, "Here are the five executive orders we want to put out on day one, here's the sequence of the policy initiatives we want to push"? What happens the day after the election with policy?

MB: The short answer to your question is yes. Immediately, the transition begins to think about what the president is going to do on the day that he or she is inaugurated. For better or for worse, America has become fixated on the first one hundred days. Whether you want it to be or not, the country, pundits, the media will be focused on that. There's also some white noise in the background saying you've got to think about that period of time. So: executive orders. You begin to look at what's happening as a matter of regulation. That's part of the importance of the agency review teams. What's been done by a prior administration that might be overturned because the new and incoming administration has strong disagreement with it?

There's also [a] focus on litigation. The government never sleeps. Litigation that was started by the previous administration that the new administration has to determine if their posture is going to change or could change on. All of those issues, in addition to what's going to happen on Capitol Hill, what will be the first pieces of legislation that a new administration wants to push for, what things were left in the hopper that still have to happen once the inauguration takes place. It is really three-dimensional chess when a new administration walks in the door, which is why those days between the election and the inauguration are so important.

DM: President Obama, when he was candidate Obama, campaigned on a number of big ideas—economic recovery, healthcare, climate change, etc. How did you choose which issues were going to go in which sequence? And in hindsight, did you make the right choice?

MB: You're exactly right about that. I think about Congress, I think about our system of government, and in spite of the impatience that most people feel, our government was designed to work slowly. It can't digest lots and lots of things at the same time. And I think about my colleague Phil Schiliro, who led legislative affairs, both during the transition and the first couple of years of the Obama administration. Phil would walk around with a three-by-five index card. On that card, he had mapped out what had to happen when and how, so that we could best utilize Congress's time and schedule to move as many things as we possibly could.

For example, for the Obama administration, the reauthorization of the Children's Health Insurance Program was something that happened very quickly. We also found space to do some things that were consistent with part of the president-elect's agenda, part of candidate Obama's set of promises that we felt would be important and that we also knew could get bipartisan support. For example, what became known as the Edward M. Kennedy Serve America Act, which focused on national service. People may say, "Why national service in a time of economic emergency?" but many of the things that happen through AmeriCorps and in national service could help the country deal with and address some of those issues. So to your question, did we make the right decisions?, I believe that we made a number of very smart decisions, one [of which was] to move very, very quickly on issues facing the economy.

Even President-elect Obama, before he took the oath of office, had to expend political capital on some of the economic issues and work in concert with the Bush administration on the planning for a stimulus bill that we believed we could move very quickly, that would be important substantively, and that would also send important signals. The last thing I will say is that I know people often questioned why this versus that. Why not do a big push on immigration coming out of the blocks? Why so big and comprehensive a healthcare bill right out of the blocks? Those were decisions that were made based on substance, based on timing, based on the fact that we believed we had political capital that we could spend and that the nation had been focused on the issue of healthcare. That also was wrapped up in the issue of the economy, given that healthcare takes up about 17 percent of American GDP. So we were thinking about all of those issues, the politics, the substance, and the signals that they were sending as those kinds of decisions were being made.

"Starting that process in the transition was not only smart, it was critical"

DM: John Podesta, who did a fantastic job on the transition, came up with this idea of developing mock councils during the transition so that the national security team would work together on policy development. He said that was a good idea to create muscle memory and process practice so that when you moved into the White House, you were ready. How did that work? Was that a good idea?

MB: It worked extremely well. First of all, you're right about John. I've worked with John now since 2003, and he is a brilliant student of government and has an understanding of what will work based on all of the experiences he's had both on the Hill and in White Houses. He was right about creating that muscle memory. I didn't realize it at the time—this was my first time going into a White House—but when I think back to the transition and the way we began to operate the process that was being put in place, my husband often laughs and says, "I never knew process could be a noun and a verb," but you know, you run a process. That's what has to happen in the White House. We were starting to do that, to build those relationships, to understand and build not only relationships with one another, but to the rest of government, to the Office of Management and Budget, for example.

That was important, particularly in a moment when we were in crisis, to be able to move as quickly as we possibly could once we walked through the doors of 1600 Pennsylvania Avenue. We had to do it because we couldn't wait until after the inaugural balls, walk in the White House on January 21 and say, "What are we going to do?" There was too much to be done and too many people—the American public—counting on us. So starting that process in the transition was not only smart, it was critical.

DM: During the preelection transition process, the transition team is basically in a bunker. Postelection, that process starts to open up, and there is just this giant spigot of input that is coiled and ready to go. How did you manage the input process from different groups, some of whom you wanted to hear from, some of whom you didn't want to hear from?

MB: You're exactly right that it is intense. As I've told people over the course of the last several months who've said: "Hey, we want to send this memo. We want to send these names. How do we do this?" I've said to people that for the transition, it feels as though several trucks back up to the transition front door and unload reports, documents, and lists of names. They just come spilling out. Like you said, there's a spigot. At the same time, the transition has objectives that they have to achieve. In this instance [Biden's transition in 2020], they're thinking about the COVID-19 task force, they're thinking about the Paris Climate Accord and World Health Organization, all the things that the president-elect has been talking about over the last few days. What they're trying to figure out is how to accomplish the goals that they have in front of them, the objectives they know they have to hit, all the things that we've talked about, and how to sift through what's coming in that may or may not be useful.

We created a process for tagging and accepting all of the reports and ideas that were coming through the door so that we would have access to them. Then there was a very organized meeting process that was put in place so we could talk to people because at the same time, what you don't want to do is look at everyone that has supported the campaign, who is enthusiastic about the Biden administration, and most importantly, all the expertise that sits on the other side of those doors and outside of government, and say, "Thank you so much, see you never." You have to be able to organize that in a way that you can either access it later on, or you can meet with people in an orderly fashion and in a way that helps you synthesize that information into the process of policymaking, planning, executive order drafting, etc. that's underway.

So that process was also put in place for us. I would imagine that the Biden-Harris transition team is doing much the same. The other thing I would just say to people who are writing those documents is, don't sit by the phone and wait for a call the next day. Draft them in a way that extremely busy people can look at them. See what's there, see what might be useful, particularly in these early weeks and months, and then be able to move forward. It's just an enormous task in a very short amount of time.

DM: What about the issue of beautiful, perfect policy and the ability to sell it?

MB: I can think of an instance where Phil [Schiliro] may have been one of the few people in the White House, along with the president, when I had an idea or believed that we could move a big piece of policy and other people are going, "I don't know about that," Phil said, "We're going to give it a run." And we did, and it's the largest reform of the higher education process that had taken place in generations. I give credit to Phil. He's got a brain for chess and being able to move the pieces around the board.

To your question, the beautiful, amazing piece of policy that doesn't have a chance. One of the things that I believed I learned working for Senator Kennedy was that the best policy processes often begin with people putting lots of ideas on the table, and some of them are, to your point, wacky, but there's the germ of something good and interesting and important there. You've got people sitting around the table who have lots of years of experience, and it is the process of running the process that refines those ideas, and engaging not only with the policy people but with the legislative affairs people, the political people, and the communications team and others so that you get to something that you believe you can push, that has a snowball's chance of getting over the finish line. That is the beauty of that process, but it does begin with people being creative, looking at the challenges and the problems and being creative.

DM: How much of the work that you did in the transition was actually relevant to your job in your first year in the administration?

MB: The vast majority. In fact, I would say almost all of the work I did in the transition was relevant because we won the election. Beginning of November, before Thanksgiving, I was tapped to be the director of the Domestic Policy Council [DPC]. We were often running and planning the Recovery Act and staffing the DPC, working on that public national service bill, the Kennedy Serve America Act, working on the CHIP reauthorization. So it was highly, highly relevant.

That also makes me think about this point in time [mid-November 2020, before GSA ascertained the apparent winner of the election] when we've got a COVID-19 crisis that was already heinous and has now almost spun out of control. It feels as though there's no one with their hand on the tiller, probably because there is no one—meaning the current president—with their hand on the tiller.

Now, for example, the Biden team not being able to meet with those at the Department of Defense [DoD] and those at the Department of Health and Human Services [HHS] on vaccine development and distribution. Even as we go through this period where the current president will not agree that President-elect Biden is, in fact, President-elect Biden, the healthcare of the nation and our national economy [are] hanging in the balance. This vaccine is critical to that. So at the very least, those teams should be able to meet with folks at DoD and HHS to do planning and work around that so that that can be executed seamlessly.

"An extraordinary moment"

DM: I think I have this right—there are five women of color that have served at the top levels of the White House: you, Condoleezza Rice, Susan Rice, Valerie Jarrett, and Alexis Herman. Five in the history of the United States. What are your feelings on the addition of Vice President–elect Kamala Harris to that group?

MB: I think about those women, and I think about colleagues like Mona Sutphen and others, what an amazing group of women to consider to be peers. I would venture to say that this is one of the proudest moments for each of us as women and of color. As a student of history, I look at it and I think it is poetic that women of color—and I think through my tradition of being an African American woman—have built and built and built on each other's work and have supported each other through that process. There is a history even before women had the right to vote—and we're celebrating the hundredth anniversary of the Nineteenth Amendment—before Black women had the right to vote, before we're considered full citizens. There is a history of political engagement and activism from antilynching campaigns to suffrage to civil rights and for so many other issues that is a *leitmotif* that plays behind the careers that you mentioned.

To see Kamala Harris standing there that night and accepting the congratulations of the crowd when the election had been called was just one of the proudest moments that I have ever had.

She's an extraordinary person, an extraordinary leader, and extraordinary woman, a sorority sister. I could not be more excited. A colleague of mine said to me that when Vice President–elect Harris was speaking that Saturday night that she was watching TV with her daughter who is eight, and her daughter walked right up to the TV screen and was just staring at Vice President–elect Harris. And when she started talking about little girls and their expectations and what they should expect for themselves, she said her daughter turned around and looked at her and said, "She's speaking to me!" And she ran back and sat on the sofa and just was enraptured listening to Vice President–elect Harris. I think about that for all little girls of all races, and little boys, and grown-up men and women and say, this is an extraordinary moment, a first that can't be the last, and I could not be more happy.

Notes

1. For the Center for Presidential Transition's best-practice recommendations on this topic, see Center for Presidential Transition, *Presidential Transition Guide*, 4th ed., April 2020, 53–54, https://presidentialtransition .org/transition-timeline-and-guide/.

2. Center for Presidential Transition, *Presidential Transition Guide*, 4th ed., chap. 6.

Bipartisanship and Cooperation

JOSH BOLTEN AND DENIS MCDONOUGH

> It was the first time in modern history that the territory of the United States was actually under threat. We cannot afford those weeks and months of people trying to learn on the job. They've got to be as well prepared . . . as we possibly can make them beginning on January 20. It was just that simple.
>
> —Josh Bolten

HISTORICALLY, PRESIDENTS have not gone out of their way to help their successors; the list of troublesome "midnight actions" has typically ranged from rushed-through regulations to controversial last-minute pardons.[1] Yet cooperation from the outgoing team is essential to any successful transition. Without it, terrible things can happen, as we saw in 1932–33 and again in 2020–21.

Josh Bolten and Denis McDonough did not need to learn this lesson. They knew it. They taught it. As chiefs of staffs to Presidents Bush and Obama during year eight of their respective presidencies, they organized the entire U.S. government to facilitate smooth transitions out of power.

Bush's transition into office, as we have seen, was a trial by fire because of the Florida recount and the subsequent 9/11 attacks. But Bush learned his lessons well, because when it came time to transition out, he made history by creating what Harry Truman had tried fifty-six years earlier: a systematic process to prepare his successor for the job—regardless of who won.

Two days after the 2008 election, George W. Bush gave a speech on the South Lawn underlining the importance of an effective handover.[2] By then, the administration's plans for a smooth transition were already well underway, thanks to Bush's chief of staff, Josh Bolten. When I interviewed Martha Kumar, a distinguished historian of transitions, I asked her to name the most influential government official in shaping the art of transition. Josh Bolten was her choice, and a wise one at that.

Here is a sampling of what Bolten did to earn that accolade. He organized committees of officials at the White House and dozens of agencies to coordinate preparation for the handover. He had staff prepare briefing materials, set up offices, and establish checklists and succession plans identifying officials who would act in place of political appointees as they departed. He instructed officials throughout the government, especially the White House and National Security Council, to be prepared to meet with and help their successors, regardless of who won. And he established a regular dialogue with representatives of both candidates—Republican John McCain and Democrat Barack Obama—on a fair, impartial, and nonpartisan basis. As described in Michèle Flournoy's interview in this volume, after the election, Bolten organized a face-to-face simulation of a potential terrorist attack with the outgoing and incoming national security teams around the same table, working together, for the benefit of the country. None of these steps had been taken before. Since then, many of these innovations have been enshrined in statute.[3]

The drivers for Bush's and Bolten's actions were based around national security, particularly the 9/11 attacks and the wars in Iraq and Afghanistan, and cooperation was particularly strong in that sphere. But the helpful attitude extended across the whole of government.[4] And these preparations soon proved their worth in a different kind of crisis, when a financial crash swept the nation in September 2008.

Even before the election, Bush, Bolten, and Treasury Secretary Hank Paulson had begun coordinating and communicating on the economic crisis with McCain, Obama, and their teams. After the election, cooperation with President-elect Obama intensified. Outgoing and incoming officials worked together on saving financial institutions and the auto industry and on preventing mass foreclosures. They collaborated in their messaging to Congress. They coordinated on use and implementation of the Troubled Assets Relief Program, a $700 billion economic recovery signed into law on October 3, 2008, just one month before the election. The result was a much smoother response to the worst economic crisis since 1932.

As a senior advisor to the Obama 2008 campaign, Denis McDonough was an early beneficiary of Bolten's magnanimous handover. Eight years later, McDonough was serving as President Obama's fourth and final chief of staff. In terms of transition planning, McDonough was determined to build on the solid foundation Bolten had laid eight years before. In essence, everything that Josh Bolten did, Denis McDonough did more.

Steve Hadley's national security team had prepared some forty memos for their successors; Susan Rice, Obama's outgoing national security advisor, had her staff prepare more than two hundred. McDonough organized more regular meetings with the leaders of the Trump and Clinton transition teams and included a broader group of agencies in transition planning. If Bolten built the gold standard, McDonough worked to move it to platinum. The ultimate expression of this: in 2016, Congress passed an amendment to the 1963 Presidential Transition Act that essentially codified the practices that Josh Bolten created and upon which Denis McDonough built.

Both are exceptional talents and, equally important, great people. For a few months during the most uncertain moments of the 2020 transition, my first call in the morning and last in the evening would be to Josh Bolten, seeking his unparalleled guidance. While he enjoys impeccable Republican credentials, he feels an even stronger obligation to the country. As a result, he became one of the unsung heroes of the 2020 transition, prodding the Trump White House to do better, advising the Biden team, and helping to shape the public narrative to allow as smooth a transition as possible, despite the mercurial and uncooperative posturing of the outgoing president. If a Presidential Transition Hall of Fame is ever created, Josh Bolten and Denis McDonough should be among the inaugural members.

"He probably set himself on a course of being determinedly gracious"

DAVID MARCHICK (DM): Josh, the transition from the Clinton administration to the Bush administration was, let's say, less than smooth. Maybe it was good with you and [outgoing chief of staff John] Podesta, but there were a lot of problems. There were a lot of stories, and I think that informed President Bush's thinking later about how he was going to hand off. But what was your recollection of some of the challenges associated with the Clinton-to-Bush transition?

JOSH BOLTEN (JB): Yeah, my recollection is that the reporting of the difficulties was exaggerated. I mean, the media was looking for that kind of thing, naturally. We did only have that truncated transition. Imagine having just run the marathon, and as soon as you hit the tape, somebody says there's a one-mile sprint coming up, and then see how your legs feel after that. So it was a pretty tired team that walked into the White House on January 20, 2001. But it was a pretty upbeat team.

I think in part because of the contested election, some of the young folks on the Clinton team were bitter. They had been strong Gore partisans, which I completely understand, so there were really minor things. It didn't come from the top. Podesta and his crew were superprofessional and gracious. The *W*s were missing from a bunch of the keyboards, that kind of thing. And kind of a funny one I experienced was I got to my desk in my office, and nobody could reach me because my phone had been forwarded to a different number. Juvenile pranks. We actually kind of laughed at it at the time. We tried to downplay it, but the press was keen on reporting some kind of conflict. It wasn't that bad, but you're right: our experience did inform some of President Bush's feeling about it. He appreciated all of the gracious stuff and was annoyed by the few bits of ungraciousness. It likely would have been his instinct anyway, but he probably set himself at that point on a course of being determinedly gracious.

DM: You set up this whole process when President Bush was leaving, to facilitate an easy entrance for either Senator Obama or Senator McCain. Denis, during this period, you were having regular conversations as part of the transition process with Steve Hadley, who was then the national security advisor.

DENIS MCDONOUGH (DMcD): Josh really set the tone at this time as he, I'm sure [he] would hasten to add, was acting at the direction of the president. Transition was happening in a state of war, and it was important to recall that and to make sure that there was no slip from cup to lips in the context of the transition. It's worth taking a moment here to just recognize that the transition [date] is set by the Constitution quite clearly, which means our adversaries know that, too. We can't give them any impression that somehow in the midst of this handoff we're losing track of important objectives of the country.

Those were the kinds of conversations that I had with the national security advisor, Steve Hadley, at the time, or the conversations that Josh was having with Rahm [Emanuel, Obama's incoming chief of staff]. And Steve was having conversations as well with Tom Donilon and Jim Jones [Obama's incoming national security advisor and deputy national security advisor, respectively]. Those are all really important things.

DM: So the handoff from the Bush administration to the Obama administration was smooth, even though essentially a large part of the campaign of then senator Obama was a repudiation of some of the Bush policies.

JB: Right. The way I remember it is that both candidates were running against the president. Both Obama and McCain were fashioning their campaigns as "not Bush," and, God bless him, George W. Bush understood that and did not take it personally—some of the rest of us did. But President Bush was sufficiently unpopular toward the end of his term that it was a political necessity for even the Republican candidate to be repudiating some of the Bush positions, in particular on what had become very unpopular conflicts in Afghanistan and Iraq. We weren't actually indifferent: we were rooting for McCain. But in the early part of 2008, Bush said: "Prepare a really good, professional, smooth transition, because this is the first transition in modern history when the United States itself is under threat. We have a national security responsibility here. Do the best possible job you can regardless of who wins this election."

DMcD: I think it's worth putting it in personal terms as Josh just has. Being at the end of the race, at the end of the campaign, and then turning the corner and realizing that the hard work is just starting. We had fresh legs to either take over things or augment the team, but the two people who don't get to slow down are the president-elect and the vice president–elect. President Obama felt that commitment that Josh has given voice to from President Bush. The fact is, as the president, you're taking over this thing and there are very few people—forty-five of them—who have been through it.

Add to that the stakes that Josh has just talked about, which is that this is in the age of al-Qaeda and the global terrorist threat that had struck right here at home, and the president himself recognizes the enormity of the challenge. So, the fact that his predecessor has teed up a process by which to make that not more challenging, but more smooth, is a very personal thing.

"Assume you're going to win, but treat it as a transition"

DM: Josh, in year four you're the director of OMB [Office of Management and Budget, a key organization within the White House], which has broad powers across the government and also was just as responsible for transition planning. And Denis, you were deputy national security advisor at the time. So are you planning for a year five in the way that you were planning for a year one? Are you thinking about personnel? Are you thinking about new policies? Are you thinking about how do we reenergize, reorient, refresh?

DMcD: On one level, your day-to-day responsibilities are no less. In fact, they're as intense as ever. So the questions about what you do every day are quite obvious. You'll recall that in September 2012 is Benghazi [an incident in which a U.S. consulate in Libya was attacked and the ambassador and several others killed], as an example of the enormity of the questions that you're wrestling every day as a matter of course. The agenda as a daily matter is plenty full, but you do have to be thinking about what the next-term priorities are. The president is out campaigning and making commitments to the voters about what it is that he will do, and you want to make sure that those commitments are able to be executed and are based on concrete executable strategies. That work is ongoing.

And then, of course, you're thinking about your team, and some of your team may have already indicated that they've got different plans. So you're making plans for them. But then you're also thinking, you've been through a transition once, you know that the stakes of the game are as high as they get. And you know that at the end of the day, personnel are key to making sure that you can execute against those challenges. So yeah, you're thinking also about people.

DM: Because the data shows that just under half the people that are secretaries, deputy secretaries, or undersecretaries turn over within the first six months of a second term, which means that's a lot of new people to bring in.

JB: I would say that the Bush administration made the converse mistake, which is that we didn't really treat it as a moment of transition. As farsighted and thoughtful as I think President Bush was in directing a robust transition in 2008, I cannot say that that was very high on the agenda in 2004. Anybody who's elected president is a competitive person and isn't inclined to say I need to plan for defeat. Right? So, the person sitting in the Oval Office is likely to have the kind of personality who's focused on, "How are we going to win and what are we going to do after we win?" There was plenty of focus on that in the Bush White House in 2004.

There was not a lot of focus in 2004 on planning for what to do if we lost. And I know Andy Card, my predecessor and our good friend, who was chief of staff at the time, tried to persuade the president to think about a second term, even in victory, as a moment of transition. The moment, even in victory, as a moment to think, just think about the staff and the cabinet from the beginning. Presidents just aren't inclined to do that. Good advice is to seize the opportunity. Assume you're going to win but treat it as a transition and make sure you're prepared and to hand off in good shape in case you don't.

"We went out of our way to demonstrate . . . that we were playing it straight"

DM: What would you advise the Trump administration to do now that they're coming up on year four, they're running for reelection? He could win, and if he does win, presumably as Americans we want him to have an effective government and plans. So what would you advise them to be doing now and into year four?

JB: Treat it like a transition. Maybe appoint a transition director of some kind, somebody that the president is close to, rethink all of your personnel and know what your priorities are. President Obama, I'm sure, was like President Bush in knowing what priorities he wanted to pursue in the beginning in year five of the presidency. But we sure weren't thinking about reshuffling the cabinet and that kind of thing. And those are all important things to think about. That would be my advice to the Trump administration, including the president; but every president, by personality, is going to be resistant to that kind of advice.

DMcD: I think a best practice is to think about how you put this somewhere where somebody you trust and who's discreet can help you give a good hard look at that. As chiefs of staff, we had strategies as to how to do that as a general planning matter, but having an expressly dedicated transition team makes sense. This is where you can use the agencies to your advantage. There's a lot of ways to do it, but very concretely, the Department of Justice in 2012 set aside a team of people to help security-clear personnel associated with the Romney transition.

DM: This was a lesson out of 9/11, when President Bush had all the secretaries in place, all the deputy secretaries, but not all of the undersecretaries and below had received their security clearances. So the 9/11 Commission said, "Let's get people cleared in." The Obama administration did a great job of saying, "We're going to set aside a team, we're going to insulate them from politics, and we're going to commit to the Romney campaign to get their people cleared and they're not going to leak." That was really a good innovation from the Obama administration.

DMcD: A lot of that now is memorialized in statute and [particularly] in the Presidential Transition Act.

DM: Josh, why did you think it was important to actually start a year ahead to get the gears of government going to hand off the government in a smooth way to either Senator Obama or Senator McCain?

JB: It's not more complicated than what the president said when he gave me the direction, which is that it was the first time in modern history that the territory of the United States was actually under threat. We cannot afford those weeks and months of people trying to learn on the job. They've got to be as well prepared and as well in place as we possibly can make them beginning on January 20. It was just that simple. So we put some effort into it. I can't say it was an exceptionally well-organized effort because we didn't have a playbook. Denis was right: there's really no manual for how to turn over government.

DM: But what did you do, which then became the playbook and then became the law?

JB: We had a transition group that cut across the government, with representatives from all of the sectors of the government and so on, that we met periodically. We showed strong White House interest in every one of the agencies preparing the next folks coming in. That's an easy thing to do in the second term, way out in the open, because you can't get reelected, so it doesn't look like you're anticipating being defeated. We invited outsiders into that process, and then we made contact with the campaigns early on and really invited them in, strongly encouraged them to come in and start reading in, start giving us names to clear.

DM: Bush was supporting McCain. How did you give the Obama team comfort that you were going to be fair?

JB: You just tell them, "We'll be fair. We'll keep your confidence." Once again, in our case it was pretty clear that both candidates were running against the president. So, we clearly had a side—we were for McCain—but we went out of our way to demonstrate to the Obama team that we were playing it straight.

DM: And you felt like they were being fair, Denis?

DMcD: Totally playing that straight. There's a kind of philosophical question, and then there's a structural question. The philosophy that Josh communicated— I'm comfortable speaking for the McCain campaign because I guarantee they had the same sense that we did. But, for example, our campaign—this is now public—our campaign was hacked in the summer of 2008. The notification of that incident came from Josh. Josh called David Plouffe [Obama's campaign manager]. Plouffe called me and said, "You're the only guy with security clearance around here, you've got to go talk to these guys."

DM: And you found that out through intelligence sources or some other manner from the FBI?

JB: From the FBI.

DMcD: For the first question: Philosophically and temperamentally, is there a reason for us to trust these guys? I mean, you know Josh. You trust him, right?

Then there's a structural question, which is, are the agencies set up? Each agency has a lead, and it's a career civil servant or a foreign service officer, and that person has her team. Once you're a president-elect, you then have an agency lead and the landing teams that marry up with those structures.

Josh did both. He communicated his interest in an effective transition, but he also built a structure that ended up being the basis now for the statute that requires a civil servant, a nonpolitical person, in each agency who's going to stay.

DM: Josh, one of the things that made the transition unique was that it was the first time actually since Truman that a two-term president was leaving office when their vice president wasn't running. If Vice President Cheney were running for office, could you have done the same thing, or would it have been difficult?

JB: Yeah, we definitely would have done the same thing. We would have had exactly the same instruction from the president. But it would have naturally been more difficult. That made our lives somewhat easier in a difficult circumstance. Though the one thing to say about the Bush-to-Obama transition, to add to what Denis said, is that, as committed as we were to doing it right, we were kind of groping along and trying to figure out how to do that.

Our counterparts on the Obama side were a really experienced, professional, and civil bunch of folks. Beginning with Chris Lu, the president's classmate from law school, who was the executive director. And then in comes John Podesta as the chairman of the transition. And lo and behold, John Podesta is the guy who was Clinton's last chief of staff and had done the last transition out, so he knew what was going on. We knew him as someone of integrity who had dealt with us fairly. It was super easy to deal with an Obama team that was so well staffed and extremely well organized.

"This is the most vulnerable time in the entire calendar"

DM: President Bush asked Andy Card to be chief of staff several weeks before the election. Did Obama ask Rahm [Emanuel] the same thing?

DMcD: I think so.

JB: As different as Rahm and I might be by disposition and as different as our vocabularies may be. . . . Well, let's just put it this way: we can both swear, but Rahm can swear for ten minutes without repeating himself. As different as he and I are by personality, we were actually friends from his service in the House Democratic leadership. In particular, he was a key contact for the White House during the financial crisis. So he was somebody we were accustomed to. And I in particular, as the chief of staff, was accustomed to working with him.

So we had the fortuity of that, but that fortuity went across a lot of the positions that were transitioning in and out. It speaks to one of the strengths of our system of democracy that people at different places on the ideological spectrum, if they're professional and experienced, have probably run into each other and know how to deal with each other. One of the concerns I have about our current environment is that that has deteriorated.

DM: Denis, when you were chief of staff, when Obama was leaving office, you essentially followed the Bolten playbook?

DMcD: Yes. I did try to just run each of the things that Josh ran. I didn't do as good a job of planning in advance, but I did try to emulate—

JB: You weren't aware it was coming? Took you by surprise?

DMcD: It shouldn't have. But I don't have a good excuse. If we do another one of these, I'll have a good excuse by then.

DM: You actually worked pretty well with both Secretary Clinton's team, whom you knew well, but also Chris Christie's team [i.e., the Trump transition preelection].

DMcD: We had a very regular meeting cadence starting after the conventions. We were making sure that the people were cleared, getting them information they needed, making sure that they had workspaces. I think this whole question of workspaces and computer infrastructure in this day and age is an important thing. Making sure that people are practicing good cyberhygiene, that people are aware of that.

DM: Because we know with 100 percent certainty that other countries are going to try to hack into the transition teams.

DMcD: They're going to try to do everything they can to disrupt, at all times, and they're going to look for times of vulnerability.

JB: This is the most vulnerable time in the entire calendar of United States governance, those few days with outgoing and incoming administrations.

DMcD: So in addition to the structure of meetings, giving the teams for Secretary Clinton and for then Mr. Trump their workspaces, getting them information—which are Josh innovations. The other two things that Josh did that we emulated were, first, that we had lunch in the chief of staff's office. I think Josh did a breakfast of four. We invited all the living chiefs of staff and Reince

[Priebus, Trump's incoming chief of staff], and we had a conversation with him over lunch. Then, in January, we also emulated another Josh innovation, which is a joint meeting of the National Security Council and Homeland Security Council personnel, a tabletop exercise [simulating a major national security crisis]. So people got to know each other; people got to brief through their colleagues. The incoming team got some familiarity with at least the flow of the meeting and the nature of the documentation. Those are all things that we quite purposely emulated after Josh.

DM: But they weren't in law as well?

JB: They were, but they were much better organized and, I think, [better] executed eight years later than they were [in 2008–9], because we were still kind of fumbling with the playbook and thanks to a lot of good work done by folks on the outside and including an organization, David, that you know well, the Partnership for Public Service.

Denis, by the time your time came around, there were statutory obligations, and there was kind of a playbook by then. So as much as I appreciate the kudos being given to the Bush administration on the way out, I think what was done in the Obama administration, and I hope what will be done at the appropriate time in the Trump administration, was much more organized and professional than we were able to accomplish in 2008.

Notes

1. William G. Howell and Kenneth R. Mayer, "The Last One Hundred Days," *Presidential Studies Quarterly* 35, no. 3 (September 2005): 533.

2. George W. Bush, Remarks to White House Staff Online by Gerhard Peters and John T. Woolley, The American Presidency Project, https://www.presidency.ucsb.edu/node/285148.

3. Center for Presidential Transition, *Presidential Transition Guide,* 4th ed., April 2020, chap. 7, https://presidentialtransition.org/transition-timeline-and-guide/.

4. Center for Presidential Transition, "Collaboration in Crisis: Examples from the 2008–2009 Presidential Transition," November 2020, https://presidentialtransition.org/wp-content/uploads/sites/6/2020/11/How-Bush-and-Obama-Collaborated-to-Address-the-Great-Recession.pdf.

Conclusion: A Republic—If You Can Keep It

Why do presidential transitions matter? Most immediately because, when they go wrong, Americans suffer. America saw that with tragic clarity in the Depression transition of 1932–33 and again in the pandemic transition of 2020–21. Viewed through a longer-term lens, the peaceful and success-ful transfer of power is a key ingredient in our democracy, a tradition that stretches back to our very first president. And if the experience of Janu-ary 2021 teaches us but one lesson, it is that we cannot take that tradition for granted. Instead, we must continue to strive toward the Constitution's vision of a "more perfect union."

When Max Stier, CEO of the Partnship for Public Service, decided, in 2008, to create a center of excellence focusing on the art of presiden-tial transitions, President George W. Bush was overseeing the smoothest handover of power in modern history—and doing so during two wars and a global financial crisis. In part thanks to the leadership of the Partner-ship for Public Service, the 2008 and 2012 election cycles saw the art of presidential transitions refined. Bush and Obama set the gold standard for modern transitions. Building on their efforts, Romney created an even more sophisticated and ambitious template.

Based on these success stories, I draw the five fundamental lessons for presidential transitions set out in more detail in the introduction to this work:

1. A presidential transition must start early, meaning in the spring of election year at the latest.
2. It must seek to learn as much as possible from their predecessors (a process with which this book should hopefully help).
3. It must hire the right team and coordinate with the campaign, which of course takes priority.

4. It must prioritize above all the selection, vetting, and training of political appointments.

5. When the time comes, an incumbent administration must be prepared to help its successor (regardless of party or faction) achieve the smoothest possible transition into office, recognizing that the work of the outgoing administration is almost as important as the work of the incoming in this regard.

Until November 2016, it seemed as if the upward trajectory represented by the Bush-to-Obama transition and Romney's preparations would continue. Both the Clinton and Trump camps built robust transition teams and plans. Unfortunately, after Trump's 2016 election victory, his transition team's leaders were fired and their meticulous plans thrown out—literally as well as figuratively. The failure to implement their plans had negative consequences on both personnel and policy throughout the Trump administration.

Bad as this was, however, few could have imagined the crisis that engulfed America four years later. Despite three acts of Congress enshrining transition best practices, substantial academic research, and dedicated sharing of experience and expertise by a bipartisan cadre of transition experts, the 2020 presidential transition almost went off the rails—threatening democracy. For the first time in our history, an outgoing president flatly denied his own election loss and impeded implementation of the Presidential Transition Act. The crisis reached its height—and turned deadly—with the Capitol insurrection of January 6, 2021.

And yet, against this backdrop, the Biden-Harris campaign proceeded to pull off what by many measures we must regard as the most effective presidential transition yet. They started early—in the spring of 2020, in fact—in line with best practice recommended by the Partnership's Center for Presidential Transition. In hindsight, an even earlier start and, more importantly, a more accelerated work plan before Election Day, would be desirable in future presidential transitions.

From the outset, Biden decided to go big on his transition, in terms of size, budget, and ambition. Ted Kaufman, Jeff Zients, and Yohannes Abraham built a large team and built it fast. The team included a huge personnel operation, one able to conduct eight thousand job interviews during the interregnum. They broke the mold by turning greater focus onto positions that do not require Senate confirmation, in order to have the maximum number of appointees ready to go on day one. Elsewhere, the transition team created new, more effective procedures for agency transition teams, for coordination between the campaign and the transition, and for preparing policy actions to hit the ground running.

This strategy paid dividends come Inauguration Day and beyond. President Biden took office accompanied by the largest White House staff ever assembled on day one, together with more than 1,100 officials already appointed throughout the government (in posts that do not require Senate confirmation). In fact, in terms of sheer numbers, Biden's staffing of the government on day one exceeded the combined staff of Presidents Obama and Trump at day one hundred of their terms. Perhaps most importantly, the Biden-Harris team built a process to distribute hundreds of millions of doses of COVID-19 vaccines developed during the Trump administration. By June 2021, 55 percent of American adults were fully vaccinated and 65 percent had received at least one shot.

Under any circumstances, this would have represented a remarkable achievement. But Biden's transition was not without its challenges, and these prove instructive in setting out improvements for the future. Most obviously, Biden was hindered by his predecessor's active obstruction of "ascertainment"—the trigger for the formal transition to begin—with the result that, for several weeks, his transition was denied access to vital resources and information.

To help ensure that this cannot happen again, Congress should clarify the standard for "ascertainment"; make fewer transition services dependent on the ascertainment decision; and bring forward the start of the formal transition process.

In parallel, the administration and Congress should work together to improve the handoff, including by vesting additional authority in career officials (in order to further depoliticize transitions); requiring the outgoing administration to cooperate with its successor on budget issues; bringing forward the statutory start date for transition planning; and mandating more sharing of intelligence with the president-elect and their team (while progress has been made on this issue, too much intelligence-sharing is still done at the discretion of the sitting president).

Biden's experience also shows that, lamentably, it remains almost impossible to staff the top ranks of the government quickly. At the one-hundred-day mark, with around 1,500 non-Senate-confirmable appointments filled, Biden still only had 44 top officials confirmed across the entire government, out of around 1,200 who require Senate confirmation. Even at two hundred days, only 127 top officials were confirmed. It almost goes without saying that a new president cannot be expected to run his or her government with less than 10 percent of its leadership in place.

Congress should therefore continue to reduce the number of Senate-confirmed officials, and both the executive branch and the legislature should work to further streamline the process and paperwork required, including the ethics review process. The relevant agencies responsible for clearing and vetting nominees should be given "surge" appropriations, allowing them to flex up for the challenge. A candidate's transition team should prepare for a variety of delays and challenges, just as Biden's team did.

Finally, the news media, academic institutions, Congress, and nonprofits like the Partnership for Public Service all must emphasize the strictly nonpartisan nature of presidential transitions and the fact that a smooth transfer of power represents one of the foundations of our democracy. Candidates can and should compete during an election, but once the votes are in, the priority must be continuity of government operations. As awful as the recent pandemic has been for millions of Americans, it would be difficult to imagine a better demonstration of why such continuity matters so much: bluntly, as Joe Biden recognized, the failure to coordinate cost thousands of lives. Transitions must therefore be considered an entirely nonpolitical exercise, building on the tradition established in the smoothest, best transitions in history.

More, perhaps, than any of the technical "fixes" recommended above, the key to the success of future transfers of power will be the American people themselves. We may well hope that "ascertainment" will not remain a household word for quite the same reasons it became so ubiquitous in late 2020. Nevertheless, it is vital that the public remain aware of and interested in the process of transition—and determined to hold public officials accountable for its success.

Asked what kind of government the Constitutional Convention had created for the new United States, Benjamin Franklin replied, "A republic—if you can keep it." With trademark pith and prescience, Franklin acknowledged that democratic traditions do not simply maintain themselves by some immutable law of nature. No matter how ingenious their design, the fate of our nation's institutions rests ultimately upon the people's active participation. All Americans have a responsibility to work together to preserve and to strengthen the peaceful transfer of power, so that it may endure for centuries to come.

INDEX

Miller Center Studies on the Presidency